TECHNOLOGY OF BIO-FUELS (ETHANOL & BIODIESEL)

TECHNOLOGY OF BIO-FUELS (ETHANOL & BIODIESEL)

Written By :

EIRI Consultants and Engineers

ENGINEERS INDIA RESEARCH INSTITUTE

4449, Nai Sarak, Main Road, Delhi-110 006 (India)

Ph. : 91-11-23918117, 23916431, 45120361

Fax : 91-11-23916431, 23918117

* **E-Mail :** eiribooks@yahoo.com

* **Website :** www.eiriindia.org

Sole Distributor :

EIRI PROJECT CONSULTANTS & PUBLISHERS

4/54, Roop Nagar, Delhi-110007

Printed and Published by :

ENGINEERS INDIA RESEARCH INSTITUTE

4449, Nai Sarak, Main Road, Delhi-110 006 (India)

Ph. : 91-11-23918117, 23916431, 45120361

Fax : 91-11-23916431, 23918117

* **E-Mail :** eiribooks@yahoo.com
* **Website :** www.eiriindia.org

Distributed by :

EIRI PROJECT CONSULTANTS & PUBLISHERS

4/54, Roop Nagar, Delhi-110007

ISBN : 978-81-89765-34-7

Printed in New Delhi (India)

Rs. 975

Printed and Published by Sudhir Gupta for "Engineers India Research Institute", 4449, Nai Sarak, Main Road, New Delhi-110 006 and Printed at Swastik Offset, Delhi

Preface

The book **'Technology of Bio-Fuels (Ethanol & Biodiesel) '** covers various methods including Bio-Fuels : Future Fuel, Marketing Strategies, Technology of Bio-Fuels, Ethanol-A Suitable Fuel, Bio-Fuel for Rural Employment, Advantages and Limitation of Bio-Fuels, Bio-Fuel Resources of Energy, Jatropha, Network of Jatropha Oil for Biodiesel, Potential for Biodiesel, Production of Bio-Fuels, Biomass Energy Technology, Jatropha Based Biodiesel, Production of Biodiesel, Blending of Easters and Diesel, Storage of Biodiesel, Handling of Biodiesel, Analysis of Technologies with Reference to Indian Resources and Requirements, Properties of Biodiesel, Biodiesel Project Report, Glycerine, Cultivation of Jatropha, Types of Lands where it can grow tih Advantage and Potential of Plantation, Bio Gas Plant, Biodiesel from Algae, Processing Technology for Biodiesel from Jatropha Seeds, Tapioca Renewable Energy Source of Bio-Fuel for India, Preparation of Biodiesel from Jatropha circus, Biodiesel Production from Jatropha Circus (SVO) Oil, Gasification of Biomass and Waste, Biodiesel from Used Soya Oil, Characterization of vegetable oils for Biodiesel production, Process of Biodiesel Production, Liquid Fuels from Biomass and Urban Waste, Ethanol (Bio-Fuel).

The book has been written for the benefit and to prove an asset and a handy reference guide in the hands of new entrepreneurs and well established industrialists.

Director

ENGINEERS INDIA RESEARCH INSTITUTE

Nai Sarak, Main Road,
Delhi-110 006 (India)
E-mail : eiribooks@yahoo.com

CONTENTS AND SUBJECT INDEX

1

Bio-Fuel : Future Fuel

INTRODUCTION

Petroleum resources are finite and therefore search for alternative is continuing all over the world. Development of bio-fuels as an alternative and renewable source of energy for transportation has become critical in the national effort towards maximum self-reliance-the corner stone of our energy security strategy. Bio-fuels like ethanol and bio–diesel being environment friendly, will help us to conform to the stricter emission norms. International experience has demonstrated the advantages of using ethanol and methanol as automotive fuel. Since blends below 10% of ethanol do not present any problem and reduce harmful emission, a decision has already been taken to blend 5% ethanol with motor spirit w.e.f. 1.1.2003 in a number of States. To achieve higher blending, a concerted programme for use of bio–mass for conversion to alcohol is essential including expansion of area under sugarcane cultivation.

High Speed Diesel (HSD) is the main transport fuel hence introduction of bio-diesel both as a diesel substitute and for blending with Petroleum diesel both as a diesel substitute and for blending with Petroleum diesel is an imperative need. Bio-diesel commands crucial advantages such as technical feasibility of blending in any ratio with petroleum diesel fuel, use of existing storage facility and infrastructure, superiority from the environment and emission reduction angle, its capacity to provide energy security to remote and rural areas and employment generation. Moreover, crops like sunflower, rapeseed and tree borne oil seeds like *Jatropha curcas* provide rich bio–mass and nutrients to the soil and check degradation of land–a major problem affecting nearly 65 million hectares of land. The nation is facing a shortage of edible and non-edible oil. The existing high price of edible oil and the full use of tree borne oil seeds for various purposes suggest that organized bio-diesel production for blending is possible only if plantation of selected species is taken up in compact areas and backed by infrastructure for procurement, primary processing, and production at the plant duly equipped to produce quality bio-diesel for the oil industry. Since the demand for diesel will continue to rise steadily with economic growth, the processing facilities as well as plantation have to necessarily expand. This will serve two important purpose e.g. blending will result in part oil substitution and thereby reduce crude oil import, save foreign exchange and help us to move towards stricter emission norms.

BIO-FUEL

The term 'Bio-Fuels' needs to be suitably defined under section 19 of the Standards of Weights and Measures Act, 1976 so as to avoid any ambiguity in this regard. Further, the term should be so defined so as to provide for necessary adjustments in its contents in respect of technological developments. Bio-fuels are alternative to conventional fuels and as such may be viewed as alternative fuels which term has been defined in Canadian Alternative Fuels Act, 1995 as follow: "alternative fuel" means any fuel that is :

(a) for use in motor vehicles to deliver direct propulsion.

(b) less damaging to the environment than conventional fuels, and

(c) prescribed by regulation, including, without limiting the generality of the foregoing, ethanol, methanol, propane gas, natural gas, hydrogen or electricity when used as a sole source of direct propulsion energy, and

(d) satisfies the specifications that may be prescribed in this behalf.

Alternative fuel shall also mean, "Such other fuel as the Central Government may specify, by notification in the Official Gazette". An alternative formulation to this can be based on the Paper "Perspective of Bio–fuel Development in India by Dr. D. N. Tiwari, Member, Planning Commission and Dr. A. P. Dikshit". Accordingly, "Bio-fuels" means plant bio-mass based fuels that can substitute petroleum based oils as motor/engine fuels and include bio-gas, producer gas, vegetable oils, alcohols, ethers, esters and other chemicals derived from cellulosic bio–mass, such as, herbaceous and woody plants, agricultural and forestry residues and such other fuels as the Central Government may specify by notification in the Official Gazette.

OVERVIEW OF BIO-FUEL

Bio-diesel is fatty acid ethyl or methyl ester made from virgin or used vegetable oils (both edible and non-edible) and animal fats. The main commodity sources for bio-diesel in India can be non-edible oils obtained from plant species such as Jatropha Curcas (Ratanjyot), Pongamia Pinnata (Karanj), Calophyllum inophyllum (Nagchampa), Hevca brasiliensis (Rubber) etc. Bio-diesel contains no petroleum, but it can be blended at any level with petroleum diesel to create a bio-diesel blend or can be used in its pure form. Just like petroleum diesel, bio-diesel operates in compression ignition engine; which essentially require very little or no engine modifications because bio-diesel has properties similar to petroleum diesel fuels. It can be stored just like the petroleum diesel fuel and hence does not require separate infrastructure. The use of bio-diesel in conventional diesel engines results in substantial reduction of un-burnt hydrocarbons, carbon monoxide and particulate matters. Bio-diesel is considered clean fuel since it has almost no sulphur, no aromatics and has about 10% built-in oxygen, which helps it to burn fully. Its higher cetane number improves the ignition quality even when blended in the petroleum diesel.

B20 (a blend of 20 per cent by volume bio-diesel with 80 per cent by volume petroleum diesel) has demonstrated significant environmental benefits in US with a minimum increase in cost for fleet operations and other consumers. Bio-diesel is registered as a fuel and fuel additive with the US Environmental Protection Agency and meets clean diesel standards established by the California Air Resources Board. Neat (100 per cent) bio-diesel has been designated as an alternative fuel by the Department of Energy and the Department of Transportation of US. Studies conducted with bio-diesel on engines have shown substantial reduction in Particulate matter (25–50%). However, a marginal increase in NOx (1–6%) is also reported; but it can be taken care of either by optimization of engine parts or by using De-NOx catalyst (De-NOx catalyst will be necessary for Bharat-III/IV compliant engines). HC and CO emissions were also reported to be lower. Non-regulated emissions like PAH etc. were also found to be lower.

TABLE 1.1

Vegetable oil production in India (2001)

Oil	Production (million tonnes)
Groundnut	1.40
Soya	0.82
Rape/Mustard	1.55
Sunflower	0.30
Sesame	0.26
Castor	0.25
Niger	0.03
Safflower	0.09
Linseed	0.10
Cottonseed	0.44
Coconut	0.55
Rice Bran	0.55
Oils from expelled cakes	0.28
Minor oilseeds	0.05
Total	**6.67**

Bio–diesel has been accepted as clean alternative fuel by US and its production presently is about 100 million Gallons. Each State has passed specific bills to promote the use of bio-diesel by reduction of taxes. Sunflower, rapeseed etc. is the raw material used in Europe whereas soyabean is used in USA. Thailand uses palm oil, Ireland uses frying oil and animal fats. Due to its favourable properties, bio-diesel can be used as fuel for diesel engines (as either, B5–a blend of 5% bio-diesel in petro-diesel fuel,) or B20 or B100). USA uses B20 and B100 bio-diesel, France uses B5 as mandatory in all diesel fuel. It can also be used as an additive to reduce the overall sulphur content of blend and to compensate for lubricity loss due to sulphur removal from diesel fuel.

PRODUCTION PROCESS OF BIO-FUEL

Bio–diesel

The chemical reaction : Bio-fuel production is a two-stage process that starts with the raw material, oilseeds, being crushed in oil mills to physically expel the oil, leaving behind the oil cake, which can be used as manure. The second stage is a chemical process involving a reaction called trans-esterification. The expelled oil is treated with an alcohol, say, methanol, and a base, say, potassium hydroxide, to convert it to fuel. This reaction removes free fatty acids and also gives off by-products glycerin and a fertilizer from the base used.

Pyrolysis: Pyrolysis refers to a chemical change caused by the application of thermal energy in the absence of air or nitrogen. The liquid fractions of the thermally decomposed vegetable oil are likely to approach diesel fuels. The pyrolyzate had lower viscosity, flash point, and pour point than diesel fuel and equivalent calorific values. The cetane number of the pyrolyzate was lower. The pyrolysed vegetable oils contain acceptable amounts of sulphur, water and sediment and give acceptable copper corrosion values but unacceptable ash, carbon residue and pour point.

Micro-emulsification: The formation of micro–emulsions (co-solvency) is one of the potential solutions for solving the problem of vegetable oil viscosity. Micro-emulsions are defined as transparent, thermodynamically stable colloidal dispersions. The droplet diameters in micro-emulsions range from 100 to 1000 Å. A micro-emulsion can be made of vegetable oils with an ester and dispersant (co-solvent), or of vegetable oils, an alcohol and a surfactant and a cetane improver, with or without diesel fuels. Water (from aqueous ethanol) may also be present in order to use lower-proof ethanol, thus increasing water tolerance of the micro-emulsions.

Transesterification : Transesterification also called alcoholysis, is the displacement of alcohol from an ester by another alcohol in a process similar to hydrolysis. This process has been widely used to reduce the viscosity of triglycerides. The transesterification reaction is represented by the general equation :

$$RCOOR' + R''OH \rightarrow + RCOOR'' + R'OH$$

Triglycerides are readily trans-esterified in the presence of alkaline catalyst at atmospheric pressure and at a temperature of approximately 60 to 70°C with an excess of methanol. The mixture at the end of reaction is allowed to settle. The lower glycerol layer is drawn off while the upper methyl ester layer is washed to remove entrained glycerol and is then processed further. The excess methanol is recovered by distillation and sent to a rectifying column for purification and recycled. The trans-esterification works well when the starting oil is of high quality. However, quite often low quality oils are used as raw materials for bio-diesel preparation. In cases where the free fatty acid content of the oil is above 1%, difficulties arise due to the formation of soap which promotes emulsification during the water washing

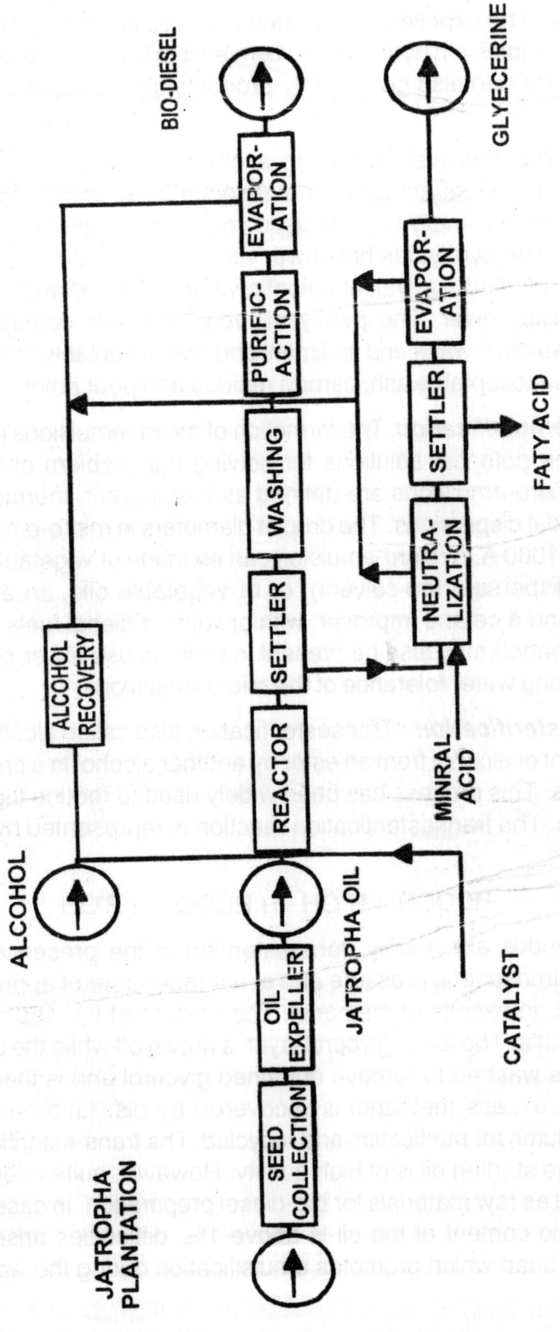

Fig. 1.1 : Production of Bio-diesel using jatropha as Feed Stock.

stage and at an FFA content above 2% the process becomes unworkable.

Ethanol

Ethanol can be extracted from three different classes of sources as follow:

(i) Starch as grain, corn and tubers like cassava.

(ii) Sugar plants (sugar beet or sugar cane).

(iii) Cellulose plants (general tree and biomass).

Process: Ethanol production is a very ancient activity linked with making potable alcohol. The liquor containing corn, grapes juice, molasses etc are fermented by adding yeast to it in batch fermentators for a number of hours (minimum 40 hours) when fermentation gets completed with no increase in alcohol content. The fermentation process consists of breaking of starch or cellulose chain into individual sugar molecules and then fermenting the sugar into ethanol and carbon dioxide. The major reaction is depicted below. The equations should show that fermentation of glucose/sugar to ethanol is energy efficient, about 93% of the feed energy is converted as ethanol and only a small amount is taken by fermenting organism (yeast).

Hydrolysis	$[C_6H_{10}O_5]n + nH_20$	→	$nC_6H_{12}O_6$ (glucose)
Fermentation	$C_6H_{12}0_6$	→	$2C_2H_5OH + 2CO_2$
Energy balance	Glucose	→	2 ethanol + 75 KJ
	180 gms		2 x 46 gms
	2.82 MJ		2 x 1.37 MJ

ENVIRONMENTAL & LEGAL ISSUES

Subsidies, incentives, etc.

Although the European Parliament in February 1994, adopted 90% exemption for Bio-diesel and the combination of legislation supporting the use of alternative fuels, differential tax incentives and oilseed production subsidies, resulted in Bio-diesel being priced competitively with diesel fuel in a number of European countries. Tax incentives take the form of significantly reduced assessments or exemption from taxes normally assessed on diesel fuel. Even recently Parliament in Denmark expressed its support for a lower tax level on Bio-fuels and on certain mineral oils containing Bio-fuels. There is a proposal by European commission according to which Bio-fuel should account for 2% of fuel sold in the Member States by 31st December, 2005 and 5.75% by 2010. However, no minimum percentage of compulsory blended fuel has been insisted upon. There is a strong backing for green fuel source to enable the European Union to fulfill its Kyoto commitments as Member States are bound to put the legislation into force by 31st December, 2004.

However, in India the cost of Bio-fuel is likely to be approximately the same as the cost of conventional petroleum fuel/ diesel and so there may be only marginal need for measures to equalize the cost. But adequate incentive may have to be provided to people to invest in producing Bio–fuels and higher returns may have to be ensured. The tax regime in respect of Bio-fuels may, therefore, have to be suitably designed. This may be taken care of through differential Excise-duty and other taxes. Any subsidies need to be excluded as they would be unsustainable in the present economic policy. It would be relevant to mention in this regard that any concession which may be provided in this regard must be in conformity with the TRIPS and WTO regimes.

CONCLUSION AND RECOMMENDATION

The envisaged bio-fuels programme is based on several compulsions and imperatives each strengthening the case for bio fuels. Some of these are :

1. the impending international oil crisis;
2. the growth momentum generated since the 1990s causing a steady spurt in oil demand for transport;
3. domestic crude oil output reaching a plateau and hence the need to reduce dependence on imported crude oil;
4. the national commitment to provide clean air to the citizens as a part of their fundamental rights by enforcement of stricter emission norms;
5. technical and economic feasibility of producing bio–fuels for blending with Motor Spirit and Diesel on a large scale due to availability of land, technology, capacity for supply of quality planting materials, positive response of the farming community, market, enterprise and financial institutions:
6. the implications of integrated bio-fuel development for upliftment of the poor, through reclamation of degraded land, drought proofing provision of income and employment opportunities in plantation, primary processing and procurement and transport; and
7. as a means to "green & rehabilitate" degraded lands on a sustainable basis.

India faces the difficult task of fine balancing the growing energy needs, the environmental damage from fossil energy sources and the energy security of the country. Worldwide concerns regarding the threat of climate change have sharpened focus on green energy as it will not only meet the goal of sustainable development but also contribute to a reduction of carbon dioxide emissions. These imperatives and the estimates of incremental demand of diesel and motor spirit in 2006-7 and 2011 suggest that a programme to produce bio-fuels which are transport fuel substitutes and blend them-ethanol with motor spirit and Bio-diesel with HSD–must be started right now to create necessary plantation base and infrastructure which takes time.

Ethanol–its Prospects

The advantages of using ethanol and methanol as blends in motor spirit are that they are oxygenates containing 35% oxygen and renewable. They reduce vehicular emission of Hydrocarbons and Carbon Monoxide and eliminate emission of lead, benzene, butadiene etc. It is technically feasible to design and run automobiles on 100% ethanol; but for the reason of availability and compatibility with vehicles presently in use, blending of ethanol with motor spirit needs to make a very modest beginning. Motor Spirit forms only 7-8% of oil consumption.

Biodiesel

Since diesel constitutes 50% of oil consumption chiefly for transportation and other purposes, its demand is integrally related to economic growth and is seen as a growth inducing factor. The estimated increase of demand for diesel from the 2001-02 level of 38.815 Million MT to 52.324 Million MT in 2006-7 and 66.095 Million MT shows a massive hike of 34% to 70% respectively over 2001-02 level in physical terms which will lead to increase of crude oil import from the present level of 85 Million MT to 147 Million MT per annum raising the oil import bill from US $ 13.3 Billion to over US $ 20 Billion. As emissions from automotive engines using diesel is a major source' of air pollution in urban areas, enforcement of stricter emission norms has become a national priority. Biodiesel has been accepted as clean alternative fuel all over the world. Though bio–diesel could be produced from soyabean, rapeseed, sunflower, the source of edible oil, existing shortage of edible oil in the country and its price, would not make these crops viable for use as feed stock for production of bio–diesel. Similarly the existing output of 5.253 Million MT of Tree borne oil seeds have been put to different uses and cannot contribute to organized production of bio–diesel on account of a number of factors including scattered location, low yield and consequently low level of seed collection of 15–20% of total exploitable seeds.

Jatropha curcas-Source of Biodiesel

There are many tree species which bear seeds rich in oil. Of these some promising tree species have been evaluated and it has been found that there are a number of them such as *Jatropha curcas* and Pongamia pinnata (Honge' or 'Karanja') which would be very suitable in our conditions. However, *Jatropha Curcas* has been found the most suitable tree specie for the reasons summarized below:

1. It can be grown as a quick yielding plant even in adverse land situations viz. degraded and barren lands under forest and non-forest use, dry and drought prone areas, marginal lands and as agroforestry crop. It can be planted on fallow lands and along farmers field boundaries as hedge because it does not grow too tall as well as on vacant lands alongside railways, highways, irrigation canals and unused lands in townships etc. under Public/Private Sector Undertakings.
2. The seeds of Jatropha are available during the non-rainy season, which facilitates better collection and processing. The cost of plantation is largely incurred in the first year and improved planting material can make a huge difference in yield.
3. Raising Jatropha plant and its maintenance creates jobs for the rural poor, particularly the landless, in plantation and primary processing through expellers.
4. It has multiple uses and after the extraction of oil from the seeds, the oil cake left behind is excellent organic manure, the bio–mass of *Jatropha curcas* enriches the soil and it can also be put to other uses.
5. Retains soil moisture and improve land capability and environment.
6. Jatropha adds to the capital stock of the farmers and the community, for sustainable generation of income and employment.

Recommendations for Bio-Fuel

A National Mission on Bio-fuel should be launched immediately with the objective of producing bio-diesel required for blending to the extent of 20% with HSD in 2011-12. As its Phase I, a demonstration project may be taken up on 4 lakh hectares in eight States. Of this area two lakh hectare of plantation may be taken up on under-stocked forest lands placed under the management of Joint Forest Management Committees in four States (Tamil Nadu, Chhattisgarh, Jharkhand and Tripura) and two lakh hectare of plantation on non–forest lands spread over four states (U.P., Madhya Pradesh, Maharashtra and Andhra Pradesh). In addition, the Ministry of Rural Development may take up plantation under the IWDP and other poverty alleviation programmes as the programme elements of the two programmes are similar.

2

Marketing Strategies

INTRODUCTION

Petroleum product consumption is increasing very fast with globalization and high technology development since last decade. Diesel consumption is about 45% of the total consumption of petroleum products. The Diesel requirements are six times to the gasoline requirement while 65% of gasoline required by two/ three wheeler vehicles only. Thus increase in vehicle population will invite fuel problems as these vehicle run designed on petroleum based fuels only. These fuels are extracted from the earth, so not immediate renewable, limited reserves. Thus fear of exhaust ultimately leads to think for eco-friendly Bio-Fuels to protect our environment from toxic emissions.

Fuels known as Bio-Fuels can be produced from many plant materials and wastes products such as agricultural wastes and municipal solid waste (MSW) that together are called bio–mass. Several oxygenated Bio-Fuels such as ethanol reduce carbon monoxide emissions when blended with gasoline. A number of Bio-Fuels can be substituted directly for conventional transportation fuels to reduce urban air pollution. Bio-Fuels can also be used in the residential, industrial, utility sectors. Substantial improvements have been made in the technology to producing the liquid and gaseous Bio-Fuels, this nation need most and these fuels now have the opportunity to make a strong impact occur fuels use.

Biodiesel markets had developed in seven primary countries (Austria, Belgium, France, Germany, Italy, Indonesia and Malaysia. Germany has been the biggest Biodiesel producer with about 2 billion liters capacity on line. France, Italy and the UK are the next largest producers. In 2001, GOI of

India launched three pilot projects in different states where supplying 5% ethanol-doped-petrol to the retail outlets under their respective areas. In 2003, the Govt. resolved that 5% ethanol blended petrol would be supplied in the nine states and four Union Territories. For Biodiesel, a National programme aims to produce enough oil seeds for the production of Biodiesel in sufficient quantities to enable its blending with diesel to the extent of 20%. Pilot projects and analysis of feedstock collection and plantation were on going.

WHAT IS BIO–MASS?

The term Bio–mass encompasses a wide spectrum of plant, materials that range from agricultural and forestry wastes to municipal wastes to crops grown especially to make Bio-Fuels, such as, bio-ethanol and Biodiesel. The technologies used to convert these bio–mass feed stocks vary and the alternative fuels produce similarly low amounts of greenhouse gas when combusted. But, by using alternative fuels, it can offset the use of petroleum products. As an example ethanol produced from plant materials (which is made from atmospheric carbon) which are not releasing carbon that has been trapped as oil for millions of years into the air.

WHAT ARE BIO-FUELS?

'Bio-Fuels' are alcohols, ethers and other chemicals made from cellulose biomass renewable resources such as fast growing trees, grasses, aquatic plants (micro algae) and waste products, such as agricultural and forestry residues and municipal and industrial wastes with further advances in technology. These domestically produced biomass resources could provide over 50% of future fuel requirements. Some of the Bio-Fuels used to fuel cars and trucks include ethanol and Biodiesel. Other alcohols fuel such as methanol which currently is produced from oil fuels can also be produced from renewable biomass and be classified as Bio-Fuels.

BIO-FUELS FROM WASTE

The paper and organic fractions of MSW comprise over 65% by volume of the waste steam. These cellulose fractions provide an excellent feedstock for conversion to bio–mass fuels. Furthermore, significant amounts of cellulose are presently being land filled due to the lack of demand for recycled paper. The utilization of cellulose waste streams would reduce the demand for land resources needed for land filling and their associated environmental impacts by reducing the amount of MWS, while at the same time producing much needed cleaner transportation fuels. Many municipalities spend anywhere from $10 to $100 per ton in tipping fees just to dispose of MWS or collect it for recycling. Alternatively, these waste feedstock may supplied to a Bio-Fuels facility with negative cost.

THE CARBON CYCLE AND BIO-FUELS

CO_2 is part of the Earth's natural carbon cycle, which circulates carbon through the atmosphere, plants, animal, oceans, soil and rocks. This cycle maintains a life-sustaining and delicate natural balance between storing, releasing and recycling carbon. By using Bio-Fuels such as bio-ethanol and Biodiesel for transportation, it can help restore the natural balance of CO_2 in the atmosphere. Besides displaying fossil fuels, the feedstock used to make Bio-Fuel require CO_2 to grown and they absorb what they need from the atmosphere. Thus, much or all of the CO_2 released when bio–mass is converted into a Bio-Fuel and burned in automobile engines is recaptured when new bio–mass is grown to produce more Bio-Fuels.

SCENARIO OF BIO-FUELS

Since the first crisis of the 1970's various alternate fuels has been investigated with the goal of replacing conventional petroleum supplies. The initial interest was mainly one of fuel supply security, but recently more attention has been focused on the use of renewable fuels in order to reduce the net production of CO_2 from combustion sources. A number of oils are being considered worldwide for use in engines. These included rice bran oil, soybean oil, palm oil, sunflower oil, rapeseed oil, neem oil, karanja oil, Jatropha oil, cotton seed oil, linseed oil, corn Stover oil etc. The usages could be in vegetable oil blends complete substitute to diesel and vegetable oil esters (Biodiesel).

The inventor of Diesel Engine, Rudolf Diesel, confidently predicted that plant based oil would be used to operate the engine.

He used Peanut oil as fuel for demonstrating his engine in 1900[1]. Esters of Rice bran oil are used as fuel in compression ignition engine and its efficiency is closes to diesel. Methanol esters of rice bran oil are of lower viscosity and low carbon residue. Delay period of raw oil is higher than diesel and esters are of lower than that of diesel and reported that smoke is higher as compared to diesel [2].

The suitability of Palm oil a compression ignition engine fuel substitute has been successfully demonstrated through field trials in Malaysia with the extensive palm tree plantation in Malaysia, the use of palm oil in compression ignition engine is proving to be fairly cost effective the country. The thermal efficiency is slightly lower than that obtained with high speed diesel, presumably due to the higher oxygen content of the palm oil. Palm oil blends are reported to be giving satisfactory result in Japan and United Kingdom [3].

Soybean oil is another vegetable oil that has been proved to be viable substitute to diesel. Studies including field trials have demonstrated soybean oil and diesel is well suitable for automotive. When pure soybean oil is used, the engine wear has been reported to be lower than that of with diesel, but carbon deposition in engine parts is higher [4].

Jatropha oil as a fuel for compression ignition engine has performance characteristics generally similar to these of diesel. Ethyl esters of Jatropha oil results in a slightly reduced thermal efficiency as compared to that of diesel. Smoke number tor the Jatropha ethyl ester was lower than of the diesel [5].

Ethanol can be deriving from Agricultural feed stocks. Recent experiments indicate that maximum concentration of ethanol emulsified in diesel fuel is about 30%. Beyond 30%, knocking combustion and misfire occur, resulting in degradation engine performance. Experiment shows that there is an increase in specific fuel consumption of emulsified fuel at higher power output. This is due to lower heat content. It may improve in thermal efficiency at higher loads for the speeds of 1200 and 1500 rpm. At 1200 rpm lower power out put there is a marginal increase in the exhaust temperature with emulsified fuels. But, at 1500 rpm there is a reduction in exhaust temperature with increase in power out put with reduction in NOx emissions [6].

Argemone Maxicana is a weed plant. It comes under the family papeveraceae. It has run down widely from America. It is available in Anantapur district of Andhra Pradesh and yield of oil is 35%. Densities of Argemone oil are slightly higher compared to diesel, calorific value is slightly lower on mass basis, viscosities at room temperature is higher, cetane number is slightly lower, flash point is higher, volatilities low and carbon residue is higher [7].

Simarouba Glauca D.C., popularly known as ACEITUNA belongs to the family of Simaroubaceae is a tall tree growing to a height of 15 meters. It is native of El Salvador in the Central America. It has been introduced into India from El Salvador by the National Bureau of Plant Genetic Resources at the regional station, Amaravati, Maharashta exclusively for soil conservation purposes for eroded waste lands, hold hills and degraded lands. In view of its excellent performance, plantation of Simarouba Glauca was propagated extensively in the States of Orissa, Bihar, Madhya Pradesh,

TABLE 2.1

Characteristics observations of various bio-fuels.

Description	Units	Diesel	Jatropha oil	Jatropha ester	Mahua oil	Argemone oil	Simarouba oil	Cotton seed oil	Palm oil	Sunflower oil	Karanja oil	Thumba oil
Specific Gravity	-	0.84	0.92	-	0.96	0.92	0.90	0.91	0.91	0.90	0.91	0.94
Heat of evaporation	BTU-lb	200	-	-	-	-	-	-	-	-	-	-
Auto ignition Temp	°C	225	-	-	-	-	-	-	-	-	-	-
Flammability Limit	%	0.6-5.5	-	-	5.92	-	-	-	-	-	-	-
Cetane Number	-	47	51	-	-	38	38	-	-	-	-	45-48
Density	Kg/m^3	840	920	880	-	-	-	-	-	-	-	-
Calorific Value	Kj/Kg	42000	36000	38450	36000	37600	37600	39400	36900	34000	34000	35800
Viscosity	cst	2.7	40.05	5.6	24.58	167.4	57.57	46.9	67.7	71.4	27.84	47.0
Flash Point	°C	46	220	175	232	262	242	-	220	190	205	230
Fire Point	°C	52	240	-	240	265	246	-	230	220	230	245
Thermal Efficiency	at 3.86 BHP	67%	-	-	-	-	26%	-	26%	24%	24%	-
Mechanical efficiency	at 3.86 BHP	67%	-	-	-	-		-	-	65%	60%	-
Specific Fuel Consumption	lt/KWh	0.461	-	-	-	-		-	-	0.446	0.435	-

West Bengal, Andhra Pradesh, Karnataka and Tamil Nadu. The generation period is about 5 years and from 6 years onwards, each tree can be grown 30-50 Kg seed per annum for 50–60 years. About 200 trees can be grown in a hectare of land. The seed is brown colour with oil content in kernel is 65.8%. It characteristics like cetane number and calorific value similar to diesel with heat contents 80–90% specific gravity 0.9062 at 30° C. It is viscous, hence preheat the oil is essential [8].

Madhuca Indica i.e. Mahua oil is found in mixed deciduous forests, usually of a some what dry type, after growing on rocky and sandy soil and thriving on the demean trap. It is commonly throughout Central India, Mumbai, Andhra Pradesh and Madhya Pradesh. The oil seed are brown with oil content kernel is 51.1%. Mahua oil is a mixture of glycerides containing fatty acid and glycerol hence it can be used as lubricant oil which is 60% less than the mineral oil with 41.2 viscosities. Fire and flash point is higher than the mineral based lubricant with 445 oleic acid which is better anti-wear characteristics. It has high heat transfer coefficient and flow ability but sticking deposit causes retardation of piston movement [9].

The investigation revealed that Cotton seed oil in general vegetable oil, can be utilized if super charging is employed at the recommended injection pressure of the engine. There is a reduction of about 15% in BSTC at full load will 0.4 bars g supercharging pressure. But, smoke density is more as the supercharging pressure is increased [10].

Thumba is classified as Citrus Cococynthis Selore (Cucurbitaecae) is a main of the gourd family. It occurs throughout India and is seen growing wild in warm, acid or sandy tracts of North West and Central South India. It is abundantly available at Gujarat and in the desert areas of Jaisalmer, Badmer, Bikaner and Jodhpur in Rajasthan. The seed content 23% oil and 18% protein. The Kernel comprises of 40% of seed with yellow colour. It shows poor performance and higher exhausts emission than diesel. The Thumba oil operation indicate 0.1 % less thermal efficiency and 0.53% BOSCH unit more compared to diesel operation at rated load with 0.18% Volume CO emission [11]. Table-1 shows the characteristics observation of various Bio-Fuels.

Nahar (Mesua ferrea L) in Hindi called as Nagaswar is very familiar tree is available in the North Eastern region of India which was used for illumination purposes in the days of Yore and its flowers were indispensable for the womenfolk of this region for their hairstyle. The Nahar seeds have immense potential of about 75% of pale yellow coloured oil that is non-edible. Approx.

one lac quintals of Nahar seeds are produced annually. Prof. K. K. Boruah and Prof. Konwar of Tezpur University those are working on NCES project said 5% of Nahar seed oil with 95% conventional diesel blended efficiently works for long duration and substitute for conventional diesel in the transportation sector. A blend of 10% with 90% diesel combined in stationary diesel engines for short term use. Laboratory experiments shows that the crude oil extracted from Nahar seed can easily blended with mineral crude oil. The experiments shows that the fraction of boiling range 37–140°C, 140–300°C and 140–370°C could be used as gasoline, kerosene and high speed diesel respectively. Fraction distilling between 370–451°C, lubricating oil and a small percentage of Wax can be obtained [12].

BIO-FUEL PRODUCTION AND GROWTH

The production process of Bio-Fuel is well known. There are three basic outs to ester production:

1. Base catalyzed transesterfication of the oil witll alcohol.
2. Direct acid catalyzed esterfication of the oil with methanol.
3. Conversion of the oil to fatty acids and then to Alkyl esters with acid catalysis.

Today alkyl esters produced with the catalyzed reaction because it has low temperature (1500 F) and pressure (20 PSI) processing; high conversion (98%) with minimal side reactions and reaction time; direct conversion to methyl ester with no intermediate step for which exotic materials of construction are not necessary. Table-2 Bio-Fuels Production in top 12 countries in the World and Table-3 Mandates of various countries in the World for Ethanol and Biodiesel blending. The ethanol industry currently employs about 2,00,000 people (directly and indirectly) and saves $2 billion a year in terms of oil imports. However, America's present trade deficit in crude oil is over $50 billion, so there is plenty of room for growth. Ethanol's total benefits in terms of farm incomes are greater about $1.5 billion. There are over 60 ethanol production plants in operation or under construction with the capacity to produce more than 2 billion gallons (7.6 billion liters) a year.

Today, about 12% of US gasoline contains ethanol as a fuel additive, which boosts octane and reduces carbon monoxide and other emissions. An estimated one billion gallons of new ethanol production capacity is already on the drawing board, about 35% of this based on non-grain feed stocks such as agricultural and forestry residues.

TABLE 2.2

Bio-Fuels Production, 2004 (Billion Litres)

Sl. No.	Country	Ethanol	Biodiesel
1.	Brazil	15	-
2.	United States	13	0.1
3.	China	2	-
4.	Germany	0.02	1.1
5.	France	0.1	0.4
6.	Italy	0.35	-
7.	Canada	0.2	-
8.	Thailand	0.2	-
9.	Spain	0.2	-
10.	Denmark	-	0.08
11.	Creche Republic	-	0.07
12.	Australia	0.07	
	World Total	**31**	**2.2**

Source : Global Status Report on Renewable, 2005.

TABLE 2.3

MANDATES FOR ETHANOL AND BIODIESEL BLENDING

Year Enacted	Country/State/Province (%)	Ethanol Blend (%)	Biodiesel Blend (%)
1975	Brazil (national)	22–25%	2% by 2005
1997	United States (state of Minnesota)	10% 20% hy 2013	2% (future)
-	Dominican Republic (national)	15% hy 2015	5% by 2015
-	China (provinces of Heilongjiang, Jilin, Liaoning, and Henan)	10%	-
2003	India (9 states and 7 federal territories)	5%	-
2004	United States (state of Hawaii)	10% by 2006	-
	Columbia (national)	10%	
2005	Canada (province of Ontario)	5% by 2007	
	United States (state of Montana)	10%	

Source: Global Status Report on Renewable, 2005.

BIO–MASS ENERGY TODAY AND TOMORROW

Bio–mass has a long history of use as a home heating fuel in wood stoves and as fuel for the forest product industry. Total estimated consumption of biomass fuels in the North East of U.S., by all energy use sectors was about 500 trillion Btus in 1993 or about 5% of the region total energy demands which is equivalent of over 235,000 barrels of oil per day and enough to heat 20–30 million homes per year and which is average world crude oil price had a value of over $1.3 billion per year.

The potential benefits of expanded biomass energy are varied from strengthening the existing forest products industry to crating new business and agricultural markets. Provided that appropriate practices are implemented,

TABLE 2.4
Key opportunities and barriers of biomass energy use.

Keys	Environmental	Economic
Opportunity	- help meet clean Air Act. Requirements. - reduce pressur on land filling. - reduce net emissions of carbon dioxide and methane, both greenhouse gases.	- build on the strengthen the forest product secotr's job/ economic base. - reduce energy costs for industries. - create new business opportunities and jobs, while keeping energy dollars in the local economic. - diversify agricultural markets.
Barriers	- perception that biomass energy is 'dirty' - potential loss fo wildlife habibat and biodiversity resulting from increased forest harvesting. - inappropriately applied regulations that limit the use of clean waste wood for energy.	- perception that biomass is not a practical, cost effective alternatives for space for process heating. - costs associated with inconsisitent or misapplied regulations. - Inability to demonstrate biomass to electricity technologies today to assure their full-scale availability in the future.

expanded use of biomass energy provides new opportunities to achieve a number of environmental objectives such as reducing air emissions and alleviating on landfills.

If these potential economic and environmental benefits are so achieved, a number of barriers associated with the development which must be recognized. To a great extend, maximizing the b nefits of biomass energy and minimizing the costs is a matter of timely support for and strategic investment in specific niches and applications. Table-4 shows the some of the Key opportunities and Barriers on Biomass Energy use.

The huge potential for Bio-Fuels for automobiles in India owing to widely cultivated high ethanol-yielding crops such as sugar cane, corn and wheat for effectively exploit the potential in the area of Bio-Fuels which would not only lower the country's dependence on imported oil but also enable it to address issues of trade balance. On the social front, Bio-Fuel production would have the potential to create large number of jobs, covering nearly 10% of the country's populations especially in the rural area with low investment per job and promote local farming and environment-friendliness. India is one of the largest producers of sugar cane in the world and has more than 400 distilleries producing alcohol by using molasses. It has surplus capacity for alcohol production and is also blessed with the cheapest carbon source for bio-refinery.

ECONOMIC BENEFITS

Establishment of major new Bio-Fuel industries in rural areas is likely to have substantial economic impacts. Oak Ridge National Laboratory of US. estimated that ethanol production from corn stover alone could result in $8.9 billion in industrial output and $3.8 billion in value added, creating about 76,000 permanent jobs. Another study, for switch grass production found that total US farm income could increase by $6 billion. USDA study estimated that a 100 million gallons/year (380 million liters/year) ethanol production facility would create 2,250 local jobs for a single community. The National Biodiesel Board estimates that inclusion of just 1 % Biodiesel (partly replacing sulfur as lubricity additive) in all road diesel fuel would generate demand for 300 million gallons (1.1 billion liters) of Biodiesel adding more than $ 800 million to gross farm incomes. Table-5 shows estimation of jobs from Renewable Energy, 2004.

ENVIRONMENTAL BENEFITS

Bio-Fuels, when blended with conventional fuels, reduce air pollutant emissions such as sulfur, particulates, carbon monoxide and hydrocarbons.

TABLE 2.5

ESTIMATION OF JOBS FROM RENEWABLE ENERGY, 2004

Technology	Global capacity (MW as of 2004)	Additional capacity in 2004 (MW)	Current employment in manufacturing (person-years in 2004)	Current employment in O&M (jobs)
Small hydropower	62,000	5,000	56,500	13,640
Wind Power	48,000	8,200	31,160-60,680	4,800-9,600
Biomass power	38,000	800	1,600-6,800	12,160-79,040
Geothermal	9,000	200	800-3,500	15,300
Solar PV	4,000	900	22,590*-29,097	4,000-10,000
Solar thermal	116 million 2ml	18 million 2ml	13,6056	381,150
Solar thermal	400	-	-	280
Ocean (tidal)	300	-	-	30
Total			**249,000-293,000**	**431,000-509,000**
Ethanol production	-	32 billon liters	902,000 direct jobs***	
Bio-diesel production		2.2 billion liters	31,000 direct jobs***	

Source : Global Status Report on Renewable, 2005

Ethanol and Biodiesel are also less of a hazard if they spill or leak, since they are rapidly biodegradable in water. Substituting Bio-Fuels for one gallon of gasoline or diesel saves up to 20 pounds of carbon dioxide emissions to the atmosphere, they are made from carbon' recycled' by plants instead of carbon dug out of the ground in the form of fossil fuels.

Growing perennial energy crops in place of surplus annual crops can reduce soil erosion and compaction, as permanent deep root systems develop and enrich the soil. Perennial crops need less tilling and less agrochemical inputs, so they may help to improve the quality of waterways. Their sturdy root systems and more permanent canopies offer a wider variety of habitats for birds and beneficial insects, compared with annual row crops. Levels of soil carbon may increase under perennial crops, helping top offset some fossil fuel carbon dioxide emissions. Table-6 shows CO_2 Emissions Reductions Targets, 2004. In the future, there may even be financial opportunities for farmers through rewards for good stewardship of the land in terms of "Carbon credits".

TABLE 2.6

CO_2 Emissions reductions targets, 2004.

City	Target
Adelaide, Australia	Zero net emissions by 2012 in buildings. Zero net emissions by 2020 in transport.
Calgary, Canada	6% reduction from 1990 levels for corporate and community emissions.
Freiburg, Germany	25% below 1992 levels by 2010.
Gwangju, Korea	20% below baseline levels by 2020.
The Hague, Netherlands	City Government "Co_2 neutral" by 2006; whole city "CO_2 neutral" in long term.
Portland (OR) United States	10% below 1990 levels by 2010.
Sapporo, Japan	10% below 1990 levels by 2012.
Sudbury, Canada	>30% reduction below 1990 levels.
Toronto, Canada	Municipal energy 20% below 1990 levels by 2005.
Vancouver (BC), Canada	6% below 1990 levels by 2012 and municipal energy 20% below by 2010.

Source : Global Status Report on Renewable, 2005.

POTENTIAL BENEFITS OF BIO-FUELS

The development of a major Bio-Fuels industry will create many domestic jobs in agribusiness, engineering, leading institutions, construction, fuel production and distribution. Bio-Fuels technologies also provide the potential of exports to other countries, where new markets exists for alternative fuels, either as a fuel extender or to address growing concerns about mobile source emissions.

Advances in genetic engineering and the growth and harvesting of feedstock will generate thousands of jobs and improve efficiencies in agriculture and in the lumber, pulp, and paper products industries. His production of high valued chemicals including ethers, solvents, and pharmaceutical will also create high paying jobs. Bio-Fuels will also revitalize the nation's rural economics by providing more farm jobs, increased equipment sales, fuel plant employment and other indirect employment and income benefits. Table-7 shows the potential benefits of Bio-fuels.

COLLABORATION WITH INDUSTRY

The Bio-Fuel system programme in collaborating with Industry, University, national laboratory and other researchers to accelerate the application of bio–mass technologies and their associated fuels, based on the Short-term, Mid–term and Long-term components of the strategic plan.

TABLE 2.7
POTENTIAL BENEFITS OF BIO-FUELS

Time	Bio–mass resources		Bio-Fuels		Displacement transportation fossil fuel use	Oil import saving	CO_2 Reduction
10^{15}	BTUx Tons	MM 10^{15}	BTUx BoE	MM (%)	LDV (%)	All Billions	$ Tons	MM
Ncar-Term (1994-2000)	3.5	219	1.5	259	11.6	5.8	5.9	146
Mid-Term (2000-2010)	6.0	375	3.0	518	21.4	10.4	15.2	292
Long-Term (2010-2030)	16.0	1,000	9.0	1,554	52.6	21.4	47.9	875

MM = Million
BTU = British Thermal Unit
BoE = Barrel of oil equivalent

Source: Department of Energy, US.

Short-term

The Short-term focus on processes that will lead to the commercial production of ethanol from waste and cellulose biomass, fuel additives and Biodiesel from plant oils. To meet these objectives transfferring technology from the laboratory to the marketplace and partnering with Industry is essential. In US 'The AMOCO" partnerships involves converting wastes into ethanol for immediate application. New Energy Company of US at Indiana is developing techno'logy for ethanol production from the residual starch and cellulose components in corn to enhance ethanol yield and decreasing production cost for corn dry milling operations.

Mid-term

The Mid-term focus is to continue improving the basic technology for the production of Bio-Fuels from wastes, as well as begin developing commercially produced dedicated energy crops for the production of alcohols, hydrocarbons, electricity and Biodiesel.

Long-term

The major long-term foci are the widespread use of energy crops for the production of Bio-Fuels for bulk transportation fuel markets, the development of aquatic micro algae, capable of rapid growth and high lipid (oil) content for processing as a diesel fuel and the economic production of bio–mass–derived fuels and chemicals, such as hydrogen.

RESEARCH TO MARKET

In the transportation sector, passenger cars and other light duty vehicles provide the best markets for alternative liquid fuel from biomass. In the last several years, as a niche market for blends, the demand for Bio-Fuels has been roughly on billion gallons. This demand has increased to 4.7 billion gallons by 1995 due to Clean Air Act. oxygenated fuel and reformulated gasoline programmes. Bio-Fuels in the near time will be used primarily as an oxygenate for gasoline, either directly or as an either derivative. By 2008, Bio-Fuels could supply 100% of the oxygenate market while providing additional neat fuel for a growing flexible and dedicated alternative fuel fleet. By 2030, Bio-fuels could provide over 50% of the light duty vehicle fleet requirement, primarily by using Bio-fuels in dedicated systems, as opposed to an oxygenate for gasoline. Table-8 shows that bio-fuels options for the market place.

ECONOMICS OF BIO-FUELS

Using present technologies and under current market conditions, transportation fuels from biomass are competitive with petroleum-based fuels in only very special circumstances (tax credits, facility add-ons for conversion, plant site, negative value waste feedstock, etc.). One or a combination of three things must happen to make Bio-Fuels reach its market potential:

TABLE 2.8
Bio Fuels options for the market place

Time Frame	Bio-fuels	Market Applications
Near Term (1994–2000)	Oxygenates Octane derivatives Fuel extenders Biodiesel (Terrestrial) Electricity	Passenger cars and light duty vehicles, Urban bruses with 25% reduction in particulars
Mid-term (2000–2010)	Ethanol Methanol Biodiesel (Terrestrial) Electricity	Flexible/dedicated vehicle Electric and Hybrid vehicle Expanded use of Bio-Fuels in mass transit
Long Term (2010–2030)	Ethanol Methanol Bio-diesel (Aquatic) Electricity Hydrogen from ethanol and methanol technologies	Flexible/dedicated vehicles Electric and Hybrid Vehicles Ful gamut of heavy, middle light duty vehicles Full cell vehicles

Source : Department of Energy US.

(1) Improvements in the technologies for both biomass and converting it to transportation fuels;

(2) Price increases in petroleum-based transportation fuels; and

(3) Internalization of the true benefits from biomass fuels. The benefits that are not currently reflected in market prices are.

the environmental benefits, especially those related to CO_2 and

the benefits from reduced oil imports.

Regarding technology improvements, the prospects are excellent that the research directions presently being pursued will result in transportation fuels from biomass at a cost competitive with petroleum-based fuels from oil at $ 20–25/barel. Although the future of world oil prices is very uncertain, most projections point to $20–25 per barrel oil very early in the 21st century. The question of internalizing costs is a public policy matter that the Bio-Fuels programme cannot address, but it does seem clear that neither the global climate change issue not the oil-import issue are going to be addressed effectively without explicit recognition of externalities.

RESOURCE BASE BIO-FUELS

Bio-Fuels programme aspiration is to foster the creation of a major Bio-Fuels industry, an industry the provides a significant fraction of the nation's transportation fuels. Biodiesel markets had developed in seven primary countries (Austria, Belgium, France, Germany, Italy, Indonesia and Malaysia. Germany has been the biggest Biodiesel producer with about 2 billion liters capacity on line. France, Italy and the UK are the next largest producers. In 2001, Government of India launched three pilot projects in different states where supplying 5% ethanol-doped-petrol to the retail outlets under their respective areas. In 2003, the Government resolved that 5% ethanol blended petrol would be supplied in the nine States and four Union Territories. For Biodiesel, a National programme aims to produce enough oil seeds for the production of Biodiesel in sufficient quantities to enable its blending with diesel to the extent of 20%. Pilot projects and analysis of feedstock collection and plantation were on going.

International Bio-Fuels trade has expended rapidly during the past few years. World ethanol trade volume hit a record level in 2004, recently nearly 4.9 billion liters, compared with 3.7 billion liters in 2003. Brazil is the biggest exporter accounting for about half of international shipments of ethanol during 2004. According to the World Energy Report, 2004, it is projected for the global market is from 60-75 billion liters per year by 2010. India has immense potential to produced ethanol and methanol from its agricultural residues with massive plantation programme in the waste land area. Table-2.9 shows the waste land scenario in India.

BIODIESEL MARKETS IN INDIA

D. I. Mohan Bio Oils Ltd., a joint venture between the Chennai-based Mohan Breweries and D I Oil Mill of UK will commercially launch the Biodiesel extracted from Jatropha, an oil bearing plant in January 2006. A Biodiesel extraction plant will soon be commissioned near Chennai with an investment of Rs. 150 million with a capacity to process 8000 tons of oil per annum. The Andhra Pradesh Government has allotted 10 districts to the company to create Jatropha nurseries.

FUTURE BIO-FUEL INDUSTRY

The current Bio-Fuels industry involves a broad spectrum of stockholders ranging from the corn/grain to ethanol, pulp/ paper, agricultural and forestry industries, as well as oil companies. In addition to the current participations, other stockholders such as fermentation equipments producers, who manufacture the needed conversion equipment for Bio-fuels and wholesale fuel distributors who will develop its accompanying infrastructure, will all apply an important role. In general, the future industry will encompass those participants who have a technical and financial interest in the development of transportation fuels on an industrial scale.

TABLE 2.9

Waste land scenario in India (as on 1984 in lac hectares)

Sl. No.	State/UT	Degraded Forest area lands	Saline & Alkaline	Eroded area by wind	Eroded area by water	Total
1.	Andra Pradesh	7.34	2.4	-	74.42	114.16
2.	Assam	7.94	2.4	-	9.35	17.30
3.	Bihar	15.62	0.04	-	38.92	54.58
4.	Gujarat	6.83	12.14	-	52.35	78.36
5.	Hariyana	0.75	5.26	7.04	2.04	24.78
6.	Himachal Pradesh	2.24	-	15.99	14.24	19.58
7.	Jammu and Kashmir	10.34	-	-	5.31	15.65
8.	Karnataka	20.43	4.04	-	67.18	91.65
9.	Kerala	2.25	0.16	-	10.37	12.79
10.	Madhya Pradesh	71.95	2.42	-	127.05	201.42
11.	Maharashtra	28.41	5.34	-	110.26	144.01
12.	Manipur	14.25	-	-	0.14	14.38
13.	Meghalaya	110.3	-	-	8.15	19.18
14.	Nagaland	8.78	-	-	5.08	13.86
15.	Orissa	30.27	4.04	-	27.53	63.84
16.	Punjab	0.79	6.88	-	4.63	12.90
17.	Rajasthan	19.33	7.28	106.23	66.59	199.34
18.	Sikkim	1.50	-	-	1.31	2.81
19.	Tamil Nadu	10.09	0.04	-	33.88	44.01
20.	Tripura	8.65	-	-	1.08	9.73
21.	Uttar Pradesh	14.26	12.95	-	53.4	80.61
22.	West Bengal	30.59	8.80	-	13.27	25.36
23.	UTs	27.15	0.16	-	8.73	36.04
	TOTAL	**358.89**	**71.65**	**129.26**	**736.00**	**1295.74**

Source : Developing India's Westelands, Ministry of Environment and Forests, GOI.

3

Technology of Bio-Fuels

INTRODUCTION

Bio–fuels has received attention because of their environment-friendliness. Biofuels are able to close the carbon-loop in a very short time. For a country like India bio-fuels have special significance due to energy security, contribution to rural economy and employment generation. For effective utilization of the vast bio–fuel potential in India, focus must be given to development of advanced technologies for biofuel production as well as their applications.

TABLE 3.1

Conventional bio-fuels, the feedstocks they use, and the production processes.

Bio-fuel	Bio–mass-Feedstock	Production Process
Straight Vegetable Oil (SVO)	Oil seeds	Cold Pressing extraction, refining.
Biodiesel from seeds	Oil seeds	Transesterification
Biodiesel from waste (oils/fats)	Waste cooking/ frying oil	Refining, transesterification
Conventional bioethanol	Sugar, Sugar beets,	Fermentation, distillation
Conventional bioethanol	Starch crops	Hydrolysis, fermentation, distillation
Bio-ETBE	Bioethanol	Chemical syntehsis
Biogas	(Wet) biomass	Digestion
Hydrogen from biogas	Biogas	Steam reforming /Wgs, CO_2 removal

TABLE 3.2

Advanced Bio–fuels

Bio-fuel	Bio–mass-Feedstock	Production process
Fischer Tropsch diesel	Lignocellulosic material	Gasification, water gas shift, synthesis, hydrocraking
Bio-metanol	Lignocellulosic material	Gasification, water gas shift, synthesis
Bio-MTBE	Lignocellulosic material	Synthesis methanol+isobutyl
Bio-DME	Lignocellulosic material	Gasification, water gas, synthetis
Alcohol from syngas	Lignocellulosic material	Gasification, synthesis ("Ecalene")
SNG from syngas	Lignocellulosic material	Gasification, water gas shift, synthesis, CO_2/H_2O removal
Hydrogen from syngas	Lignocellulosic material	Wet bio–mass materials
Bioethanol	Lignocellulosic material	Advanced hydrolysis, fermentation
HTU-diesel	Lignocellulosic material	HTU, HDU, refining
Pyrolysis diesel material	Lignocellulosic material	Pyrolysis HDC refining Super/subcritical gasification
SNG from wet	Wet Biomass materials	
Bio-hydrogen	Wet biomass materials	Supercritical gasification, or Dark/photofermentation

[HTU : Hydrothermal upgrading; HDO : Catalytic hydro de-oxygenation]

ADVANCED BIO-FUEL TECHNOLOGIES

Bioethanol from lignocellulosic bio–mass: High cost of sugar or starch based bioethanol has driven efforts towards ethanol from lignocellulosic biomass. These technologies are in the phase of R & D, pre-pilot and pilot phase. Production of bioethanol can be through two different routes–hydrolysis and fermentation; and gasification or syngas route. Lignocellulosic biomass contains cellulose, hemicellulose and lignin. In the bioethanol production from lignocellulosic feedstock as against from conventional feedstocks, there are major differences in the pretreatment, and hydrolysis section, as well as in the fermentation of C5 sugars.

Pretreatment technologies: Pretreatment of biomass is required for increasing the effectiveness of hydrolysis or fermentation methods. Pretreatment research is focused on developing processes that would result in reduced bioconversion lime, lower cellulose enzyme usage, and/ or higher ethanol yields. Current pretreatment researches are directed towards approaches that primarily support the subsequent enzymatic hydrolysis of treated biomass. The main idea has shifted to producing a solid sut·strate that is accessible to action of cellulase enzymes, at the same time preventing any loss of hemicellulose.

There are broadly four categories of pretreatment technologies:

1. Physical Pretreatment: This process includes Mechanical and Pyrolysis.
2. Physico-chemical Pretreatment: Includes Steam explosion, Ammonia fibre explosion, CO_2 explosion.
3. Chemical Pretreatment: This involves Ozonolysis, Acid hydrolysis (dilute acid), Alkaline hydrolysis, Oxidative delignification, Organosolv process.
4. Biological pretreatment

The Steam explosion process is considered as most effective for hard wood and agricultural residues because of its low energy requirement compared to mechanical comminution. Also, there is no recycling and environmental costs.

Hydrolysis: Hydrolysis is catalyzed by dilute acid, concentrated acid or enzymes (cellulase). In the long term enzymatic hydrolysis is viewed as the most cost-effective ethanol production. It has advantages like mild conditions, high yields and low maintenance costs due to low corrosion problems. Enzymatic hydrolysis of sugar oligomers using cellulase enzymes to fermentable monomeric sugars, mainly glucose (C6) and xylose (C5) is called saccharification. To avoid the undesirable effect in the increase of amount of sugars during the saccharification of lignocellulosic biomass, simultaneous saccharification and fermentation technology is being developed. Research efforts are directed towards finding suitable thermotolerant micro–organisms for this process.

Fermentation and distillation: The conversion of glucose has been known for at least 6000 years. The conversion of xylose (pentose) is more complicated and research has only lately obtained success. This issue is still an important R & D field to increase ethanol yield and thereby enhance chances of commercialization. Utilization of residue lignin is also an important aspect.

Gasification or Syngas route: Partial oxidation of biomass by addition of sub-stoichiometric oxygen at high temperature produce a mixture of carbon monoxide, carbon dioxide, methane, hydrogen, water and nitrogen. Gas cleaning needs to be developed further in gasification technology.

Some efforts in bioethanol production from lignocellulosic ethanol:

Bioengineering Resources Inc. (BRI), Arkansas, USA : Pilot plant for fermentation of syngas operating since four years. BRI will begin the construction of their first commercial plants.

Ethanol Teknik (ETEK), Ornskoldsvik, Sweden: Hydrolysis and fermentation of softwood residues. Producing ethanol since spring 2005.

Fuel Cell Energy, Lakewood, CO : Pilot plant for thermo chemical gasification with catalytic conversion.

Iogen, Ottawa, ON, Canada : Enzymatic hydrolysis and fermentation of straw. Steam explosion pretreatment. Pilot plant operated since 1985.

National Renewable Energy Laboratory (NREL), Colorado, USA : Three different pretreatment technologies for different feedstocks may be adjusted as per requirement–commercial dilute acid, counter current shrinking bed and steam explosion.

BC International, Louisiana: Two stage hydrolysis C5 sugars with metabolic engineering of microorganisms capable of fermenting all sugars from all types of cellulosic biomass. Technology established in two pilot plants, commercial plant under development.

Pure Vision Technology, Ft. Lupton, CO: Enzymatic hydrolysis of wood. The technology is proven at bench scale level. Constructing the pilot plant.

Vogelbusch Gmbh, Austria: Starch, sugarcane are used as feedstocks. Molecular sieve dehydration technology adapted to replace distillation.

The Fisher Tropsch (Ff) Process

In the FT route gasification of the biomass is followed by synthesis process. Depending on the composition of syngas and the process control parameters, the final products are kerosene, petrol and diesel like products. Liquid fuels are produced from syngas and the products are long chain paraffins, free of sulfur. FT processes using natural gas or coal as feedstocks are relatively well established technologies. Shell (natural gas feedstocks) and Sasol (coal feed stock) have commercialized the FT technology. A number of pilot and demonstration projects with woody biomass feedstocks are at various stages of development. Daimler Chrysler and Volkswagen are involved in production projects and demonstration of BTL fuels.

Adaptation of FT synthesis to syngas of different origins is focused on purity, cleanliness, and CO/H_2 ratio of the product gas.

Two main characteristics of FT synthesis are. unavoidable production of a wide range of hydrocarbon products (olefins, paraffins and oxygenated products) and liberation of heat from the highly exothermic synthesis reaction. The catalysts used in the FT synthesis are intrinsically very sensitive to small amount of poison. For the gasification stage, the important issues are optimization of operating pressure and minimization of 0xygen consumption and high syngas yield by maximum carbon conversion and low residual concentration of hydrocarbons in the syngas.

Energy Research Centre of the Netherlands (ECN) has demonstrated an integrated system of gasification of willow, cleaning of bio-syngas to FT specifications and operating a small FT unit on the cleaned gas. Some other gasification plants are Güssing-Chore, Värnam-Sweden and Choren, Freiberg.

Bio-oil (pyrolysis oil)

Biomass is first dried and grinded and then pyrolysed. Very rapid flash pyrolysis process is most relevant for bio- oil production. In this process the production of gaseous components is maximized and a liquid fuel is produced by cooling these gases. Fast reactors for bio-oil production are still at an early stage of development at pilot/demonstration phase. The current bottleneck of pyrolysis technologies concern upscaling the reactors and meeting the desired oil quality through condensation and treatment of the desired tar fraction, product cleaning and modification, and upgrading techniques.

Bio-oil is also important source for production of fine chemicals and R & D efforts have been directed towards that.

Hydro Thermal Upgrading (HTU)

The biomass is decomposed in water to produce a crude-oil like liquid called "bio-crude". The dry or wet biomass reacts with liquid water at a high pressure and a relatively low temperature. This process can be used for the conversion of a broad range of biomass feedstocks, including municipal solid wastes and agricultural wastes. The biomass need not be dried first-very wet mixtures with 10–30% organic materials are a suitable feedstock. The biocrude can be separated into light and heavy biocrude.

Research in this area concentrates on complex chemical properties of the reactions and the testing of several feedstock types. Other critical aspects are the introduction of the feed, the heating of the reactants and the treating of the waste water. Best process conditions for the Hydro-De-Oxygenation are still unknown. So far the technology has been proven at experimental level by Shell.

The HTU technology currently exists in pilot scale in Appledoom. The conversion process has not been demonstrated for all feedstocks yet. A demonstration plant of 3000 T per annum is being built.

Bio–methanol

Bio-methanol can be produced by fermentation or from the syngas. Development of catalysts with higher methanol producing capacity at lower temperature and pressure required.

Dimethyl ether (DME)

DME can be produced directly from synthesis gas, a mixture of CO and H_2. The technology for producing DME from biomass as a raw material is still in the development phase.

Bio-butanol

Bio-butanol can be produced by fermenting sugar just as ethanol, due to its higher energy density (20 per cent higher energy density than ethanol closer to gasoline). It has a greater energy content (125,000) as compared to bio-ethanol (101,000).

The companies Du-Pont -BP are working with British Sugar, part of Associated British Foods, to convert the country's first bioethanol fermentation plant at Wissington in Norfolk, to produce biobutanol with sugar beet as the feedstock.

Biomass to Hydrogen

Hydrogen can be produced from biomass through syngas or fermentation route. The fermentation process seems to be a long term prospect since this process does not produce CO_2. However the major bottlenecks are lower rate of hydrogen production and its low yield by this process.

Biorefinery concept

Research is also ongoing towards the so-called 'biorefinery' concept, with integrated facilities for multiple fuels and chemicals from biomass feedstocks. The benefit of biomass refineries is that the primary product selling price can be lowered significantly by co–producing higher value, lower volume products. Also, it provides economies of scale that reduce the cost of making such products below levels that can be achieved through dedicated production.

APPLICATIONS

The application of conventional biofuels like bioethanol and biodiesel have been established in different countries.

FT diesel

FT diesel is similar to mineral oil diesel with regard to its energy content, density, viscosity and flash point and is at liquid phase at ambient conditions. The fuel has even some more favourable characteristics like higher cetane number and low aromatic content. This means that particles and NOx exhaust emissions are lower. FT diesel is free from sulfur, thus sulfur emission is avoided. As FT diesel is completely miscible with conventional diesel, it can be applied in current diesel engines and the existing diesel distribution infrastructure almost without any modifications.

Methanol

Methanol has a high octane rating (RON over 100 and low cetane number - 5, compared to 50 of fossil diesel). Up to 15% methanol can be used in regular spark-ignition engines with existing infrastructure for petrol without any adaptations.

Bio butanol

Biobutanol has certain advantages over bioethanol– in particular it is compatible with existing fuel supply and distribution systems since it has low vapour pressure and is tolerant to contamination by water. It can be blended in higher concentrations without requiring vehicle modifications, has better fuel efficiency characteristics and does not require modifications to storage tanks or retail station pumps. It also compliments ethanol blends, improving ethanol vapour pressure and water absorption, which has prohibited wider adoption of ethanol.

Di-methyl ether

Oi-methyl ether (DME) can only be used in adapted diesel engines using fuel storage technology and infrastructure similar to or modified from that of LPG. It can also be used as an ignition improver in methanol engines. It is suitable as a diesel engine fuel on account of its low self-ignition temperature and appropriate cetane number. Another favourable quality of DME is that it burns without producing soot. Moreover, engines using DME produce less noise. A disadvantage is that the energy content of DME is lower than that of diesel.

Bio-MTBE (Methyl Tertiary Butyl Ether)

Bio-MTBE can be produced from biomethanol and isobutylene. MTBE is an octane enhancer and formerly used in petrol, however, it is hazardous and several studies detected ground water contamination by MTBE throughout the USA.

Bio-oil

Bio-oil can be applied as a fuel for co-firing in an electric power plant or as a raw material for synthesis gas production, where it is gasified with enriched air and pure oxygen. If desired it can then be converted to automotive fuels such as methanol or Fischer–Tropsch fuels. For direct application as a diesel substitute in vehicle engines, bio-oil needs to be upgraded (by using catalytic upgrading or hydrogenation processes) and stabilized first. The technology is still in the laboratory/pilot phase. Technical barriers include removal of contaminants from the product and acidity of the oil which causes corrosion of the engine. Bio-oil contains less nitrogen than fossil fuels and almost no metal and sulfur compounds. It can be stored, pumped and transported like petroleum based products.

Bio-crude from HTU

The heavy bio-crude can be used for co-firing in coal based electric power plants and as naphtha for production of chemicals. The clean lighter fraction can be used for production of diesel fuel components. For converting bio-crude into a transportation fuel of diesel quality, it must be upgraded by means of hydrogenation techniques. Requirement of large amount of hydrogen is energetically and economically unfavourable aspect. Removal of contaminants from the product still needs to be resolved.

Bio fuel and Advanced Technologies

The use of bio–fuels for transport is still rather low compared with petroleum in almost all countries. Main reason has been the high production costs resulting in low market acceptance. However production costs have decreased somewhat during the past decade and will probably continue to drop in future.

Recently use of bio–fuels in advanced engine technologies like Homogenous Charge Compression Ignition (HCCI) engines have received attention. HCCI uses a premixed fuel and air mixture like a gasoline engine, but the mixture is ignited through compression. This technology promises low emissions and high efficiency. An HCCI engine precisely controls the amount and distribution of fuel in each cylinder to allow rising the heat of compression to ignite the fuel/ air mixture instead of relying on a conventional sparkplug to do the job.

There are some efforts to utilize specific properties of alcohol fuels for HCCI combustion. One example is to use flash boiling of methanol as a means of improving mixture preparation and combustion. The potential of using DME, mixtures of DME and methanol or reformate from DME and / or methanol in HCCI engines has been investigated. DME has a very high cetane number and methanol and reformate of DME and methanol has very low cetane number. By using two fuels, the problems of controlling the combustion in a HCCI engine may perhaps be overcome. Japanese universities and institutes tried to exploit this idea.

FT-BTL fuels could also form a key element in the development of HCCI engines.

Spark-Ignited Direct Injection engine can provide optimum combustion for ethanol blended petrol and improves cold start performance. Flexi-fuel vehicles, that can run at different compression ratios, can utilize different fuels like gasoline and ethanol. This technology will enhance the use of ethanol in IC engines.

Certain studies have shown higher NOx emissions from use of biodiesel in IC engine. Studies have suggested that retarding of the injection timing or addition of heavy alkylate could reduce the NOx emissions.

INDIAN PRIORITIES

India is deficient in edible oils and at the same time has vast area of wasteland where tree-born oils like Jatropha, Karnja, Neem etc. may be cultivated. A National Mission on Biodiesel has already been initiated by the Planning Commission. There are certain issues for biodiesel which need for R & D efforts. These include oxidation stability, toxicity studies, efficient use of by-products, engine modifications required for higher blends of biodiesel, additive response etc. In the trans-esterification process development of continuous process, use of heterogeneous catalysts, development of lipase catalysts for trans-esterification are important.

The Government of India has mandated the blending of 5% ethanol in petrol in 10 states and 3 Union Territories since 2004. In the Indian context, bioethanol from lignocellulosic biomass has special significance. The crops residues such as rice straw, bagasse etc, are not currently used to derive desired economic and environmental benefits and thus they could be important resource bases for bioethanol production.

The surplus sugar production in the country makes sugar–ethanol co-product complexes relevant. Sweet sorghum to ethanol production. Molecular sieve dehydration technology, effective pretreatment processes including enzymes for pretreatment and conversion processes.

Use of SVO will have potential impact on rural economy. Although it has been observed worldwide that using SVO in automobiles have difficult challenges. Some of the problems are the high viscosity, acid composition, free fatty acid content, and gum formation due to oxidation and polymerization during storage and combustion, carbon deposits and lubricating oil thickening. However, there is potential for use of SVO in agricultural pumps, stationary engines etc. At the same time, fundamental work on spray, injection and combustion aspects along with other engine and fuel system modifications may bring out suitable technology for use of SVO in automobile engines. Development of flexi-fuel vehicles is also required for higher utilization of ethanol.

4

Ethanol–A Suitable Fuel

INTRODUCTION

With a threat of global warming and energy crises in today's environment the need for clean, "green" fuels is quickly becoming a necessity. Ethanol is an environmentally friendly fuel, and with a 90% blend of Ethanol with no-lead gas it is an approved fuel in Canada. Ethanol is a liquid Ethanol that is manufactured by the fermentation of grains such as corn, wheat and barley. It is a high octane fuel with high oxygen content and when blended properly in gasoline produces a cleaner and more complete combustion. The effect of adding Ethanol to gasoline on environmental quality includes reducing air toxins, reduced carbon monoxide, reduced ozone formation, and the potential to reduce net carbon dioxided emissions to the atmosphere.

Ethanol is an Ethanol-based alternative fuel produced by fermenting and distilling starch crops that have been converted into simple sugars. Ethanol can also be produced from "cellulosic biomass" such as trees and grasses and is called Bio–Ethanol. Ethanol is most commonly used to increase octane and improve the emissions quality of gasoline. Ethanol is blended with gasoline to form an E90 blend (90% Ethanol and 5% gasoline), but it can be used in higher concentrations such as E95 or E100.

OBJECTIVE

The main objective of our project is to convert existing single cylinder petrol engine (Enfield Engine 350cc) in to Ethanol fueled vehicle. Conducting and comparing the performance test results of petrol and Ethanol Fuel (E75 and E90).

DESIGN CHALLENGES

The starting performance of gasoline depends on its forerunning point and the temperature at which 10% distillate is released. The starting performance of the blend fuel mainly depends on the performance of Ethanol vapourization.

The latent heat of Ethanol is about 216 Kcal/Kg, while that of gasoline is 80 Kcal/Kg. Besides, the latent heat of Ethanol also increases with the proportion of water in Ethanol. This makes Ethanol absorb much more heat than gasoline does during vapourization, thus reducing the admission temperature in engine, and causing difficulty in starting the engine. The specific heat of Ethanol is (0.65 Kcal/Kg°C) at 20°C, which is higher than fact of gasoline (0.58 Kcal/Kg°C). It increases too with the proportion of water in Ethanol, leading to low temperature at the end of compression stroke and making it difficult for the engine to start. This means that the starting performance of blend fuel is poor.

METHODOLOGY

a. Modified compression Ratio

For Ethanol, C.R. (Compression Ratio) has to be increases.

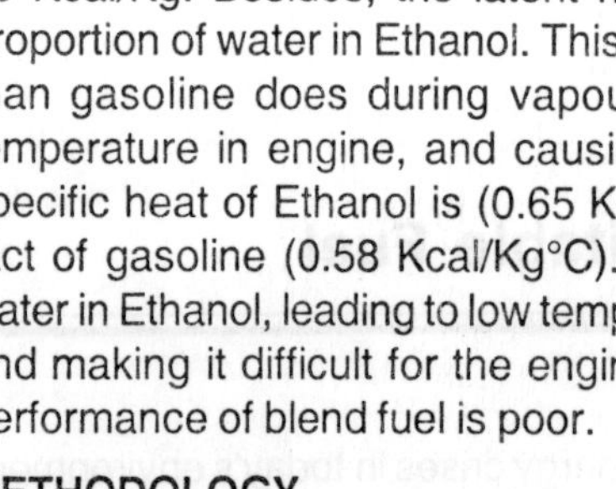

Fig. 4.1 Cylinder Head.

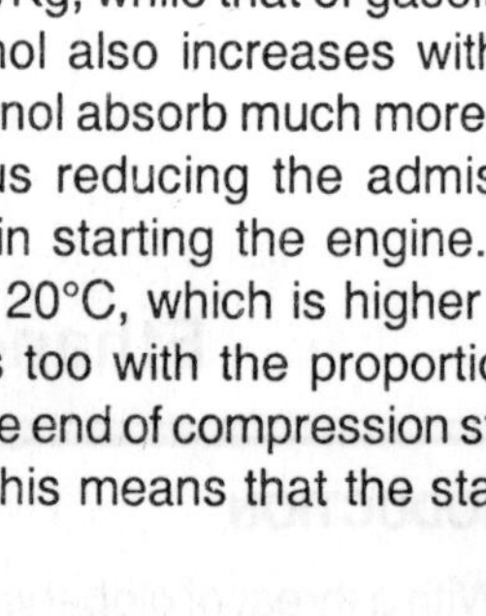

Fig. 4.2 Cylinder Block.

One way of increasing compression ratio slightly is by "milling" (planing) the surface of the cylinder head and/or block. The cylinder head and the cylinder of Bullet Engine are shown above. The blue shaded portion of cylinder head and green shaded portion of cylinder are machined by 2 mm each. Thus reduces clearance volume. Clearance volume is calculated as

$V_c = 54\ cm^3$. Now CR becomes, CR = (Vc+Vs)/Vs

= (54 + 346)/54

= 7.5:1

Hence CR is increased from 6.5:1 to 7.5:1. Beyond 2 mm it's not possible to increase CR in bullet engine.

b. Advanced ignition timing

In Bullet Engine ignition timing is advanced by 4° before TDC (top dead centre). Beyond 4° the engine gets overheated. But for Ethanol ignition timing can be advanced by 22 degree before TDC. Care should be taken while adjust the timing, since a 22 deg, advance might be excessive. It;s not safe to be just short of detonation, since inaudible knocking also can damage the engine. The best procedure is to set the distributor timing at least two degrees retarded from the point of detonation.

Fig. 4.3 Ignition Timing Wheel.

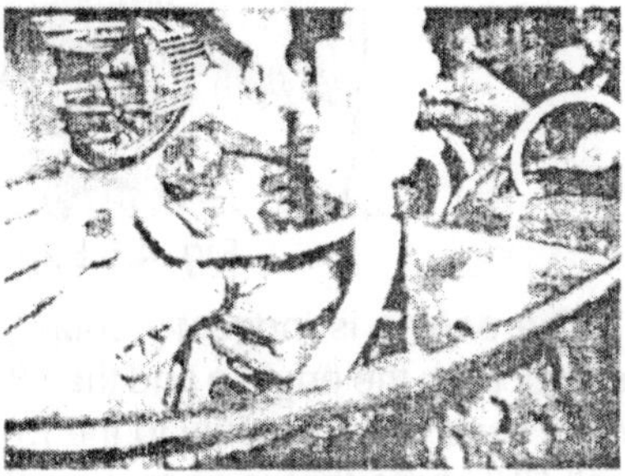

Fig. 4.4. Preheating Coil Setup.

c. Fuel preheating

In extremely cold climates, it may be ncecssary to preheat Ethanol fuel before it enters the carburetor float bowl. A fuel heater is fabricated in a matter of minutes by winding a section of copper around cylinder by head, and solder it in position if possible.

Initially bullet engine is started with petrol. As the engine reaches the operating temperature, the hot coil wounded around the cylinder head, supplies the heat to the container where Ethanol is stored.

d. Increasing carburettor jet size.

In bullet engine is jet size is 90 means 0.9 mm and it is increased to 105 means 1.05 mm. It is available as a standard in market. Or else multiply the jet sizes by the conversion factor. Often the jets will not be available as standard one in market, and it has to be drilled out the old jets.

EXPERIMENTAL SETUP

This experimental setup is made to conduct performance test for petrol and Ethanol blended petrol with various properties as follows,

- 75% Ethanol and 25% Petrol
- 90% Ethanol and 10% Petrol

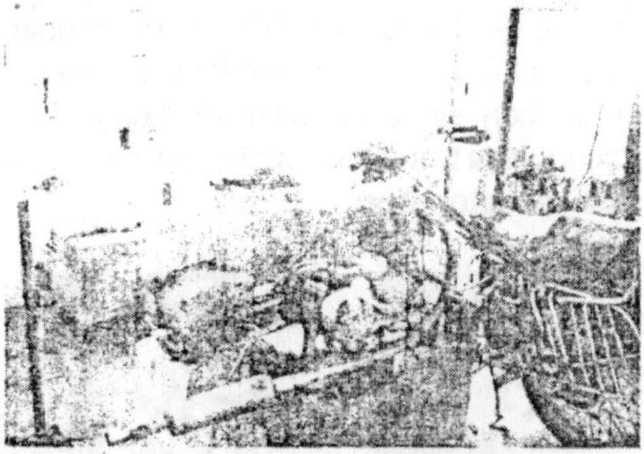

Fig. 4.5 Experimental Setup.

The engine is indirectly coupled with the alternator using chain drive method. Both the engline and the Alternator are rigidly fixed on the bed. Fuel tank is used to supply fuel to the Engine. The fuel is supplied by means of small PVC tube that is shown in the Figure. Burette is provided so as to measure the fuel consumed by the engine for a certain amount of time. In this case fuel consumption is measured for 5 cm rise in the burrette.

There is a separate loading device available which is used for loading the Engine. The type of loading done is water rheostat loading. Voltmeter and ammeter are used for calculating the input power and the brake power of the Engine. Initial spark is given to the Engine by means of a battery.

BULLET ENGINE SPECIFICATIONS

No. of cylinder	-	One
Engine Types	-	4 Stroke Petrol
Bore	-	70mm
Stroke Length	-	70mm
Displacement Volume-	-	350 CC
Engine Speed	-	5600 RPM
BHP	-	18 BHP
Valve Types	-	Over Head Valve
Jet Size	-	90 (.9mm)
Compression Ratio	-	6.5:1

RESULTS AND DISCUSSIONS

a. Performance test for petrol

TABLE 4.1
Measurement using petrol.

S. No.	Voltage (Volts)	Current (AMPS)	Time (Sec.)	Engine Speed (RPM)
1	110	0	12	1634
2.	80	3	14	1212
3.	70	3.5	17	1186
4.	65	4	19	1076

TABLE 4.2
Performance results.

S. No.	Brake power (KW)	Fuel consumption (Kg/Sec.) *10-4	BMEP BAR	SFC (Kg/KW/Hr)	Thermal Efficiency
1.	0	2.958	0	0	0
2.	0.37	2.536	1.45	2.48	14
3.	0.38	2.086	1.84	1.98	17
1.	0.40	1.868	2.39	1.68	20

Graph 4.1 shows the variation of Brake Power with SFC. As SFC increases Brake Power also increases, after certain stage SFC starts falling whereas Brake Power increases.

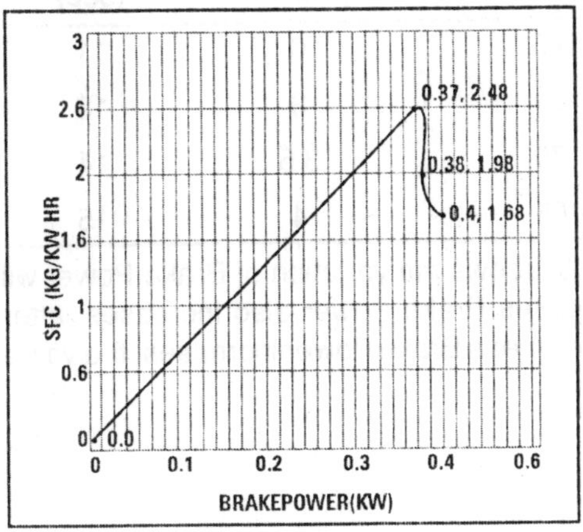

Fig. 4.1 Brake Power vs SEC.

Graph-4.2, shows the variation of Brake Power with thermal efficiency. As Thermal efficiency increases, Brake Power also starts increasing steeply. After a certain range, there is a sudden increase in Thermal efficiency with fewer increases in Brake Power.

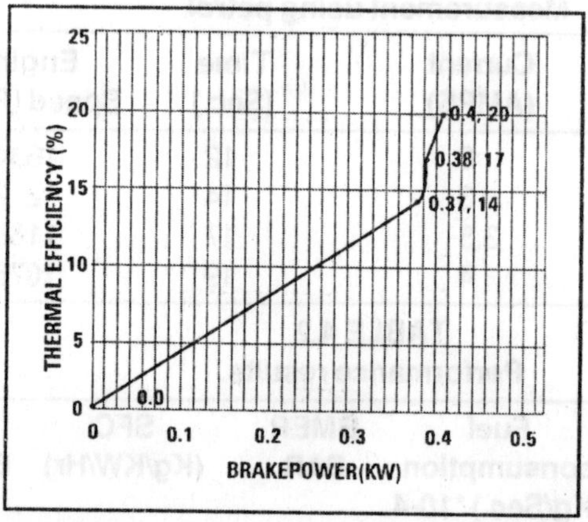

Fig. 4.2 Brake Power vs Thermal efficiency.

b. Performance test for e75 (ethanol 75% & 25% gasoline)

TABLE 4.3

Measurement using E75

S. no.	Voltage (Volts)	Current (AMPS)	Time (5cc)	Engine Speed (RRM)
1.	120	0	11	1402
2.	80	3	13	1148
3.	70	3.5	14	1108
4.	65	4	15	972

Graph-4.3, shows the variation of Brake Power with SFC for E75 fuel, As SFC increases Brake Power also increases, after certain stage SFC starts falling whereas Brake Power increases, the values are more than that of gasoline.

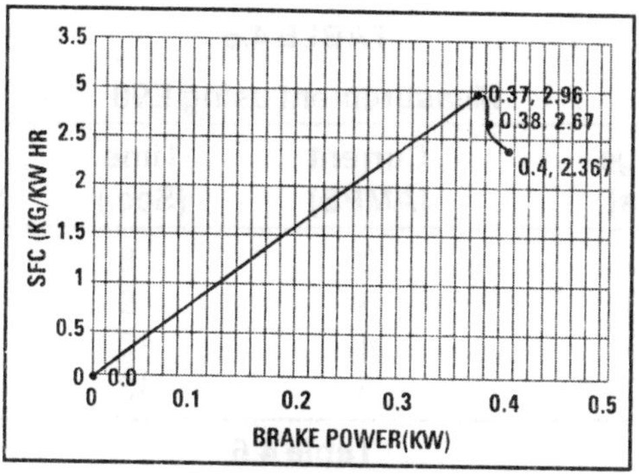

Graph 4.3 : Brake power vs SFC.

Table 4.4
Performance results of E75

S. No.	Brake Power (Kw)	Fuel Consumption (Kg/Sec.) *10-4	BMEP BAR	SFC (Kg/Kw/Hr)	Thermal Efficiency (%)
1	0	3.590	0	∝	0
2.	0.37	3.038	1.27	2.96	16
3.	0.38	2.830	1.46	2.67	18
4.	0.40	2.630	1.87	2.37	20

Graph 4.4, shows the variation of Brake power with Thermal efficiency for E75. As Thermal efficiency increaes, brake power also starts increasing as similar to gasoline.

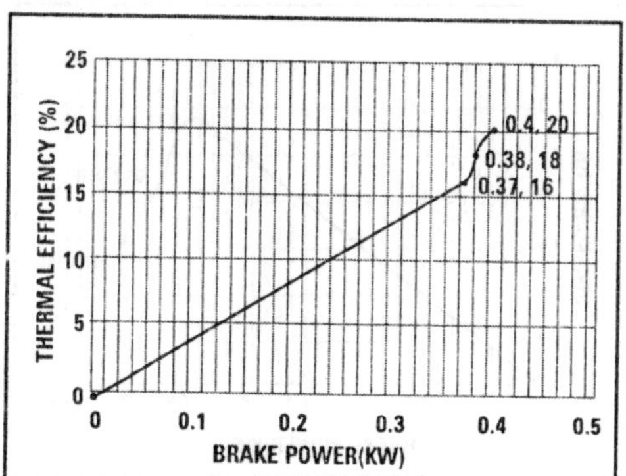

Fig. 4.4 Brake Power vs Thermal Efficiency

TABLE 4.5

Measurement using E90

S. No.	Voltage (Volts)	Current (AMPS)	Time (Sec.)	Engine Speed (RRM)
1.	140	0	8	1770
2.	120	3	9	1702
3.	100	4	10	1560
4.	90	5	13	1194

Table 4.6

Performance results of E90

S. No.	Brake Power (Kw)	Fuel Consumption (Kg/Sec.) *10-4	BMEP BAR	SFC (Kg/Kw/Hr)	Thermal Efficiency (%)
1.	0	4.938	0	∝	0
2.	0.55	4.389	0.89	2.87	18
3.	0.62	3.95	1.21	2.29	23
4.	0.69	3.038	2.28	1.585	33

Graph-4.5, shows the variation of Brake power with SFC for E90 fuel. As SFC increases Brake Power also increases, after certain stage SFC starts falling whereas Break Power increases, the values are more than that of gasoline and E75.

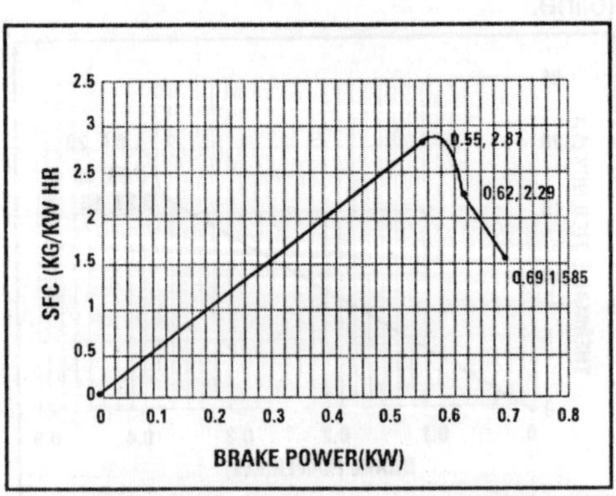

Graph 4.5 : Brake Power vs SFC.

Graph-4.6, shows the variation of Brake Power with thermal efficiency for E90. As Thermal efficiency increases, Breake Power also starts increases as similar to gasoline. And it is much more efficiency than both gasoline and E75.

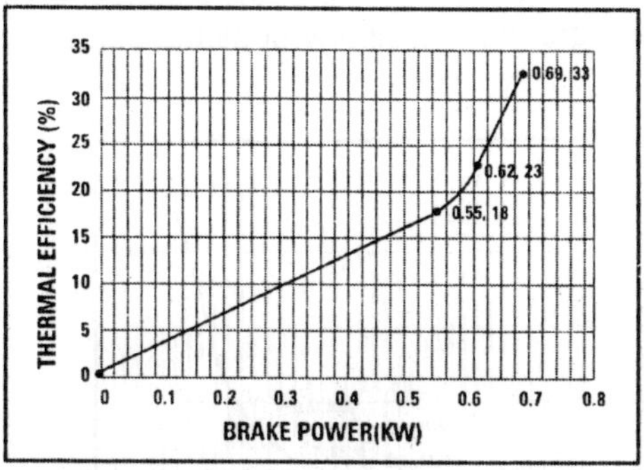

Graph 4.6 : Brake Power vs Thermal Efficiency.

Comparison Gasoline Vs E75 Vs E90

Here all the three combinations are compared, the efficiencies of Gasoline, E75 and E95 are compared and plotted to slow clearly the variations among them and from these graphs it is clearly depicted that E90 is efficient than E75 and Gasoline.

Graph-4.7, shows the variation of Brake Power with SFC for Gasoline, E75 and E90 fuel. As SFC increases Brake Power also increases, after certain stage SFC starts falling whereas Brake Power increases, the curves shows that E90 is much efficient than the other two.

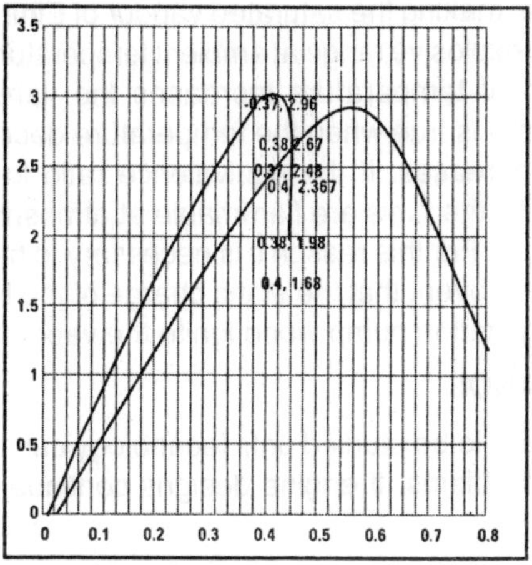

Graph 4.7 : Brake Power vs SFC

Graph-4.8 shows the variation of Brake Power with Thermal Efficiency for Gasoline, E75 and E90 fuel. As Thermal Efficiency increases, Brake Power also starts increases as similar to gasoline. the efficiencies of Gasoline, E75 and E95 compared and plotted to show clearly the variations among them and form these graphs it is clearly depicted that E90 is efficient than E75 and Gasoline.

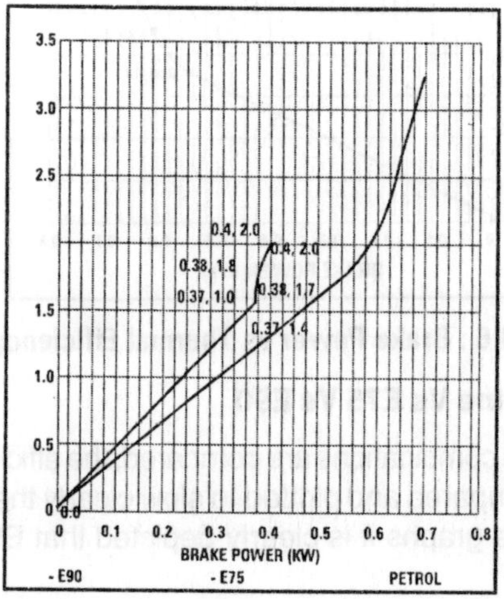

Graph 4.8 : Brake Power vs Thermal Efficiency

SAFETY OF E90

Successful conversion of Ethanol vehicle will incorporate the safety concerns associated with Ethanol. Ethanol's have much wider flammability limits than gasoline, making the saturated vapour of Ethanol in a fuel tank on a vehicle within the explosive range at ambient temperature. The equivalence ratio is a function of temperature increases the flammability limit also increases. The same is true when the temperature deceases and the Reid vapour pressure increases. If the equivalence ratio fo these varpours is between 0.6 and 2.5 the fuels are flammable at atmospheric pressure and ambient temperature. For this reason it is necessary to have flame arrestors in fuel fill tubes in the event that the static charge of the fuel travelling to the tank from the filling station pump world ignite the vapours in the tank.

FUTURE OF ETHANOL

E90 will continue to be studied until technology can solve its emissions and cold starting problems. If engine designs continue to improve overall efficiency, E90 powered engines may soon be able to produce fuel mileage that is comparable to today's E10 standards. Mileage, performance, and emissions are all goals of studnets competitions such as the 2005 EVC.

Fig. 4.5

The future 2020 EVC will yield many new ideas and help promote the growth of Ethanol research in industry as well as educational institutions. Events such as the Ethanol Vehicle Challenge are needed and are very important for obtaining the interests of young engineers to work on the fuel of the future-E90.

CONCLUSION

Mixing gasoline with 90% Ethanol is a suitable choice for popularizing the use of blended fuel in the gasoline engine in India. Burning a mixture of lead free low octane gasoline can not only make the best use of high-octane value of Ethanol but also reduce fuel cost. No appreciable corrosion and unnatural wearing down in the main engine parts were observed. Reduce the dependence on foreign oil, Improves Indian economy by means of producing Ethanol fuel and creates employment opportunities and enhances agriculture-backbone of our country. When a gasoline engine is converted to Ethanol/gasoline blended fuel, it is crucial to maintain the stability to ratio between Ethanol and gasoline during the operation of the engine. The cost of the conversion is low. And the engine performance is satisfactory and stable (increased thermal efficiency and brake power). At the some time, the converted engine can be switched over to gasoline alone when there is no Ethanol available.

5

Bio-fuel for Rural Employment

INTRODUCTION

The study has been under taken for finding out the improved production techniques for *Jatropha curcas* (Ratanjot) plants for arid and semi-arid areas where it is well produces under technical expertise and also plays a vivacious role to generate better rural employment. It gives continues producing for more than 40 years after the plantation. Still the farmers are much dependent upon the traditional crops which consume more time and money and contribute less economic value as compare to the cash crops. So in this present scenario Bio-fuel plant acts as a substitute to these traditional crops in arid and semi arid areas and generates better employment opportunities for the rural people.

OBJECTIVES OF THE STUDY

1. To find out improved production techniques for the Bio-fuel plant.
2. To find our various ways and means for rural employment by the cultivation of Bio-fuel plant.

METHODOLOGY

Study methodology is based upon the secondary data, which have been collected from the agricultural journals, agriculture department and website.

LIMITATION OF THE STUDY

Although the researcher has tried to collect relevant informations for the concerned subject but result may differ according to the demographic characteristics.

RESULTS AND DISSCUSSION

1. To find out improved production techniques for the Bio-fuel plant

A. Climatic Condition: Bio-fuel plant grows well through out India as semi-wild bush or shrub and also as hedge vegetation and not browsed by the cattles. Bio-fuel plant requires dry climate and grows well in arid and semi-arid regions. For healthy germination hot and humid atmosphere is required. Dormancy period starts from December and it remains till April. Sprouting will appear in the month of April and flowering will appear in July-August. Fruiting period is October to December.

B. Sowing: Sowing pattern of Bio-fuel is categorized into three forms.

By the Seeds–3-4 Kg/ha seeds are required if the proper irrigation facility is available and 6–8 Kg/ha is for dry fields where irrigation facility is improper. The numbers of plants are 2500/ha and 5000/ha are recommended in irrigated and non-irrigated fields respectively.

Proper spacing of seeds — 2 x 2 meter in irrigated condition 2 x 1 meter in non-irrigated condition.

After one month of sowing the germination occurs and it is recommended to remove all the plants except the healthy one for healthy plantation.

By the nurseny plantation– Pockets should be prepared having the mixture of soil, red soil and FYM with the proportion of 1 :1:1 in the month of April. Seeds should be placed in these pockets @ 2 seeds, pockets with depth of 6 cm in the same month. When the plants attain the height of 1½ feet in these pockets, should be replaced in the fields.

By the Vegetative propagation–The age of these plants is less as compare to others and also less productive. The lateral shoots which are having a length of 1 to 1½ feet should be cut properly from the main stem and placed in the boundary of the field in the April month and this propagation requires less irrigation as 40°C temperature is conducive for growth.

C. Fertilizers application: Bio-fuel plantation requires 40 Kg Nitrogen and 40 Kg Phosphorus per hectare. Half dose of Nitrogen and full dose of phosphorus are placed at the time of sowing and remaining half dose of Nitrogen is placed after two months of sowing.

D. Irrigation: Bio-fuel plant is tolerant from the dry condition and is less affected with harsh atmosphere. If the proper irrigation facility is available than three irrigation are imperative for healthy crops mainly in the month of December and at end of April and May month.

E. Inter-culturing and weeding: Annually 4-5 weeding as per required may be carried out during the initial stage of the crop for healthy produce.

F. Flowering and Fruiting : In India, it flowers between September - December. The fruits mature 2–4 months flowering.

G. Economic Aspects : The yield of seeds of Bio-fuel plant is measured up to 25 qtl./hac. And it contributes 20 to 25,000 Rs./year/hac. In seeds, oil contents range from 30–40%, kernels constitute 55–60% of seed by weight and oil content 50% and are white in colour. So Bio-fuel plant acts as a commercial crop in arid and semi, arid region and by the proper technical knows how cultivator can earn better as compare to others traditional crops.

H. Yield : With proper technical know how and proper irrigation condition the expected seed yield is as under-

Year of planting	Seed yield Kg./Ha/Year
1.	-
2.	250
3.	1000
4.	1250
5.	2000
6.	2500

2. To find our various ways and means for rural employment by the cultivation of Bio-fuel plant

As India is deficient in edible oils, non-edible oils are the main source for producing the bio-diesel. According to the Indian Government and Indian Technology some development works have been carried out to produce bio diesel from the Jetroppha plant and it may be very potential and usefull source of earning for arid and semi–arid farmers.

The commission agents sell traditional agricultural commodities in local mandis through auction. In case of bio-fuel produce, there are no as such routine practices for sale in mandis as cultivation of the bio-fuel is recently started. But the value of the produce is high and the commission agents directly purchase it from the village sites. After purchasing commission agents transfer these materials to the other parties who are basically facilitate this for value addition and further used in preparation of bio-diesel. As it is high value crop and used in the raw material for diesel so it is sold on cash basis.

Farmer's returns depend upon mainly two factors-

1. Technical support and know- how– Farmers should have technical and scientific knowledge to solve out cultivation problem for better produce.

2. Pricing policy– There should be financial agreement with the purchaser at which price the seeds or oil will be purchased for better earning.

A. Economic Viability: The main factors, which are imperative for returns in value terms, are as follows-

1. Expenses during the cultivation*- Jatropha plants require minimum investment and less maintenance. Inputs for one hectare cultivation of the Jatropha plant is as under-

	Unit	Rate (Rs.)	Total (Rs.)
Land	1 hac	0.00	0.00
Planting material and overheads	2,500.00	2.50	6250
Manure and fertilizer	2,870.00	2,870.00	2,870.00
Labor and others	175.00	70.00	12250.00
Irrigation, Weeding	3,000.00	3,000.00	3,000.00
TOTAL			**24,370.00**

2. Returns in value terms- After the continues cultivation for five years the returns are as follows :-

	Expen.(Rs.)	Output (Rs.)	Income (Rs.)
Year 1	24,370.00	1,500.00	-22,870.00
Year 2	5,000.00	4,500.00	-500.00
Year 3	5,000.00	25,000.00	20,000.00
Year 4	5,000.00	40,000.00	35,000.0
Year 5	5,000.00	62,500.00	57,500.00

After three years break-even point will be achieved and fourth year onwards continue return exists.

*Data' may vary according to cultivation expertise and local climatic conditions.

B. Distribution Channel for Jatropha Plant : Unlike the traditional crop, farmers may contract with the regional parties for purchasing the seeds with the prior agreements of prices. Alternative distribution channel may be adopted

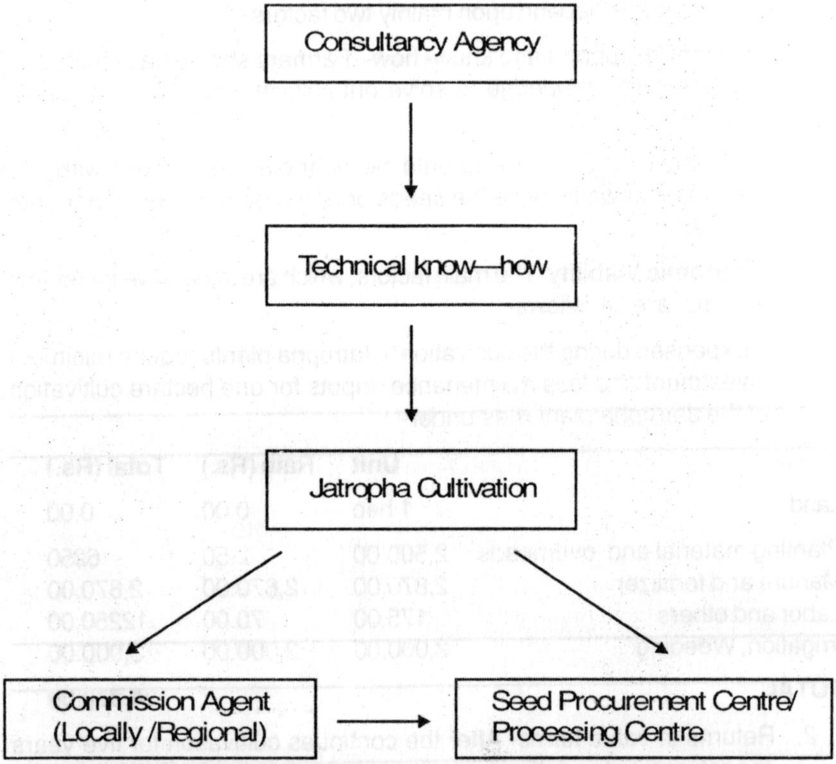

by the farmers to sale their material in market in the following way :

As it is new crop, farmers require technical support and know how for producing optimum production and they also require where to sale this material. In this regard farmers may get knowledge from consultancy agencies. Unlike the traditional mandis purchasing, farmers should undergo some pricing agreement to the commission agent who will purchase their material and then transferred to the procurement center. In this way the whole process will be carried out and farmers will able to fetch their commodity in cash form.

6

Advantages and Limitations of Bio-fuels

INTRODUCTION

Bio-fuels are extracted from plants viz. Saffola, Sun flower, Soya bean in developed countries like Australia, France, Germany and United States. But these are edible oils in India. However, climatic conditions of India offer suitable environment for cultivating non-edible oil producing plants such as Jatropha curcas, Pongamia pinnata and Madhuca indica. Oils derived from these plants can be used as bio-fuels. Like most countries of the world India is still dependent upon the crude oil imported from other countries. Since India has the vast potential of agricultural resources, therefore, different agricultural oil bearing crops can be used as the source of fuel oil generation. Moreover, India's economy depend mainly on agriculture, the utilization of country's resources for energy production could be an extremely important step in the overall development of the nation.

Keeping in view the economy and environment friendly benefits of bio-fuels, bio-fuels production is of great importance and in this paper some of the important bio-fuels have been highlighted.

FACTORS TO BE CONSIDERED

(i) Modification of Existing Engine

Engine modification should be simple, inexpensive and easily reversible. Such modification should not affect the use of traditional diesel fuel in order to preserve engine compatibility for the use of dual fuels.

(ii) Investment Cost

Eventual add-on cost necessary to ensure normal engine performance with alternative must be small to ensure that the operation is competitive with petroleum based fuels.

(iii) Environmental Compatibility

Engine performance, while using an alternative fuel is expected to improve significantly with regard to regulated emission, already subjected to limitations. However, unregulated emission such as benzene, aldehydes and noise emission are yet be monitored properly.

(iv) Additional Requirements

The alternative fuel must guarantee that the life time of equipment, its reliability and operational capability is not altered. Maintenance, repair and fuel cost must be almost similar to that of conventional fuels. Moreover, alternative fuel must be easily available.

MANUFACTURING OF ALTERNATIVE FUELS

Among the various alternative fuels, the derivative of plants and tree oils has shown a great potential as diesel substitute. Therefore they are known as bio-fuels. At present, the most common bio-fuels are ethanol, ethyl tertiary-butyl ether derived from ethanol and bio-diesel. Ethanol, the most widely used bio-fuel, is currently produced by fermentation of grain or sugar crops. In the future, ethanol may also be produced by from lignocellulosic bio-mass such as woody or herbaceous crops. Bio-diesel can be used directly or mixed with conventional fuel for diesel engines as well as a heating fuel. Bio-diesel is synthesized from direct trans-esterification of vegetables oils, where the corresponding triglycerides react with a short-chain alcohol, usually methanol in the presence of a catalyst. Trans-esterification reaction can be represented as:

Triglyceride + Methanol → Methyl esters + Glycerin

Glycerol is obtained as a by-product of the trans-esterification and is separated from the reaction mixture. It has a number of applications in pharmaceutical, cosmetics, food and plastic industries.

ECO AND NATIONAL IMPORTANCE

India, the world's second most populous country, has been its population explodes from 300 million in 1947 to approximately one billion today. India's per capita energy consumption and carbon emissions, while lower than the world average, result in a substantial percentage of world energy use and carbon emission, due to country's large population and heavy reliance on coal. Increased use of renewable energy is one of the means of the reducing carbon emission. India's five year plan for 2002–2007 calls for 10% of new electric generating capacity to come from renewable sources, India faces great challenges in energy and environment as it enters the 21st century. As in the year 2002-2003, the consumption of diesel was 35% of total petroleum product consumption. Therefore, immediate attention has to be paid towards searching the viable alternative fuels for diesel engine. In this direction, non-edible oil producing plants play an important role in imparting clean and environment friendly fuels.

FEED-STOCKS FOR BIO-DIESEL PRODUCTION

Vegetable oils are the main raw materials for the production of bio-diesels e.g. rape seed oil account for 80%, soy for 10% and sun flower seed oil for 10% of the total bio-diesel feed stock. However, in India, main problem arises from the high cost of vegetable oils. In order to make bio-diesel cost effective and more competitive, one of the option to make effective use of waste cooking oil to cater to the demand of industries generating bio-fuels. Lot of waste cooking oil from big restaurants, shops, hotels and other food processing units, which otherwise goes to the drains as waste and causes a lot of environmental problems, collection of this waste cooking oil and its further processing in industries to produce bio-fuels can add more towards the improvement of our eco-system as well as economy of the nation. Moreover, waste cooking oil proves to be fatal to the aquatic life if it goes to the water sources.

ADVANTAGES OF BIO-FUELS

From an environment point of view, bio-fuels show clear advantages over petroleum fuels. Some of the advantages are given below:

- Since it is plant derived, so its combustion does not increase net atmospheric levels of CO_2 i.e. reduction in Green House Effect. CO_2 is recycled in the atmosphere during photosynthesis occurring in plants used as raw material for bio-diesel production.
- It can be produces at domestic level, thereby reducing burden on petroleum imports.
- It is bio-degradable.
- In comparison to petroleum fuels, its combustion reduces the level of CO_2, particulate matter, SO_2, hydrocarbons, soot, pqlyaromatics and NO_x.

- Bio-fuels contribution to the Green House Effect is quite significant.

Other more scientific advantages of bio-fuels productior include:

- New avenues and markets for agriculture.
- Cost saving in agriculture policies.
- Securing jobs in agriculture, creating jobs at the post-harvest production stages.
- Additional macro-economic demand induced by multiplier affects, thus creating more jobs.
- Less consumption of environmental resources compared to fossil diesel and, therefore, lower environmental protection cost.
- Reduction in mineral oil imports and petroleum diesel fuel imports.
- Less import of oil seed residue (for fodder) and raw glycerin because these are by-products of bio-diesel production.
- A movement towards independence of exhaustible fossil fuels.

LIMITATIONS OF BIO-FUELS

Though bio-fuels have been accepted as renewable sources of energy but it has been found that bio-fuels suffer from certain limitations such as:

- Poor stability in comparison with petro-diesel. Poor stability of bio-fuel is because of presence of double bonds in the fatty acid chains and because of presence of functional groups.
- Bio-fuels and their blends can't be stored for more than six months because of stability.
- In presence of moisture, bio-fuels get hydrolyzed to alcohols and acids. Presence of alcohol reduces the flash point of the fuel and presence of acids will increase its acid number which may cause corrosion of the engine parts.

Taking in to consideration the stability factor of the bio-fuels, it is important to increase its oxidation stability by blending it with certain additives so that it may come under required specifications.

CONCLUSION

In developed countries, bio-mass accounts towards one third of the total renewable energy sources. Feed–stock for bio-fuels are mainly vegetable oils. However, cost of the vegetable oils makes their restricted use. Cheap and best sources of raw materials for bio-fuels production are the waste cooking oils from food manufacturing centers. Though bio-fuels are clean sources of energy but they suffer from certain limitations such as poor oxidation stability, therefore they have to be blended anti-oxidants so as enhance the oxidation stability.

7

Bio-fuel Resources of Energy

INTRODUCTION

The process of economic development is largely related and dependent on the energy consumption in the present day context. Everyday effort to exploit energy for benefit of mankind has become thus a day-to-day necessity of subsistence and an important subject of national planning process.

The present day national energy scenario looms around 65% of fossil fuel contributing to power generation. It is interesting to go through the following statistical data:

- 131,000 MW cumulative generation capacity. Mainly based on coal thermal and hydro. Total generation 633 bu.
- Per capita energy consumption 520 kgoe which is 30% world average.
- About 80% of total rural energy consumption comes from non-commercial energy.
- 125,000 villages still remain to be electrified. Only 43.5% of rural households use electricity.
- Over the next 25 years, six fold increase projected in electricity and four fold increase in crude oil requirements.

The increasing requirement of energy has led to the non-conservative exploitation of fossil fuel resulting in a large-scale pollution, they being emissionery of toxic gases. It is thus imperative requires diversification of energy-mix with larger and accelerated harnessing of new and renewable energy specially when it is known that:

- Renewable are indigenous, non-depleting, modular and environment-friendly.
- Renewable can meet a broad spectrum of energy demand.
- They can provide energy access and meet unmet demand.
- Provide captive energy thus conserving fossil fuels and electricity
- Supplement fossil fuels in transportation.
- Augment grid power.
- Renewables can contribute to energy security in a sustainable manner

Indian power generation capacity is expected vide long term energy scenario (2031-32) to reach 62700–77800 MW for sustaining 7-8% economic growth. In achieving this fossil fuel would remain dominant with six fold increase in CO_2 emmision to about 6 billion tons per year. It is envisaged that with R & D thrust and more responsive policy in relation to environment, renewable can contribute :

- 100,000–120,000 MW grid power.8–10%of electricity generation

  Wp* : 40000

  BMP: 30000

  SP : 20000

  SHP : 15000

  WTE : 7000

* 10% fossil fuel substitution.

- Energy excess and unmet demand in 2 lakh villages. 100 million rural population to be served.
- Solar water heating systems and waste-to-energy projects in all major cities. Captive energy for SMEs.

*WP- Wind Power; BMP- Biomass Power, SP–Solar power; SHP–Small hydro power and, WTE–Waste to energy

RURAL ENERGY SCENARIO

70% of the population of India–700 million people residing in the villages, subsists on non-commercial energy from biomass resources. This, thus, should form one of important bases for energy scenario planning. Further, only 43.5% of rural household use electricity where energy services are unreliable and of poor quality. In addition majority of villages that remain to be electrified are remote to where extension of centralized grid be grossly uneconomical.

RENEWABLE ENERGY STATUS AND POTENTIAL

The national estimated potentials of sources are:

- Solar Power 40,000 MW
- Bio–mass Power 88,000 MW
- Agro residues 16,000 MW
- Bagasse 5,000 MW
- Plantations 60,000 MW
- WTE 60,000 MW
- Wind Power 45,000 MW
- Small Hydro Power 15,000 MW
- Biogas plants 12 million
- Bio-fuels 20 MMT / annum

Thus renewable energy is poised to meet broad spectrum of energy demand in a sustainable manner for which provisions have been made in the National Electricity Policy.

A publication made by Connemann 1995 in which a long-term energy mix in global energy scenario has been predicted. To me his prediction of renewables contributing 80% of the energy requirement by 2050 appear to be required foreseable possibility specially with the concern of cleaner and agreeable environment. I understand that western counh'ies led by Germany, Sweden and U.S.A. have already started investing huge financial and technical resources towards this goal. In our country also there is an emerging need for similar efforts in this direction.

RAJASTHAN: RENEWABLE ENERGY HUB/HABITAT

With regards to Rajasthan, the largest State of India with 60% arid and semi–arid areas with sparse population of 165 per sq km, it is characterized by low erratic rainfall and recurring droughts, limited surface water, proof hydropower potentials and high cost of power distribution due to sparse and scattered loads. In addition there is heavy power requirement for agriculture and drinking water due to high dependence on ground water. A cursory glance of the power scenario of the State gives the following picture:

- Installed capacity	:	5300 MW
• Thermal	:	3200
• Hydro	:	1300
• Nuclear	:	800
- Likely capacity addition	:	580 MW
- Energy shortage	:	22 %
- Households electrified	:	44 %

- High ATC losses, low cost recovery.

In long and near terms the state of Rajasthan in view of its renewable energy potential it could be summarized as follows:

1. Long–term
   - Solar power : 20000 MW
2. Near term
2. Biomass

- Surplus Agro Residues 600 MW
- Plantations: 1500 MW
  - Wind power : 1000 MW
  - Small Hydro: 27 MW (49 sites)

The installed capacity and power generation with major production from hydro (27.5%), thermal coal and gas (72%) and wind sources (0.5%) presently fall short by 12% with respect to demand of power in the state. In order to ameliorate the scenario after Administrative Reforms Commission (2001) and Government initiates varying reforms including segregating, transmission and distribution systems of autonomous nature and privatization as well as reduction of A % T losses due subsidy on consumption and thefts of power supply, have yields results. Actions are afloat to reduce the staggering A & T losses from 66% to 22% through technological advancements and for reducing the theft of power through feeder improvement, the motto being unit saved is equal to unit generated.

A seminar of national level on Oil, Gas and Lignite Scenario held on 20th and 21st April, 2005 at SPRL, Jaipur was attended by 100 and odd national scientist, social scientists and implementing authorities of Government of India and Rajasthan. They concluded that ample fossil fuel resources exist in Rajasthan for generating power from lignite, heavy oil gas being exploited by NLC, ONGC, OIL and CAIRAN not only to provide with requirement of the state but export the same to neighbouring States. R & D Thrust by MRPL has further indicated that 1200 MW of power could be annually generated from the heavy bottom residue of the upcoming refineries of Barmer.

Another seminar on Energy Sector in Rajasthan–Strategies and Policy Options held on 11th and 12th March, 2006 was deliberated by several visionaries of our countries and 70 and odd scientists and others related to Energy Sector. They opined that in addition to fossil fuels, renewables specially, wind, biomass, bio-fuel and solar resources are available in plenty, the exploitation of which along with R & D thrust could be a boon in achieving the distributed generation for decentralized rural need of Rajasthan.

ROLE OF BIO-FUELS IN RAJASTHAN

Having understood the importance of renewables as the potential future energy source, the scenario discussed above would entail concentration on the exploitation of wind and solar energy resources. An intrinsic analysis would however, reveal that wind energy is a portable source for grid quality power generations in the locales falling in the" Wind tunnel" extending eastward from Jaisalmer to Sikar-Jhunjhunu. But for a distributed generation for a decentialized rural need of the hour of this State only Solar or Bio-fuel resources have to be looked into. Solar Energy though available for 300 of sunny days in a year need more R & D for production of affordable power for the common mass. Thus the analysis makes us to ruminate on Bio-fuel resources, more so with the reasons that:

(a) The rural mass are agricultures and would understand this as a gullible source of energy.

(b) Could be beneficially developed as a cooperative movement.

(c) Would be affordable and adaptable since it is a means of profit in the place of its production from which the people could generate employment and means of livelihood.

In addition to above the bio-fuels are potential solution to address the twin issue:

- Potential solution to address the twin issues of fast depleting fossil fuel (short, unreliable supplies and increasing prices of petroleum products) and environmental degradation.

- For a rural dominating population of India (70%) decentralized renewable bio-fuel production by rural community offers an impending way out to meet their energy needs in a sustainable way.

DEFINITION OF BIO-FUEL ENERGY

The use of vegetable oils for engine oil is predicted to be as important as petroleum and coal tar products. The source of raw material are animal fats, vegetable oil edible and non-edible–from plants crops or tree-borne. Many TBO's are non-edible viz., karanja, wild castor or ratanjot (Jatropha).

SOURCES OF RAW MATERIAL

The preparation of bio-fuel, the only liquid renewable energy source from the raw material such as seeds from plant crops or tree borne is a simple process. Manual or mechanical crushers produce vegetable oil (upto 38% from seeds of Jatrophas) and oil cakes on line similar to edible oils ("Khal" from" gtianees").

The feedstock is converted through a base catalysed trans-esterification process at low temperature (65°C) and atmospheric pressure. The oil is reacted with alcohol (like methanol) in the presence of a catalyst (NaOH or KOH mixed with methanol) to produce glycerol and methyl ester or bio–diesel.

Depending on the feedstock the bio–diesel, which is a mixture of Methyl or Ethyl esters obtained by esterification and trans-esterification of vegetable oils or animal fat, may be referred as:

- Soybean methyl ester- SME or SOME
- Rape methyl ester-RME
- Fatty acid methyl ester-FAME
- Vegetable oil methyl ester- VOME

DRIVING FORCES OF DEVELOPMENT OF BIO-FUELS

The most important consideration is an assessment of the potential for a technology is to relate to the future, especially so for long-term thinking for an illustrated economic assessment. Practically speaking economics is not only about money but about the sensible use of resources. With the increase in demand for liquid resource of energy specially in the currently poor and populous countries and not to far in future the current supply of fossil fuels will become unavailable, one has to search foreseeable possibilities of energy resources more so for decentralized energy needs. For a considered step for such a development several forces need to be promulgated for fruitful outcome.

Global Forces: Bio-fuel–Biodiesel resource is now recognized globally as a sensible renewable fuel diversity from which an energy security could be apprehended. Studies conducted world over conclude:

- Bio-fuels can be produced in tropical countries on a significant scale. Primarily from TBO's.
- There is a significant advantage over fossil fuel in terms of reducing atmospheric pollution.
- Biodiesel could be used in place of fossil diesel without modification to modern diesel engines.
- Biodiesel has definite advantage with regards to fuel consumption, lubricity, emission, toxicity, cold flow properties etc.
- Liquid bio-fuel are insurance against catastrophic interruption of imported or even home produced fossil derived oil supplies.
- It has been recognized that further R & D will markedly change all existing significant parameters and thus the economic outlook.

Simple process of crushing seeds of TBO's to produce raw bio-fuel oil, its esterification to biodiesel at its *in-situ* rural site thus make availability of an amenable energy source of clean, eco–friendly nature providing rural energy security. It is not out of context to say that it most warranted in the regions of developing countries now targeted for socia-economic development of the needy populace.

Local force: The analysis of the social structures of the rural areas show that these regions require a fillip for their economic growth through the sustainable and sensible use of resources of energy so intimately connected with development. The local forces such as job creation and job retention, income generation through rural diversification need to be addressed to. There are no two ways about this fact that such concerns are intimately related to the availability of indigenous energy which in itself would not only provide avenues for jobs and income generation through community participation and awareness but also supply of power which forms the basic need of any plausible pathway of development.

Hurdles: All said and done the statistical data indicate that in the initial stages the techno-economics of renewable energy resource of biodieselj bio-fuel is established. A recognized methodology however with enhanced R & D for affordable production of usable energy on a large scale from resources need to be pursued.

Farms are businesses and products will only be produced if : (1) there is a demand for them, and (2) if a profit can be made from growing them.

The important aspects of information, knowledge of technological advancement and dissemination to achieve users through institutional support for making Bio-fuels as gullible profitable projects would be the prime necessity in making this resource viable proposition.

ADVANTAGES OF BIO-FUEL AS ENERGY RESOURCE

In the presentations made by Dr. A.K. Lyall in the seminar on Energy Sector in Rajasthan–Strategies and Policy Options, it broadly summarised that :

- 100 kg of oil (from 400 kg of seeds) +12 kg of methanol + 1 kg of catalyst yields approx. 98 kg. of Biodiesel + 9 kg. of Glycerine +4 kg of Methanol, and 300 kgs. of oil cake (fertilizer).
- COSTS: Investments of seeds, @ Rs. 4/kg, Methanol @ Rs. 19/ kg, NaOH (Catalyst) @ Rs. 12/kg, processing = Rs. 4 kg produces oilcake recovery @ Rs. 2/kg, Glycerine (raw) @ Rs. la/kg
- Biodiesel @ Rs. I5/kg.
- Recent (APJAKs) figure is Rs. 20 per liter.

Hence developing a strong biodiesel industry would have large economic benefits distributed in our country. Investment in this technology ensures an indigenous transport fuel option and energy security. The key benefits are several, however one need overcome many barriers:

Key benefits:

- An increased level of understanding and commitment to Renewable Energy.
- Use degraded or less fertile land.
- Profits and benefits retained locally thus supporting local economy.
- Huge potential for jobs creation.
- Reduce vulnerability to climate change and other disasters.
- Offer a source of income.
- Create opportunities for new businesses, especially for women.
- Improve health.
- It enables the point of production to be nearer to the point consumption.

Barriers of Concern:

- Logistics and agricultural production for large scale jatropha and other TBO cultivation.
- Efficient use of biodiesel in India villages.
- Formation of institutional capacity, regulatory framework and incentive measures.
- Gaining people confidence in biodisesl.
- Educate and motivate small entrepreneurs.
- Affordable indigenous biodiesel production technology.
- Setting up co-ordination mechanisms for project replicability major areas of the India but also in other countries in the region.

ACTION PLANS

It is known well that production of bio-fuels "coming from the earths current energy account rather than its caption account" is poised to seek to reduce the vulnerability of a serious shortage of fossil derived fuels in near future. There are suggestions from visionaries that the one way could be to reduce the use of oill–gas for non-vehicular purpose which could be fed by resources of wind, tide and solar radiation for heating and cooking.

However, there remain a demand for fuel for roadl rail transport. The question is to what extent could home-produced fuel crop reduce this dependence, Bio-fuels as the only liquid renewable resource are the promising alternatives.

Short and long–term targets in a well thought out action could help in assessing to what extent it is possible to await the opportunities provided by these liquid renewable energy resources of bio-fuel.

Short Term Goals

- Enhanced utilization of TBO and other non edible oils.
- R & D of superior production technologies.
- Technology h'ansfer (low cost Transesterification units) from national international quarters.
- Bio–technological research to match agro-climatic conditions.
- Demonstration projects of economy based technologies.
- Incentive for operating plant using biodiesel in agriculture, farm machinery and pump sets.

- Waste land development.
- Support research into uses for Biodiesel co-products such as cattle fodder and oil cake as fertilizers.

Long Term

- Exploration of partnerships for commercial scale Biodiesel ventures
- Infrastructure Development.
- Institutions and policies for competitive community Biodiesel production system.
- Advanced integrated cooperative Biodiesel system from farm to service.

COOPERA TIVE MOVEMENT FOR BIO-FUEL RESOURCE EXPLOITATION

Though the benefits of bio-fuel energy resource are established, nevertheless, there are many hurdles for its real implementation, main aspect being the wait of 3, 4 years for actually drawing the product from TBO's in their agricultural land and wait for 3-4 years to reap the harvest of the seeds when otherwise he has to wait maximum a season 3-4 months for other agricultural products. For him even a cash crop does not require this long time to harvest then why risk TBO's cultivation; further the type of yield of the crop is also not assured/uncertain till the fruiting starts after 3 years.

To remove this major hurdle, agencies Government or other have to give relative priority to such crop which is an uphill task. The only inevitable limitation on land area would be land unsuitable for growing the crop for food. Further the yield in such land, probably agro nomical research may provide the basics for increased yield herein (genetic improvement, genetically modified crop or hybrid species). Cost and benefit, the main guiding factors governing the economy have to be overseen by national legislation. The financial reward for growing the crop are adequate, it is likely that it would be grown, but the scale on which this would happen can only assessed by creating the conditions first. Probably a demonstration on a smaller scale to realize the potential could be an important step to mitigate apprehensions. Insurance against future hazards may be one of the possibility.

Bio-fuel resource exploitation thus requires exploration of partnerships for commercial scale, biodiesel ventures and befitting infrastructure development. In the democratic set up, establishment of large scale biodiesel farms from dedicated investors for national set up, national cause has limited choices. Economic considerations for such entrepreneurs would be cost, benefits and funds involved and not sensible use of resources. Thus the success of such projects need creation of logistics for large scale Jatrophas and other bio-cultivation and formation of institutional capacity, regulatory framework and incentive measures by competent authorities of the Government of India and state. Nevertheless, such a development is a long drawn process.

In a thought provoking study, it is considered that a co–operative movement supported by government could remove the apprehensions of an individual on cost and benefit aspects of bio-fuel large operations for a community based decentralized system enabling point of production of crude vegetable oil for cooking stoves, biodiesel for running tractors/pumpsets and oil cake residue for fertilizer to be nearer point of consumption tailored to the size of the demand. This would have a greater acceptability in rural India where profits and benefits are retained locally thus not only supporting local economy and job creations but providing a sense of individuals having a real stake in their local renewable energy project.

Several ways and means of such a cooperative movement could be considered:

- Cooperatives for collection of seeds in already existing forest areas
- Barter system of exchange.
- Agriculture in wasteland.
- Fencing for fuel.
- Production system.

  1 Crushers,

  2 Biodiesel esterification.

(A) **Collection centers**: While travelling in the forest area of Kumbalgarh and environ where Jatropha grows wild, I am happy to find that local villagers and triblas are bearing fruits of their labour in collecting the seeds of this bio-fuel crop and earns rumeration through the panchayats who accumulates the product; and in turn distributes the proceeds, many-a-times to the tune of a lakh by selling it to the buyers exporting it for medicinal requirement. I would like to support the usage of this collection for running a local cooperative run by the villagers including the tribals actually collecting the seeds for manufacture of crude vegetable oil, biodiesel and oil cake for their own as a step for amelioration of their socio-economic livelihood.

(B) **Barter System:** Another step may be providing cooking oil for burning stove as a barter of the seed by the collection center following the prevalent system of bartering amongst the tribals of the region. Such an initiative would not only provide better proceeds of their labour of collecting the seeds and stimulate many more to get involved in such an activity but help in using a clean, non-polluted method of cooking rather than the firewood an unhealthy smoking environ for their women folk and children.

(C) Agriculture in Wasteland: Agriculture in wasteland is considered as a possible alternative of growing TBO's, however, undertaking it on a large scale through regulatory framework and incentive measures have till now remained on paper. Probably a national zeal and national cause have not overcome the cost and benefit consideration of the entrepreneurs. Competent authorities at central and state level have to motivate the entrepreneurs through designs and dissemination of awareness that projection on present day may be totally irrevelant to future conditions and thus projects allotted to them need to be implemented soon. One could not be allowed to sit on wasteland provided to them immemorial. The project need to be time bound.

(D) Fence for Fuel: An alternative to the cost-benefit consideration of an agriculturist for TBO cultivation in his farms is "fence for fuel". SPRI is involved in a project with HPPL in providing technical assistance for the agronomical research in the interested yield of Jatropha seeds being grown in the fences of the agricultural farms in Viratnagar. This project is not of creating business opportunities for the village but also educate and disseminate the public awareness of TBO's for a source of income, gaining people confidence in biodiesel/bio-fuel and a demonstration project for the utilities of bio-fuels in the socio-economic development of rural India.

(E) Bio-fuel Production Systems: The next cooperative involvement would be in decentralized biodiesel production system through placement of mechanical or electrical crushers and the biodiesel makers. This would provide means for the rural population to not only become self–sufficient in understanding the total gamut of bio-fuels as the clear choice of an alternative source of energy but also for distributed generation and decentralized rural energy need. In adition this would make the rural India gain confidence on the bio-fuels as means of supporting local economy, source of income and huge potentials of job creation.

BIO-FUEL AS A TOOL TO REMOVE INDOOR POLLUTION

SPRI is also choosen as a partner of HPPL, to initiate and provide supervision on a most innovative World Bank aided project of bio-fuel as an alternative to indoor pollution. The later is a recognized slow killer of the women and their offsprings in rural India due to smoke inhaled by them in their ill ventilated dwelling sited. This project would demonstrate how the health of the rural populace would improve with the implementation of bio-fuel projects as an alternative source of energy

8

Jatropha

INTRODUCTION

India is emerging very fast as a major force in the global economy. During the present phase of accelerated development, it is inevitable that energy consumption increases many folds as compared to the present per capita energy consumption which is very low in comparison to the other developed countries. India's total energy requirement has doubled over the last three decades, from 147.05 million tones of oil to 437.69. However, the scenario is bound to change very fast and the gap between demand and supply of crude oil will exert a recurrent pressure on the import bills. On the other hand, non-renewable fossil fuels are getting reduced at a faster rate than ever before pushing the resources at the brink of exhaustion. There has been a renewed interest in bio–fuels in the past two years as government looks for alternatives to increasingly expensive oil-based fuels.

Depleting reserves of fossil fuel and increasing effects of pollution from these fuels demand eco-friendly alternatives, which can supplement or replace fossil fuels. In recent years, research has been directed to explore 'biofuels' -plant based fuel sources as a supplement or substitute of fossil fuel. Bio–fuels are renewable and environmentally safe. The most common types of biofuels that are being developed and used at present are bioethanol and bodiesel. Since these biofuels, are derived from cellulosic biomass such as herbaceous and woody plants, agricultural and forestry residues, a prefix 'bio' is added before their names. At present biodiesel is reported to substitute about 10% of the world diesel consumption. Low cost labour, high unemployment, high cost of delivered petroleum products, and unfavourable balance of payments are some of the serious concerns which make biofuels an attractive option for India. In view of a strong agricultural and forestry base, both these biofuels-ethanol and biodiesel–are likely to emerge as an alternative transportation fuel, beneficial for the environment and economy, in India. Ethanol has been explored in many countries as a potential fuel to reduce harmful emissions. Brazil has been producing ethanol from sugarcane molasses and juice for more than forty years. Ethanol thus produced is being used as transport fuel as a blend (24%) in petrol (gasoline) and in the neat form (alcohol) in Brazil (Jagadeesan, 2001). Similarly, in the US, the use of ethanol produced by corn maize as an oxygenate in Reformulated Gasoline (RFG) is well established. Other countries, which have experience of using ethanol as a transport fuel, include France, Indonesia, the Philippines, Guatemala, Costa Rica, Argentina, The Republic of South Africa, Kenya, Thailand and Sudan.

BIODIESEL

Biodiesel is a fuel produced by a chemical process between vegetable (virgin or used) oil or animal fats and alcohol in the presence of a catalyst.

Biodiesel development worldwide is well documented (Korbitz, 1998). Biodiesel has acquired respectability among diesel fuel producers, diesel engine manufacturers and end users. In the last 15 years, 28 countries have embarked on biodiesel projects and bodiesel production has grown from trials at pilot plant scale to full industrial production. To date a total of 85 production plants of biodiesel have been identified, with capacities ranging from pilot plant to industrial scales up to 1,20,000 t/year (Choo and Ma, 2000). Biodiesel is currently used commercially in France, Germany, Italy, Australia, Sweeden the Czech Republic, Slovakia and the USA.

Biodiesel (fatty acid alkyl esters) is a cleaner-burning diesel replacement fuel made from natural, renewable resources such as new and used vegetable oils and animal fats. Vegetable oils/fats are triglycerides of fatty acids, which on trans–esterification are converted into their alkyl esters to produce biodiesel (Sonntag, 1982). Esters of vegetable oils and fats are used because they have a low viscosity and better fuel properties than pure vegetable oils and fats. Thus biodiesel is a mixture of methyl or ethyl esters of C_{16} to C_{18} fatty acids. Just like petroleum diesel, biodiesel operates in combustionignition engines (Choo *et al,* 1997). Blend of upto 20% biodiesel (mixed with petroleum diesel fuels) can be used in nearly all diesel equipment. These low level blends (20% and less) don't require any modifications and can provide the same payload capacity and range as diesel.

- Biodiesel is environmentally friendly: it is renewable, "more biodegradable than sugar and less toxic than table salt" (US National Biodiesel Board).

- Biodiesel can be used in any diesel engine
- Fuel economy is the same as conventional diesel fuel
- Biodiesel is a much better lubricant than conventional diesel fuel and extends engine life - a German truck won an entry in the Guinness Book of Records by travelling more than 1.25 million km (780,000 miles) on biodiesel with its original engine
- Biodiesel has a high cetane rating, which improves engine performance: 20% biodiesel added to conventional diesel fuel improves the cetane rating 3 points, making it a Premium fuel
- Biodiesel can be mixed with ordinary petroleum diesel fuel in any proportion, with no need for a mixing additive.
- Even a small amount of biodiesel means cleaner emissions and better engine lubrication: 1% biodiesel will increase lubricity by 65%

The current industry recommendation in the USA is that biodiesel be used within six months or reanalyzed aiter six months to ensure that the stored fuel meets ASTM specifications. A longer shelf life is possible depending upon the fuel composition and the use of storage enhancing additives such as anti–oxidants, Generally standard conditions used for storage and handling of diesel can be used for biodiesel. It could be stored in tanks made of aluminium or steel under clean, dry and dark environment. To avoid growth of algae in fuel, water contamination need to be minimized, and if necessary, some biocide should be added.

Several studies (e.g. in Mali, Nicaragua, India, Zimbabwe) have indicated that the *Jatropha curcas* plant shows promise for use as an oil crop for biodiesel (Foidl and Elder, 1997; Henning, 1998). The *Jatropha* plant is Latin American in origin and is closely related to the Castor plant. It is a large shrub/small tree able to thrive in a number of climatic zones in arid and semi-arid tropical regions of the world. An easy to establish perennial, it can grow in areas of rainfall of 400–1200mm and is drought resistant. In addition it is valued for crop protection, prevents wind/water erosion, is not browsed by animals, reaches maximum productivity by year five, and has a 50-year life span. Planting is usually done at a density of about 2500 plants per ha.

Realising the convenience of raising plantations of *Jatropha curcas* as a pure crop with or without irrigation, projections for cultivation on wasteland has been made and it is estimated that cultivation of *J. curcas* on 2.67 million hectare would suffice to meet the target (5%) replacement by biodiesel (Table 8.1). The target is achievable in view of availability of about 175 million ha wastelands.

TABLE 8.1
Projections for raising plantations of *Jatropha curcas* on wastelands

S. No.	Items	Yield/ requirement
1.	A verage fruit yield per plant (kg) after 5th year	2.0
2.	A verage seed yield per plant (kg); 50–60% of fruits	1-1.2
3.	Number of plants per hectare (2 x 2m spacing)	2500
4.	Average oil yield (litres) per hectare (30% of oil on seed basis)	750
5.	Biodiesel yield (litres) per ha (95% efficiency)	712.50
6.	Annual biodiesel requirement for 5% replacement (lakh tones)	20.0
7	10% replacement	40.0
8.	Wasteland required for cultivation of Jatropha (million hectare) to meet 5% replacement	2.67
9.	10% replacement	5.34

As shown in Table 8.1, the cultivation of *Jatropha* on about 5.34 million, ha of wastelands would make the country self–sufficient in meeting its biodiesel needs. However, raising of mixed plantations over monoculture should be preferred in view of ecological sustainability and multifeed technology to sustain the supply of feedstock.

Other species of forest origin seeds which contain fatty oils in significant quantities and having adaptability of growing on wastelands need to be identified and suitable site-specific ecologically sustainable and economically viable plantation models with peoples' participation for wasteland, un-cropped marginal lands/degraded forest lands may be developed for the production of biodiesel in the country. No doubt the gestation period in case of oil seed trees will be longer, the benefits once start accruing will be available for a much longer period without much efforts and investment. For the purpose, besides launching a nation wide campaign to educate the masses, particularly the rural masses, under peoples' participation programme and wasteland development programme, improved and high yielding plant material could be supplied in rural areas free of cost with other essential inputs and technical know-how for planting them on community wastelands, and degraded forest lands. The villages in return for raising and maintaining these plantations may be given exclusive rights for collection of the produce at nominal royalty. Moreover, to promote the use of biodiesel in the country, policy should be made to provide the subsidies initially for cultivation of energy plants and production of biodiesel from them.

SOCIO-ECONOMIC AND ENVIRONMENT AL CONSIDERATIONS OF USING BIODIESEL IN THE COUNTRY

Local production of bio energy is projected to have a broad range of positive economic, social and environmental implications. Upgrading eroded and deforested land, creation of employment and income is part of the argument. The national programme wants to stop soil and forest degradation and its environmental implications, generate employment for the poor, in particular for women, reduce climatic change and improve energy security.

While the country is short of petroleum reserve, it has large Arabic land as well as good climatic conditions, potential to produce biomass to be processed into bio-fuels. Instrument to promote non-edible oils is hoped to be buy-back arrangements with oil companies to be put in place and mandatory use of bio–diesel blends. The Jatropha programme is to be combined with other programmes of the Ministry of Rural Development to attract growers, entrepreneurs and financial institutions so that a "self–sustaining programme of expansion takes off on its own, with the Government playing mainly the role of a facilitator. Hence, for the expansion phase, the Government will need "to give only marginal financial support". The rural community will have the first right of access to the oil for its own use. Responsibility for availability of sufficient processing units will be with the Ministry of Petroleum. Studies have revealed that "direct and indirect impact of bio–diesel e.g. employment generation, balance of trade, emission benefits etc. are substantial and need to be accounted for" while considering the duty structure on bio–diesel and HSD.

Economics of production of biodiesel is a determining factor in making bio–fuel programme successful. Production economics though dependent upon several factors is essentially and basically guided by the sustainable availability of the feed stock! raw material. Raw materials being exploited commercially by the biodiesel producing countries constitute the edible fatty oils derived from rapeseed, soybean, palm, sunflower, coconut, linseed etc. (Reed, 1993). Use of such fatty oils to produce biodiesel in India will not be feasible in view of a big gap in demand and supply of such oils in the country as the gap is presently met by huge imports. Increased pressure to augment production of edible oils has also put imitations on the use of these oils for production of biodiesel. Under Indian conditions only such plant sources can be considered for bio–fuel, which produce non-edible oil in appreciable quantity and can be grown in large scale on non-cropped marginal and wastelands. Seeds of more than 100 species of forest plants have been identified as source of fatty oils with an estimated potential of 11.3 lakh tones (Gulati *et ai.,* 1984; Dayal *et ai.,* 1999; Juyal *et al.,* 1995; Rajak, 1995). However, the realized potential of such oils is 6.6 lakh tones (Anon., 1994). It has been reported (Foidl and Elder, 1997; Srinivasa, 2001) that fatty oils derived from *Jatropha curcas* (Ratanjyot) and *Pongamia pinnata* (Karanj) are excellent feedstock for biodiesel production. A World Bank Study Reports that developing countries will not be able to leave themselves out of poverty without increased use of energy (Anon., 1999). Rural electrification has long been recognized as needed to improve conditions in rural areas and help stem migration of people to already over crowded cities. According to the Central Electricity Board in India, about 15% of villages were not electrified by March 1998 (Menon, 1999).

Biodiesel can be made through a simple chemical process technology. It could be made accessible to rural communities. It provides opportunity for immediately addressing benefits of energy needs particularly of remote areas where access to conventional sources of energy is not always possible and affordable. More reliable electricity can be produced from mini-grid system than central grid extension. On the basis of the study conducted (Rosenblum, 2000) energy benefits of biodiesel in the country are seen for decentralized micro-grid electricity generation at village level as well as a replacement for diesel fuel in small scale application such as irrigation pump sets, etc.

There is potential to generate an additional 12.58 crore new well-paid jobs in agri–business and textile export. Our oil companies should create a bioenergy clusters in each village. The cluster will use locally available feedstock to produce biogas, biodiesel and ethanol. Rural people for cooking, running agricultural pumps, energising cold storages and powering transport vehicles, can use biogas. It can also produce electricity, bio-fertilisers and bio-pesticides. Waste heat from the generating set can boil drinking water for health and hygiene. Biodiesel and ethanol can be sold to oil companies for further processing and blending with diesel and petrol. Carbon credits under Kyoto Protocol will improve the clusters economic viability.

Ready energy at reasonable cost will induce the farmer to opt for mechanization and improve productivity. A rural woman can add to her family income by taking up a job in a local agri–business unit. India has 108 million hectares of non-irrigated farmland where farmer's earnings are rather low. On a part of this land they can grow sweet sorghum, corn or similar energy-rich plants or grass and sell to the cluster at a good profit. Such feedstock can produce enough ethanol to meet out petrol needs.

Domestic production and utilization of biodiesel will result in significant economic benefits to both the urban and rural sectors, and the balance of trade. The employment generated by nursery raising, site preparation, planting, maintenance and seed collection activities of Jatropha raising on wasteland are shown in Table 8.2, 8.3 and 8.4 respectively.

TABLE 8.2

Cost of nursery raising
(2500 seedlings per hectare of plantation)

S. No.	Item	In Rs.
1.	Cost of Polythene bags 10 kg (Rs. 60/Kg)	600.00
2.	Cost of collection of seeds (3 kg)	45.00
3.	Cost of soil, sand and FYM	1250.00
4.	Cost of filling of 3000 polybags excluding cost of soil–fertilizer mixture and sowing two seeds in each (200 polybags / MD) i.e. 15 MD @ Rs. 89.00/MD	1335.00
5.	Maintenance for 4 months total 30 MD @ Rs. 89.00 / MD	2670.00

TABLE 8.3
Cost of planting and maintenance of Jatropha plantation (per/ha)

S. No	Particulars	Year of Plantation 1	2	3	Total	Employment Generation in MD 1	2	3
1.	**Site preparation**							
i.	Site Clearing (7 MD)	623.00	-	-	623.00	7	-	-
i.	One ploughing (Rs. 1000.00)	1000.00	-	-	1000.00		-	- iii
	Alighment and Stacking (3 MD)	267.00	-	-	267.00	3	-	-

Contd. TABLE 8.3
Cost of planting and maintenance of Jatropha plantation (per/ha)

S. No	Particulars	Year of Plantation			Total	Employment Generation in MD		
		1	2	3		1	2	3
iv	Digging pits (2,500 *No.)* of 45 cm @40 pits/MD-62.5 MD	5563.00	-	-	5563.00	62.5	-	-
v	Cost of FYM/Compost: 1 kg/pit @Rs. 400/MT	1600.00	-	-	1200.00	-	-	-
vi	Cost of pesticides	1250.00	-	-	1000.00	-	-	-
vii	Cost of biofertilizer including application 1.00/pit	2500.00						
2.	**Transportation and Planting**							
i.	Cost of Transportation @Rs. 0.50 / seedling	1250.00	-	-	1250.00	7	-	-
ii.	Planting cost including application of pesticide (100 pits/MD), 25 MD	2225.00	-	-	2225.00	25	-	-
iii.	Mortality replacements 500 pits/MD : 5 MD	445.00	-	-	445.00	5	-	-
3.	**Inter-culture opertions**							
i.	Weedling and Soil work : twice in1st year & once in subsequent year @ 30 MD / weedling	5340.00	2670.00		8010.00	60	30	-
ii.	*Irrigation; three irrigation in 1st year & one irrigation in 2nd year @ Rs. 500 per irrigation	1500.00	500.00	-	2000	14	5	-
4.	**Tending operation**							
	Cut back at a height of about 30 to 45 cm in 1st year. Prunning side branches in 2nd year ; 500 plants/MD; 5 MD	445.00	445.00	-	890.00	5	5	-
	Total	**24.008.00**	**3615.00**	**-**	**27623.00**	**189**	**40**	**40**

Basis of calculation:Spacing: 2m x 2m; No. of plants per ha : 2500; Mortality replacements : 20 %; wage rate : Rs. 89 per manday (MD) vide Government of India Ministry of Labour/ notification No. S.O. 09(E) & 113(E) dated 3rd and 26th Jan., 2002.

* Irrigation is applicable in arid and semi–arid areas where it is essential for earlier establishment phase.

Note

- In hilly terrain, the expenditure of Rs. 6,000.00 should be incurred for digging/preparation of contour trenches and other soil conservation structures in place of ploughing and digging pits.
- In case of termite infected soils, termiticide to be mixed with soil mixture before filling the pits.
- The above estimate has been prepared on the basis of Rs. 89.00 per manday, which may vary as per prevailing rates of daily wages in different states.

Table 8.4

Employment generation in raising plantations of *Jatropha curcas* on wastelands

S. No.	Items	Mandays generated (Millions)
1.	Wasteland required for replacing 5% diesel (million ha)	2.67
2.	Raising of nursery, 2500 plants/ha; 45 mandaysjha	120.15
3.	Plantation activity; 2500 plants/ha; 189 mandaysjha	504.63
4.	Maintenance of plantation; 2500 plants/ha; 40 mandays	106.8
5.	Seed collection and other activities; 66 mandaysjha	176.22
6.	Total employment generated for raising 2.67 million wasteland with Jatropha till 2nd year (274 mandays)	731.58
7.	Continuous employment till 30 years for seed handling and maintenance activities (66 mandays)	176.22

Thus the cost of raising one hectare *Jatropha* plantation and its maintenance upto 2nd Year at considering espacement 2 m x 2 m including nursery cost is estimated at Rs. 33,523.00 only. The activity may be viewed mainly as rural employment generation programme. During the first year itself 234 mandays per hectare would be generated with 40 mandays per hectare during the second year onwards. From 4th year onwards, as seed yield gets stabilized, 66 mandays are supposed to be generated per year per hectare which may extend up to 30 to 40 years of fruiting span of plantations. Implementation of similar projects in Mali and other countries have shown that proposed activities have high financial viability taking in to account end uses of products and by-products of the different components.

In addition to generate the employment opportunities, there are other financial benefits of raising these plantations. The oil cake left as residue after extraction of oil from the oil seeds of *Jatropha* is rich in nitrogen and are excellent organic fertilizers. Organic biofertilizers in form of these cakes will not only be available to the farmers right at their doorstep but also help to reduce huge import bill and subsidies make on chemical fertilizers.

High unemployment, low cost labour, high cost of delivered petroleum products and unfavourable balance of payments make biodiesel production an economic and environmentally lucrative venture. Domestic production of biodiesel starting from large scale plantation, collection of seeds, their processing into fatty oils and their conversion into bio–diesel will generate more employment as it is three to six times more labour intensive per unit of production than fossil fuels. Further, utilization of the by products (e.g. glycerine) and residual products (e.g. seed cake, a good source of organic fertilizer) left after fatty oil extraction would offset the production cost of biodiesel.

CARBON TRADING POTENTIAL

India can tap the $52–billion global market for carbon trading by encouraging production and use of bio–fuels. Bio–fuels, apart from enhancing energy security, ensuring employment and development and mitigation environmental pollution, can be instrumental in carbon trading if certain criteria of the clean development mechanism (CMD) of the Kyoto Protocol of the United Nations Framework Convention on Climate Change (UNFCCC) are fulfilled.

According to a recent study by Point Carbon, the potential of global carbon market over the next several years is around $52 billion per annum. Growing at a rate of 4% per year, India, the sixth largest producer of greenhouse gases (GHGs), contributing almost 3% of the world's total emissions (including CH_4 from waste generated by cattle) is seen as one of the most attractive destinations for CMD linked investments. Estimates put the cumulative foreign direct investment (FDI) on account of such projects at about $2 billion, growing at the rate of $200 per year.

In light of increased evidences of climate change effects and their mitigation methodologies, several carbon market and investment mechanisms are slowly evolving. Though the carbon market dynamics are not transparent, the scenario indicates a huge potential in future. Till January 2004, the total volume traded in project-based transactions is 78 million tonne of carbon dioxide emissions ($C0_2$e). The buyer side included Japan with 41 per cent, The Netherlands and CFB with 23% each. According to estimates, if the CMD captures at least 35% of the global market, the estimated value to the concerned countries would be $18 billion.

Reductions in GHG emissions can be accumulated and traded as carbon credits. The CMD facilitates selling of these reductions in terms of certified emission reductions (CERs), a unit of which equals to one tonne of CO_2e.

The present market price of carbon credits is around $5 per CER, which translates into additional revenue of Rs 690 per tonne of bio–diesel consumed. This additional revenue from sale of carbon credits can be used to raise plantations of trees having oil-bearing seeds and materials or meet unforeseen expenses during stabilization period of bio-diesel technology. Large-scale plantation of trees having oil-bearing seeds and materials, like Jatropha and Pongamia species will fix carbon by photosynthesis via the carbon cycle. Thus the consumption of bio–diesel as an energy source either in stationery or mobile combustion leads to "no net-addition of CO_2 to the atmosphere."

Apart from making India self–sufficient in meeting energy needs, reducing the import bill and generating employment, environmental benefits of using biodiesel in the country are seen significant. Biodiesel is considered "Climate neutral" because all of the CO_2 released during consumption is sequestered out of the atmosphere during crop growth. Combustion of on litre of diesel fuel results in the emission of about 2.6 kg of CO_2, a gas responsible for 'Green House Effect' (Anon., 1997). Combustion of biodiesel has been reported in a number of sources to have lowest emissions compared with petroleum diesel as presented in Table 8.5. Environmental benefits from using biodiesel depend upon how much of it is blended into regular diesel fuel.

Thus the development of biodiesel will help the country not only in balancing the huge import bill on account of petroleum products but also in generation of employment opportunities and meeting the environmental obligations such as reductions of GHGs, exhaust emissions, carbon sequestration etc. Under the Kyoto Protocol regulations Euro-III norms will be implemented in the entire country by 2010. In order to meet these emissions requirements, drastic reduction in sulphur content <350 ppm) and higher cetane number (>51) will be required. Biodiesel meets all these important specifications and would help in improving the lubricity of low sulphur diesel (Laucey, 1998).

TABLE 8.5

Average biodiesel emissions compared with conventional diesel

S. No.	Emission type	Percent reduction/increase in emissions Biodiesel*(100%)	Biodiesel* (5%)
1	CO_2	-78.0	-3.90
2	CO	-44.0	-2.25
3	Total unburned hydrocarbons	-68.0	-3.50
4	Ozone depleting potential of certain hydrocarbons	-50.0	-2.50
5	Sulfates	-100.0	-5.00
6	Particulate matter	-40.0	-2.0
7	Polycyclic aromatic hydrocarbons	-80.0	-4.0
8	Nox	+6	+0.25

* National Biodiesel Board, USA.

** Projected from B_{100} results

In the Indian context, biodiesel would not only serve to reduce import of petro-diesel but also facilitate large-scale employment and accelerated ruritl development. Further large wastelands could be utilized for the cultivation of non-edible oil producing trees/shrubs for production of biodiesel. However, current literature on environmental impacts is limited, and there is a need to carry out extensive studies from all possible feedstocks and generate comprehensive data on environmental impacts including pollutant emission, global warming potential, and energy efficiency.

9

Network of Jatropha Oil for Biodiesel

INTRODUCTION

Diesel Engines have become indispensable prinle movers in the organized and unorganized sectors. They are mainly used on Industries, Power, Transport and Commercial sectors as power drives. Due to the rapid depletion of oil reserves and uncertainty in crude oil supply, many countries have started using alternate fuels like Hydrogen, CNG, LPG, Ethanol, Methanol and biodiesel as an alternate fuel. Recently, CNG has been introduced in automotive vehicles in New Delhi, Mumbai and Gujarat. Similarly, LPG has been introduced as alternate fuel in the automotive vehicles in Bangalore. The inventor of diesel engine, Dr.Rudolf Diesel used peanut oil as a fuel in 1885 and demonstrated at the 1900 World Exhibition in Paris speaking to the Engineering Society of St. Louis Missouri in 1902, Diesel said, "The use of vegetable oil for engine fuels may seem insignificant today but such oil may become in course of time as important as Petroleum and the coal tar products of present times."

It is only in recent years that systematic efforts have been made to utilize vegetable oils as fuels in engines (1).

A review of literature shows that European Countries and USA have mainly concentrated on Saffola, Sunflower oils as alternate fuels for diesel engines, which are edible in nature. In India, only non–edible oils can be seriously considered as alternate fuel for IC Engines because the edible oils are in great demand and expensive at present.

India has a large potential of using biodiesel because it could be easily and largely procured in our country. Biodiesel in a renewable fuel and can be produced from any vegetable oil or animal fats. Due to this, employment opportunities will also be more in our country because of large agricultural lands available.

Non–edible oils can be produced to a great extent from the oil seeds of Jatropha, Pongamma (Karang), and Cotton etc. These non–edible oils can be converted to biodiesel through esterification process. The present work is to assess the supply chain of Jatropha Oil seed, which is presently considered as main oil seed for biodiesel production in our country.

BIODIESEL PRODUCTION

Vegetable Oils have higher viscosity and longer hydrocarbon chains. This will lead to produce poor combustion characteristics when they are used as directly used as fuels in Diesel Engines.

To overcome these problems, various techniques have been successfully tried out. They are :

(i) Dilution; (ii) Drier emulsification; (iii) Esterification; (iv) Pyrolysis.

Among the all above, esterification is the most adoptable process. It refers to the conversion of an organic acid into another ester of same acid. It is the process of reaching a triglycerol and fatty acid enters. The vegetable oil based esterified fuels are popularly known as biodiesel and these commercially available in the developed countries.

Jatropha grows in vicinity of villages and towns throughout India. It is cultivated as drought resistant plant in marginal areas to prevent soil erosion. It has a small height multi branched bushy shrub 3-4 m high found in different forms. White (Dhalabaigaba), black (Kala baigaba) and red (Nali baigaba). Black ones are more wild and growing in waste lands, orad and rail sides. The white forms is taller used as hedge plant (fencing plant). The baigabas are medicinal value plants. Planting of any form of Seeds or cuttings are best accomplished early in rainy season.

Recently, private sector giant Reliance Industries Limited (RIL) set aside \$ 500 mm to set up a biodiesel refining plant and earmarked 200 acres of land at Kakinada in Andhra Pradesh as a pilot project to cultivate Jatropha shrubs. The Indian Government has identified 39 mm hectares (almost 100 mm acres) of land suitable for growing Jatropha, cheerily termed "the wonder plant" by Rajasthan State's "Centre of Excellence for Jatropha Biodiesel Promotion."

TABLE 9.1
Jatropha Species in India

Specific Name	Common Name	Distribution In India	Desirable attributes
J. Curcas L.	Pinhao, French physic nut, purging nut, Sabudam, Barbados Nut	South America (Peru)	High oil content, drought resistant frost tolerant less attacked by insects and pests
J. Integerrima Jacq, (J. Panduraefolia Andr, J. Acuminata Desv, J. Hastala Griseb, Manihot diversifolia Sweet)	Fiddle-leave Jatropha	Through out the country	Xerophylic adaptation, resistant to diseases and pests excepts leaf webber and scale, photoperiod insensitive.
J. Gllanduliferra Roxb (J. Glauca Vahl.)	-	S. India, Uttar Pradesh, Bengal	Resistant to pests and diseases
J. Gossypfolia L.	Bellyache Bush, Cotton leafed physic nut	Through out the country	Resistant to scale, miles and leaf eating caterpillars, tolerant to saline soils.
J. Multifida L.	Coral Plant, Finton, Spansih physic Nut	Through out the country	Oranamental, photoperiod insensitive, non dehiscent capsules
J. Heterophylia (J.Heynil)	-	S. India	Ephemeral
J. Nana	-	Pune, Mumbai	-
J. Podagrica Hook	Guatemala Bhubarb, Tartago or Gouly-stemmed Jatropha Hanuman Nagtaen	Thorugh out the Country	Ornamental and adapts well to xerophyic conditions, photoperiod insensitive
J. Wightiana (J. Peltata) J. villosa)	-	Deccan Peninsula Coimbatore	-

The government claims that, if fully exploited, the said 100 mm acres could produce biodiesel that can substitute for 20% of the country's diesel consumption in five years, far higher than the present 2%. Some of the Jatropha species found in India are given in Table 9.1.

Among all the species *Jatropha curcas* and *Jatropha gossypifolia* have potential for exporation in commercial scale. The comparisons of these two are given below in Table 9.2.

TABLE 9.2

Comparisons of Jatropha and Gossypifolia

Character	Jatropha curcas	J. gossypifolia
Fruit bearing	Long juvenile stage full bearing after 3rd year	Short juvenile stage (8 to 10 months)
Capsule dehiscence	Slight	Violent
Dormancy	Absent	Present
Reaction to pests/ diseases	Resistant to disease but susceptible to leaf miner	Resistant to insect and pests
Oil (%)	High (48.5)	Low (28.5)
Life span	Up to 50 years	15 to 20 years.

Though *J. gossypifolia* has heavy fruit bearing it has the serious limitation of violently exploding capsules which makes seed collection labour intensive and not commercially feasible till such time he drawback is overcome. The requirement of Jatropha oil for blending of bio–diesel in India is given in Table 9.3.

TABLE 9.3

Jatropha oil required for blending of biodiesel in India

Year	Diesel Demand Million Tones	Jatropha Oil required for biodiesel blending million tons		
		5%	10%	20%
2006-07	52.33	2.62	5.24	10.47
2007-08	54.95	2.75	5.50	10.99
2008-09	57.70	2.89	5.77	11.54
2009-10	60.59	3.03	6.06	12.12
2010-11	63.62	3.18	6.36	12.72

The above data is based on 5% growth in fuel consumption. The other characters of jatropha seed has to be identified.

CHARACTERS OF JATROPHA

The wood hnd fruit of Jatropha can be used for numerous purposes including fuel. The seed of Jatropha contains (50% by weight) viscous oil, which can be used for manufacture of candles and soap, in the cosmetics industry, for cooking and lighting by itself or as a diesel/paraffin substitute or extender. This latter use has important implications for meeting the demand for rural energy services and also exploring practical substitutes for fossil fuels to counter greenhouse gas accumulation in the atmosphere. These characteristics along with its versatility make it of vital importance to developing countries subjected to decreasing tree cover and soil fertility because of increasing population and development pressures. Nearly half the world's poorest people live on marginal lands with the number expected to increase from 500 million to 800 million by 2020. These areas are by definition isolated and fragile, with soils susceptible to erosion and subjected to environmental stresses of deforestation, prolonged droughts, and decreasing soil and ground water.

The recommended spacing for soil conservation is 15 cm - 25 cm x 15cm–25cm in one or two rows respectively and 2m x 105m to 3m x 3m for plantations (Jones N, Miller J.H. 1992). Jatropha shrubs can deliver 1,600 to 3,000 liters of biodiesel per hectare, depending on irrigation conditions and the number of shrubs planted per hectare. The important Jatropha Curcas is given in Table 9.4 below

Table 9.4

The important Jatropha curcas

Promising states	Sowing time	Climate	Seed	Collection period
AP, Gujarat Rajasthan, Kamataka and Maharashtra	February-March	Grows in arid and semi arid, Tropical and semi tropical environment with average rainfall 480 mm to 2380 mm.	Sep.-Dec. 1.8 cm long Oil content 30–40% Driage 20-35%	October-November February - March Collection per person per day-2.5 g.fruit.

India's motor vehicle industry is growing very fast. There are over 8 mm vehicles sold per year. The vehicle includes :

- Passenger cars,
- Utility vehicles,
- Commercial trucks,

- Two-wheeled *vehicles.*
- Three-wheeled vehicles.

THE SUPPLY CHAIN NETWORK

"Colllectivity for the billion people is *the connectivity of the planet; it means we are connecting* 600,000 *villages in a single country. This experience will become the foundation for other continents." -* ***A.P.J. Abdul Kalam.,*** *President of India on his Address to the General Assembly of Intenational Union of Radio Science (URSI) on 25-10-2005: New Delhi.*

The distribution of the seeds to the extraction units and the oil to the respective factories to biodiesel now plays a important role in the economic issue of the product. The methodology of the distribution system and use of modern technology are to be considered for the effective supply chain of the system.

"SCM is a Management philosophy of systemic, strategic coordination of the business functions within the organisation and across the entire Supply Chain for improving long term preformance of all Supply Chain Partners"*

-Mentzer

It is very hard to deliver enough seeds to the expeller units and to the biodiesel plants because:

- There are not enough vehicles that can be committed to this purpose for long periods of time.
- Limitations on the number of available drivers.
- Rail cars are not easily obtained and converted to this purpose in the short run.
- Pipeline, Storage, Facilities.

The distribution market, like other petroleum markets, is not regulated economically. The decisions about how much inventory to maintain are wholly within the discretion of the distributor and his retailers. Large inventories are desirable to avoid fuel outages. But there is no way for the state to require distributors to maintain a given quantity of fuel on hand. To improve the efficiency and effectiveness of an organization network supply chain optimizes a variety of business processes. It provides decision support capabilities in the areas of material and capacity requirements planning, Inventory analysis of seeds and oils, financial analysis and product life cycle management. It also balances any MRP /ERP investment. The schematic representation of the supply chain network of Jatropha oil is as shown in Figure 9.1.

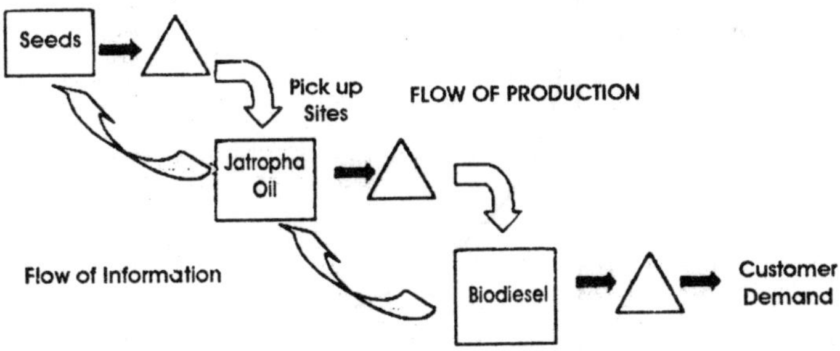

Fig. 9.1 : Supply Chain Network of Jatropha.

When product ownership transfer occurs and that firms are linked together in cooperative vertical marketing systems providing total channel-wide performance. Langley (1992) suggests four stages of development: (i) cost control, (ii) profit-centre orientation recognizing the positive impact on sales, (iii) view of logistics as key to product differentiation, and (iv) as a principal strategic advantage. The supply chain network design requires data for the system setup and during system operation. The data is grouped into three categories : (1) Reference, (2) Demand, (3) Supply. This is given in Table 9.5.

Table 9.5

Data base for supply chain

Reference	Demand	Supply
-Production data -Cost element -Work centres -Substitution rules	-Customer (biodiesel plant) order -Inter site demand order -Forecast on each manufacturing facility	- Purchase order -Inventory -Work orders -Purchase Requisitions

This data base would provide the decision on the number of pick up sites and distribution centers.

SERVICE AND NUMBER OF FACILITIES

The transportation management would be efficient when the numbers of facilities are high (Figure 9.2). Hence the response time has to reduce both at the pick sites and distribution centers. When the number of facilities increases the response time decreases and vice versa. Figure 9.2 shows the relationship between response and number of facilities.

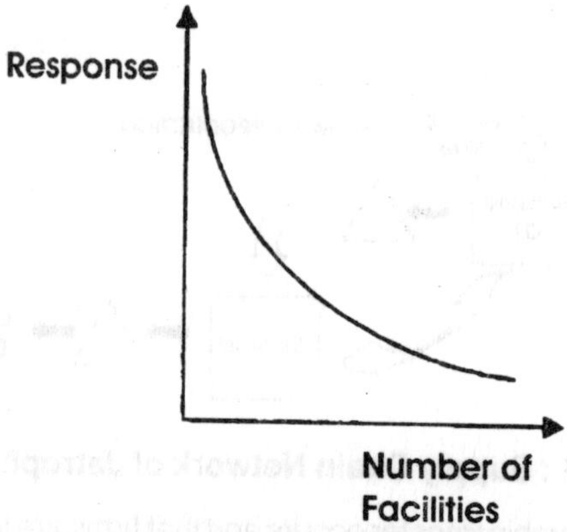

Fig. 9.2 : Response time vs. Facilities

The service factor is affecting the effectiveness of supply chain. In the supply chain features include options on serving size, promptness of service, and ambience of location. The number of pickup sites locations to be serviced in a day, coupled with the customer's demands for delivery timings makes optimizing the transportation routes a unique challenge.

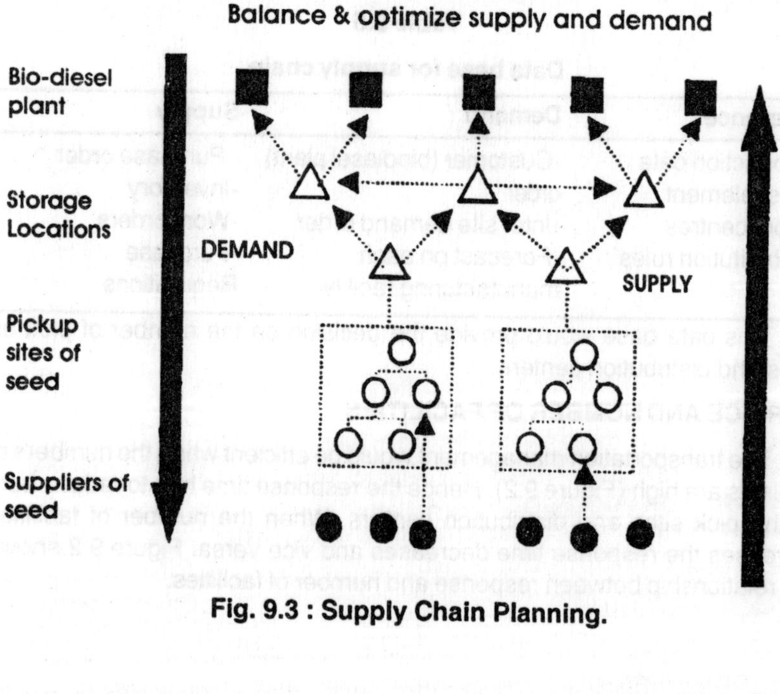

Fig. 9.3 : Supply Chain Planning.

The permissible delivery times to each pick up sites is often fixed in the industry, because the supply is not to meet an immediate demand - it is to replenish stock at the immediate pickup sites location, which in turn will be used to fulfill demand. The number of pickup sites locations to be serviced in a day, coupled with the customer's demands for delivery timings makes optimizing the transportation routes a unique challenge. Based on the number of pickup sites the cost related to the issue will change. The Fig. 9.4 gives the detail about total cost compared with facilities.

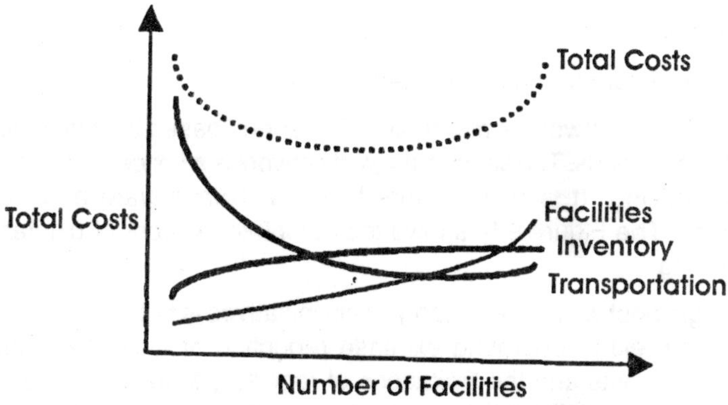

Fig. 9.4. Total Costs Related of Number of Facilities

As the demand expands internationally, additional functionality, not available in their existing methods, was needed to continue effective support of operations. The existing methods was becoming difficult and time intensive to navigate due to the high volume of customisations that had to be created to keep up with the growing business. One of the most important steps has to be taken in deciding how to proceed with adding additional functionality and streamlining our system to perform a business optimisation analysis (BOA). This process enables to see exactly where and what needed to upgrade as well as how to best go about it. An inefficient and poorly functioning supply chain can negatively impact every aspect of an organization. Here are four trends that will re-evaluate current processes and performance.

Trend 1 — Demand Planning of seeds Begins at the End of the Cycle.

Trend 2 — Globalisalion.

Trend 3 — Outsourcing.

Trend 4 — Collaboration between Stakeholders in the Extended Supply Chain.

Problems in the regular supply of seeds are:

1. Low yields.
2. Significant yield variability.
3. Poor roads and Limited freight.
4. High procurement cost.
5. Poor storage facility.
6. High interest costs.
7. Lack of supply chain management tools.

In the existing network of plantation it is planned based on their types of seed and farming lands. The second stage of network is a concentrate towards the oil processing. It is being carried out by both private and public organizations. The Figure 9.5 shows the complete network of plantations and processing.

The single best way to sell supply chain initiatives is to forecast positive cash flow from either operating expense reduction or increase in sales. Understanding costs and the limitations of reporting them is an important SCM skill. Performing the "make or buy" decisions to determine functions that might be outsourced.

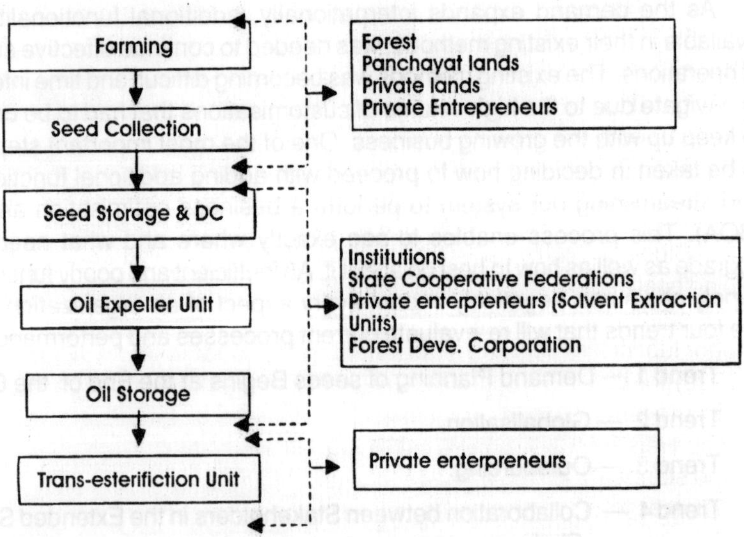

Fig. 9.5 : Existing Network of Plantation and Oil Processing.

10

Potential for Biodiesel

ADVANTAGES OF BIODIESEL

Biodiesel offers many advantages

- It is renewable.
- It is energy efficient.
- It displaces petroleum derived diesel fuel.
- It can be used in most diesel equipment with no or only minor modifications.
- It can reduce global warming gas emissions.
- It can reduce tailpipe emissions, including air toxics.
- It is non–toxic, biodegradable, and suitable for sensitive environments.
- It is made from either agricultural or recycled resources.
- It can be easy to use if you follow these guidelines.

Biodiesel can be used in several different ways such as use 1% to 2% biodiesel as a lubricity additive, which could be especially important for ultra low sulfur diesel fuels (ULSD, less than 15 ppm sulfur), which may have poor lubricating properties. It can blend 20% biodiesel with 80% diesel fuel (B20) for use in most applications that use diesel fuel. It can even use it in its pure form (B100) with take proper precautions. The word biodiesel in this report refers to the pure fuel– B100 - that meets the specific biodiesel definition and standards approved by ASTM International. A number following the "B" indicates the percentage of biodiesel in a gallon of fuel, where the remainder of the gallon can be No.1 or No.2 diesel, kerosene, jet A, JP8, heating oil, or any other distillate fuel. The use of Bio diesel are tested for various parameters and blending of Bio–Diesel up to 18–20 % is found most efficient for the running of the vehicle and also pollution limits due to hydrocarbon (HC), Carbon-mono oxide (CO) and nitrogen (NOx) are found well within the emission limits prescribed by EPA in 1995.

ASTM D-6751 standards for biodiesel [5]

Flash point (closed cup)	130°C min (150°C average)
Water and sediment	0.050% by vo, max
Kinematic viscosity at 40°C	1.9-6.0 mm ^{2}/s
Ramsbottom carbon residue, % mass	0.10
Sulfated ash	0.020% mass, max.
Sulfur	0.05% by mass, max.
Copper strip corrosion	No. 3 max.
Cetane	47 min.
Carbon residue	0.050% by mass, max.
Acid number - mg KOH/g	0.80 max.
Free glycerin	0.020% mass
Total glycerine (free glycerine and unconverted glycerides combined)	0.240% by mass, max.
Phosphorus content	0.001 max. % mass
Distillation	90% @ 360°C

SIGNIFICANT BENEFITS OF BIODIESEL [5]

Environmental Benefits

In 2000, biodiesel became the only alternative fuel in the country to have successfully completed the EPA-required Tier I and Tier II health effects testing under the Clean Air Act. These independent tests conclusively demonstrated biodiesel's significant reduction of virtually all regulated emissions, and showed biodiesel does not pose a threat to human health.

Biodiesel contains no sulfur or aromatics, and use of biodiesel in a conventional diesel engine results in substantial reduction of unburned hydrocarbons, carbon monoxide and particulate matter. A U.S. Department of Energy Study showed that the production and use of biodiesel, compared to petroleum diesel, resulted in a 78.5% reduction in carbon dioxide emissions. Moreover, biodiesel has a positive energy balance. For every unit of energy needed to produce a gallon of biodiesel, 3.24 units of energy are gained [5].

Energy Security Benefits

With agricultural commodity prices approaching record lows, and petroleum prices approaching record highs, it is clear that more can be done to utilize domestic surpluses of vegetable oils while enhancing our energy security. Because biodiesel can be manufactured using existing industrial production capacity, and used with conventional equipment, it provides substantial opportunity for *immediately* addressing our energy security issues.

If the true cost of using foreign oil were imposed on the price of imported fuel, renewable fuels, such as biodiesel, probably would be the most viable option. For instance, in 1996, it was estimated that the military costs of securing foreign oil was $57 billion annually. Foreign tax credits accounted for another estimated $4 billion annually and environmental costs were estimated at $45 per barrel. For every billion dollars spent on foreign oil, America lost 10,000 - 25,000 jobs [5].

Economic Benefits

Increased utilization of renewable bio–fuels results in significant microeconomic benefits to both the urban and rural sectors, and the balance of trade. A study completed in 2001 by the US. Department of Agriculture found that an average annual increase of the equivalent of 200 million gallons of soy-based biodiesel demand would boost total crop cash receipts by $5.2 billion cumulatively by 2010, resulting in an average net farm income increase of $300 million per year. The price for a bushel of soybeans would increase by an average of 17 cents annually during the ten-year period.

In addition to being a domestically produced, renewable alternative fuel for diesel engines, biodiesel has positive performance attributes such as increased cetane, high fuel lubricity, and high oxygen content, which may make it a preferred blending stock with future ultra-clean diesel [5].

Quality Benefits

Biodiesel is registered as a fuel and fuel additive with the EPA and meets clean diesel standards established by the California Air Resources Board (CARB). B100 (100 per cent biodiesel) has been designated as an alternative fuel by the US. Department of Energy and the US. Department of Transportation. Moreover, in December, 2001, the American Society of Testing and Materials (ASTM) approved a specification (D6751) for biodiesel fuel. This development was crucial in standardizing fuel quality for biodiesel in the U.S. market.

The National Biodiesel Board, the trade association for the biodiesel industry, has formed the National Biodiesel Accreditation Commission (NBAC) to audit fuel producers and marketers in order to enforce fuel quality standards in the US. NBAC issues a 'Certified Biodiesel Marketer' seal of approval for biodiesel marketers that have met all requirements of fuel accreditation audits. This seal of approval will provide added assurance to customers, as well as engine manufacturers, that the biodiesel marketed by these companies meets the ASTM standards for biodiesel and that the fuel supplier will stand behind its products [5].

EP Act Benefits

Effective November 1998, Congress approved the use of biodiesel as an Energy Policy Act (EPAct) compliance strategy. The legislation allows EPAct-covered fleets (federal, state and public utility fleets) to meet their alternative fuel vehicle purchase requirements simply by buying 450 gallons of pure biodiesel and burning it in new or existing diesel vehicles in at least a 20% blend with diesel fuel. The Congressional Budget Office and the US. Department of Agriculture have confirmed that the biodiesel option is the least-cost alternative fuel option for meeting the Federal Government's EPAct compliance requirements. Because it works with existing diesel engines, biodiesel offers an immediate and seamless way to transition existing diesel vehicles into a cleaner burning fleet [5].

SCOPE OF PRODUCTION OF BIODIESEL IN INDIA

India has nearly 60 million hectares of wasteland, of which 30 million hectares are available for energy plantations like" Jatropha". Once grown, the crop has a life of 50 years. Each acre will produce about 2 tonnes of biodiesel at about Rs. 20 per litre. Biodiesel is carbon neutral and many valuable by-products flow from this agro-industry. Intensive research is needed to burn bio-fuel in internal combustion engines with high efficiency, and this needs to be a urgent R & D programme. India has a potential to produce nearly 60 million tones of bio-fuel annually, thus making a significant and important contribution to the goal of Energy Independence. Indian Railways has already taken a significant step of running two passenger locomotives (Thanjavur to Nagore Section) and six trains of diesel multiple units (Tiruchirapalli to Lalgudi, Dindigul and Karur Sections) with a 5% blend of bio-fuel sourced from its in-house esterification plants. In addition, they have planted 75 lakh Jatropha saplings in Railway land which is expected to give yields from the current year onwards. This is a pioneering example for many other organisations to follow. Similarly many states in our country have energy plantations. What is needed is a full economic chain from farming, harvesting, extraction to esterification, blending and marketing. Apart from employment generation, bio-fuel has a significant potential to lead our country towards Energy Independence [9].

CULTIVATION OF JATROPHA AND OTHER SEEDS IN INDIA

President of India Plants Jatropha Saplings in Mugal Gardens of Rashtrapati Bhavan (Presidential Palace)

Dr. A.P.J. Abdul Kalam has planted Jatropha sapling in Mugal Gardens of Rashtrapati Bhavan. To begin with 800 plants are being planted for educational purposes to promote the use of herbal plants for extracting oil from which biodiesel can be produced. This is being done in collaboration with G.B. Pant Agricultural University, Pantnagar and National Botanical Research Institute, Lucknow. A demonstration of Agricultural implements being operated by biodiesel was also made before the President. President of India Dr. A.P.J. Abdul Kalam always emphasizes on plantation of *Jatropha curcas* [1].

Every State Government if taking steps to promote *Jatropha curcas* and *Pomgamia pinatta*.

Chhattisgarh

The government has planted in 2005, 80 million saplings of Jatropha, a source of bio-fuel, as the state attempts to tap non-conventional energy sources. It has set a target of cultivating Jatropha plantations in one million hectares in 2006, covering 20,000 hectares in the first phase. The government would work with NGOs for starting 350 Jatropha nurseries, each spread over a maximum of 500 hectares, in 2005.

Andhra Pradesh

State has taken the lead in Jatropha Plantation. The State Government has set up a separate department for bringing into productive use the 728,000 hectare cultivable wasteland available for cultivation of Jatropha plantation for production of biodiesel. The State Government is drawing up a roadmap, which will see the involvement of oil majors like Indian Oil Corporation (IOC) and Reliance Industries, to make the state the biggest producer of biodiesel. It is planning to bring between 4 and 5 million acres of land in seven to eight districts of the state under biodiesel plantations and ensure that micro-irrigation is used in a big way in these areas. This will change the ecology of the area.

Tamil Nadu

Underutilised lands could turn into fertile farms and farmers can be assured of a price for their produce. This is a project to produce 100 per cent biodiesel from Jatropha. D1-Mohan Bio Oils Limited (a joint venture of Mohan Breweries and Distilleries and U.K. based D1 Oils Plc) plans to bring one lakh hectares under Jatropha cultivation in Tamil Nadu. Indian Overseas Bank signed an agreement with Coimbatore based Classic Jatropha Oil (India) Ltd. for promoting cultivation of Jatropha curcas in Tamil Nadu under contract farming. Classic Jatropha Oil, a subsidiary of Tirupur based major knitwear exporters, has been involved in developing the Jatropha cultivation for a long time.

(**D1 Oil pic:** A UK producer of green fuel, Newcastle-based D1 Oil plc, has 10,000 hectares of the crop planted in India and its target of 267,000 hectares by the end of 2006 is on track.)

Uttar Pradesh

State is also taking lead in Jatropha plantation in district Basti, Bahraich, Gonda and Barabanki. Formers have started cultivating the Jatropha in big way. Atleast 200 acres land is initially being used for its cultivation. So far there is no plant for producing biodiesel from Jatropha seeds.

Reliance Industries Ltd to Enter Bio-Fuel

Reliance Industries Ltd. (RIL) is planning to enter the bio-fuel segment in a big way. To begin with, the company has earmarked 200 acres of land at Kakinada in Andhra Pradesh to cultivate Jatropha, which can yield high quality biodiesel. The area of cultivation will be increased to many thousands of acres depending on the progress of the project. The project is being implemented by Reliance Life Sciences, a subsidiary of RIL.

Several smaller Indian companies are already working towards developing biodiesel

Companies like Nandan Bioagro and Labland Biotech have tied up with British Oil Company D1 Oils to produce Jatropha and trade in it. The company will encourage hundreds of farmers to cultivate the crop under an arrangement with the company. A Jatropha seed contains 31 to 37 per cent extractable oil. A Jatropha plantation over 100,000 hectares is expected to yield 250,000-300,000 tons of crude Jatropha oil per annum. It is estimated that an initial 100,000 hectare Jatropha farm will yield revenues of $100 million per annum. Reliance is also in talks with Maharashtra, Gujarat, Andhra Pradesh and Rajasthan Governments, to get access to land for contract farming.

Godrej plans Indian Rupees 5 billion for bio-fuel projects

Godrej Agrovet Ltd. is planning to invest over Indian Rupees 5 billion, for Jatropha and palm oil cultivation in the States of Gujarat and Mizoram. The company would cultivate Jatropha or palm oil according to the nature of the wasteland in these states. According to industry sources, Godrej Agrovet would invest Indian Rupees 2.5 billion for bio-fuel plant cultivation along with the palm oil processing and plant cultivation project in Gujarat while it would invest Indian Rupees 2.5 billion for both Jatropha and palm oil cultivation in Mizoram. Godrej would be cultivating both Jatropha and palm oil in an area over 10,000 acres in Mizoram as per the fertility of the land. The company is also in the process of setting up mills in Walia (Gujarat) at an estimated cost of $ 10 million.

Emami Ltd.

One of the leading toiletries outfit in the country, is planning to enter into the farming of Jatropha, a source of biodiesel. The company might float a joint venture outfit with a leading European company in the field of biodiesel for the new business. Emami group is now talking to some companies in United States, UK and Austria for technical collaboration for the extraction of oil from Jatropha. The project will be first of its kind in the Eastern India. The company will start farming of Jatropha in Suri in West Bengal and Balasore in Orissa.

Plantation of Other Seeds

In India from old days oil from Mahua, Neem, Soybean seeds were extracted and being used for domestic purposes for lighting lamps, heating stoves[7] etc. The potential now be utilized for this by getting the plantation again done which may help in ecological balances and may bee used as renewable energy source.

BIODIESEL POLICY

Price Policy for Biodiesel

Public Sector oil firms have announced a price of Indian Rupees 25 (US$ 0.56) per liter for procuring biodiesel extracted from non-edible oilseeds for mixing in diesel. The programme to sell diesel mixed with non-edible oil extracted from *Jatropha curcas* and *Pongamia pinnata*, which could cut India's import dependence, but would take 4-5 years to launch on commercial scale. It will take time for adequate quantities of *Jatropha curcas* and *Pongamia* pinnata to be planted and oil extracted for mixing in diesel.

Biodiesel Credit Bank

Petroleum Conservation Research Association (PCRA), www.pcra.org, launched Biodiesel Credit Bank. It will co-ordinate activities relating to Carbon Credit.

Field Trials: Several Field trials have been performed.

1. Indian Oil Corporation, (IOC) had placed an order of 450 kiloliters of biodiesel in 2004, for field trials with the Indian Railways and State Roadways. IOC will be able to supplement 5% of diesel with biodiesel in three years.
2. The first phase of the project, by Daimler-chrysler India, in 2003-04 saw production of the indigenous biodiesel and completion of road trials on two C-Class Mercedes-Benz cars. The cars, powered by pure (neat) Biodiesel, traversed the rugged terrain of the country in April-May, 2004, and clocked over 5,900 kilo meters under very hot and humid conditions.
3. The Council for Scientific and Industrial Research (CSIR) is now in talks with country's biggest truck and bus maker Tata Motors and Indian Oil to take its bio–fuel project to the next stage, for testing its vehicles on biodiesel developed from Jatropha plant.

Bio–fuel Policy in India

1. **Centre may clear bio-fuel policy by 2006** : The Center is likely to come up with a clear-cut biodiesel policy by end of 2006. The Energy Policy Committee has submitted its report to the government by November 30, 2005. An in-principle approval is expected to be given by that time, which will be worked into a formal bio-fuel policy later. The report from the committee has made specific proposals which will then be forwarded to the Energy Co-ordination Committee for final acceptance by the government.
2. **Zero excise duty for bio-fuels on cards** : The government is likely to change the excise duty structure for bio–fuels in the next Budget to make their use attractive. Petroleum Ministry officials said the excise duty on biodiesel and ethanol is likely to be made nil and states would be asked to have a favourable sales tax regime.
3. **Government to assist, encourage states in biodiesel production**: The government will assist states promote Jatropha cultivation for increasing biodiesel production in the country under the National Rural Employment Guarantee Scheme, the Rajya Sabha was informed on 7th December 2005.

4. **Andhra Pradesh State Government Introduces Draft Industrial Policy**: The Andhra Pradesh Government has introduced a draft biodiesel policy to facilitate both investors and farmers to plant oil-bearing trees in 1.5 million acre in the next four years. Also, a risk fund of Indian Rupees 2 Billion is expected to be created, as loan to the State Government, to support small and marginal farmers with maximum five acre land holding. There is also a proposal for constituting a biodiesel board, which would be an autonomous board for integrated development of Jatropha cultivation and biodiesel oil in the state. The proposed board, having legal authority, will monitor the tripartite agreement signed between the stake holders, besides assisting, encouraging, and promoting Jatropha cultivation, according to the officials involved in preparing the draft policy said. Following the constitution of policy, the government is determined to promote contract farming for buyback of Jatropha seeds. The minimum buy-back price will be fixed considering the different variables including the quality and quantity of the produce. i\ special department called the Rain Shadow Area Department has been created as a special purpose vehicle for planning, coordination, monitoring and implementation of the biodiesel programme.

COMMERCIAL PRODUCTION IN INDIA

Two small units are already in production

1. Aatmiya Bio–fuels Pvt. Ltd., 68,G.I.D.C POI' Ramangamdi Taluka, and District Vadodara, Gujarat- 391243, Phone No : 0265 2885009, Mobile No: 09879359010, has commercialized the production of biodiesel in Gujarat on 8th March, 2005 and now producing 1000 liters/day. The company is promoted by Mr. Umakant Joshi, umakanljoshi@hotmail.ccm a Chemical Engineer who did his graduation from M.S.University of Vadodara, then post graduate in Chemical Engineering from Delaware University, USA specialized in Bio–energy.
2. Gujarat Oelo Chem Limited (GOCL), a Panoli-based firm started on 12th of March 2005, producing biodiesel from vegetable based feedstock. It released the first commercial consignment of biodiesel to Indian Oil Corporation (IOC). Head Office: Gujarat Oleo Chem. Ltd., D-315, Crystal Plaza, Oshiwara Link Road, Andheri(W), Mumbai- 400053, Tel: 91-22-2673 3369 / 70 / 71, Fax: 91-22-2634 9195. E-mail: gocl@bom5.vsnl.net.in, Website: www. gujaratoleochem.com. Regd. Off. and Works: Plot No. 631–639, GIDC, Panoli, 394 116, Tel: 91-2646-271 730 / 731 / 647, Fax: 91-2646-272195.

Production Plans

Number of companies are planning to setup new units.

1. Kochi Refineries Ltd. (KRL) is setting up a pilot plant with a US firm to extract biodiesel from rubber seed oil. An R & D exercise, the company proposed to look at the feasibility of the project and would initially have a pilot plant setup with a daily capacity of 100 liters. The company has initiated studies into the availability of rubber seed oil from neighboring Tamil Nadu, especially from the Nagercoil belt.
2. Another Kochi-based company, TeamSustain Ltd, a division of US-based Dewcon Instruments Inc, is in talks with a US firm for setting up a biodiesel plant in Kochi.
3. Pune-based Shirke Biohealthcare Pvt. Lld., 11, Navrang Plaza, Tingre Nagar, Vishrantwadi, Airport Road, Pune, India, 411 015. Tel: 91-20-5623 3110, Cell: 91-9422010236, Fax: 91-20-2581 3993, jetindia@rediffmail.com, is setting up a refinery at Hinjewadi, with a capacity to process 5,000 liters biodiesel per day from Jatropha plant. The refinery will also produce 1 MW power with the oil cake, apart from natural gas which will be used to run the power plant.
4. Renewable energy company Bhoruka Power Corporation Ltd, has received a grant of 100,000 dollars from the US government to conduct a detailed feasibility report for a biodiesel project in State of Karnataka. The study envisages use of Neem or Pongamia non-edible oilseeds for production of biodiesel as well as power.
5. The Southern Online Biotechnologies Limited, which is setting up a biodiesel project in Andhra Pradesh, has signed MOU with several government bodies and non-governmental organisations, for procuring raw material like *Pongomia pinnata* (Karanja or Kanuga) and Jatropha seed. The oil extracted from this seed is used to produce biodiesel. The company is setting up the biodiesel project at an estimated cost of Indian Rupees 150 million at Choutuppal in Andhra Pradesh, with technology from a German company named Lurgi. The plant capacity is 30 tons per day or 90,000 tons per annum. It would require around 100 tons of seeds per day. The annual requirement of seeds is around 32,000 tons. As the current availability of seeds in the state is less than 4,000 tons, company will use other raw materials like acid oils, distilled fatty acids, animal fatty acids and non-edible vegetable oils like neem, rice bran etc.

6. Jain Irrigation System Ltd. has plans to set up a Indian Rupees 480 million large-scale commercial biodiesel plant, with a capacity of 150,000 tons per day in Chattisgarh by 2008. R & D works at 3 tons per day biodiesel pilot plant at Jalgaon, built at a cost of Indian Rupees 5 million. This will be followed by another biodiesel plant with a capacity of 10 tons per day at Jalgaon. The current concern in the biodiesel industry is finding adequate farmland to make sure our industry receives a regular supply of feedstock.

7. Nova Bio Fuels Pvt. Ltd, is setting up a Indian Rupees 200 million, biodiesel plant with a capacity of 30 tons per day in Panipat in 2006. Their plant would also supply glycerine to local pharma companies.

8. Naturol Bioenergy Limited is setting up an integrated biodiesel facility in Andhra Pradesh. The 300 tons per day biodiesel plant will come up in the port town of Kakinada at an estimated cost of Indian Rupees 1.4 billion and would be a 100 per cent export-oriented unit.

9. An Indian Rupees 9 million biodiesel plant is coming up in Ganapathipalayam village, about 20 km away from Pollachi. KTK German Bio Energies India is all set to commence commercial production of bio–fuel from January 2006. The plant will use rubber seeds for extraction biodiesei.

10. Biodiesel extracted from *Pongamlia pinnnta* (Karanj) seeds, was commercially launched in Pune in January 2006. The fuel has been produced and marketed by Pune-based Mint Bio–fuels, Though the plant initially had a capacity of 100 litres per day, it was scaled up to 400 lih'es per day. The company will set up a Indian Rupees 300 million plant at Chiplun, which will have a capacity of producing 5,000 tons of fuel per day. Plans are afoot to increase the capacity of the plant to 1,00,000 tons within a period of four years.

11. Vijayawada based Sagar Jatropha Oil Extractions Private Limited is setting up an Indian Rupees 100 million Jatropha oil extraction unit at Gannavaram. The company has also experienced success with contract farming of the Jatropha plant in the state. Jatropha oil is mixed with diesel to produce biodiesel.

12. British Petroleum on Feb. 2, 2006, declared that it would fund a $9.4 million project in India to see if biodiesel can be produced from a non-edible oil bearing crop. The project by The Energy and Resources Institute in the southern state of Andhra Pradesh will study the

feasibility of producing biodiesel from the crop Jatropha Curcas. The 10-year project will cultivate around 8,000 hectares of wasteland with the crop and install equipment needed for seed crushing, oil extraction and processing, to produce 9 million liters of biodiesel per year. The project will also include an environmental and social impact assessment. TFRI will run the project's daily operations.

RISING CRUDE PRICE

The rising crude oil prices will lead to higher usage of vegetable oils and fats as alternative fuel. Demand for bio-fuels will invariably increase, it is expected that the demand for bio-fuel from vegetable oils and fats will shoot up to 3 million tons a day.

Biodiesel will have a pronounced impact on edible oil prices

Prices of both palm and soy oils will firm up in the coming months, with demand for biodiesel alone grabbing at least six million tons of oils despite the slower growth of the economy. Crude Palm Oil futures have gone up from 1,300-1,500 ringgit to a new higher range of 1,400 to 1,600. As the period October to February advances, prices will creep towards the upper end of this range. Crude de-gummed soy oil would be in the range of $460–500 per tone free on board, while RBD palm olein will be in the $400–450 band and crude palm oil will be between $370–420 free on board. Malaysia and Indonesia are the world's largest producers and exporters of palm oil, while Brazil and Argentina are among the top soy oil producers. From mid-2006, the use of soy oil for biodiesel will have a pronounced impact on prices, and the total biodiesel capacity coming on stream by the end of 2006/07 will require 1.6 million tons of soya oil. Edible oil imports by India, the world's leading buyer, in 2005–06 could remain flat at around 5.65 million tons, but imports of soy oil will go up at the expense of palm oil.

OPPORTUNITIES TO EMPLOYMENT

There are new work opportunities in Jatropha cultivation and biodiesel production related sectors and the industry can be grown in a manner that favours many prosperous independent farmers and farming communities specially Promotion of *Women* employment .

11

Production of Bio-fuels

INTRODUCTION

Fast acceleration growth in population has led to strive for survival. In the processes of developmental growth, the urbanization and industrilization has also increased drastically. Without energy no industry can run, no transportation in possible and ultimately survival will be difficult.

The requirement of fossile diesel (also called petrodiesel) is expected to grow from 39.815 MMT in 2001-2002 to 52.324 MMT in 2006-07 and just over 66 MMT in 2011-12. At present from domestic resources of crude oil, only about 22% of demand can be fulfilled and for the rest 78% we have to depend on importing countries. The import of crude oil is not only money drain out of India but also causes restrictions in many forms especially in case of mobilization. Presently there is annual expenditure of 16 Kharab Rupees on important of crude oil.

The Biodiesel is domestically produced, renewable fuel that can be manufactured from vegetable oils, animal fats or recycled restaurant grease. Biodiesel is safe, bio-degradable and reduces serious air pollutants such as particulates carbon monooxide, hydrocarbon and air toxins. Biodiesel can be used as pure fuel or blended with petroleum in any percentage. Compared to edible oils, the use of non-edible oils is very significant in developing countries like India because of the tremendious demand for edible oil as food and they are far too expensive to be used as fuel.

BIODIESEL PRODUCTION

Biodiesel production consists of two stages. The first stage is to extract oil and then second stage to convert the vegetable oil into Biodiesel through transesterification. The disdavantages of vegetable oil (as diesel fuel substitute) are: high visocity, lower volatility and the reactivity of unsaturated hydrocarbon chain.

METHODS OF OIL EXTRACTION

The popular methods are: Mechanical Press, Solvent Extraction, Hot Water Extraction Soxhlet Extraction, Ultrasonication and Enzymatic Oil extraction.

Each one of the stated method has got some advantages disadvantage over others. For example Mechanical Press is most conventional but it requirs further filterization and degumming. In Enzymatic oil extraction method suitable enzymes are used to liberate oil from crushed seeds. This methods is environment friendly and does not produce volatile organic compound as atmospheric pollutents. However it takes long process time for enzymes to liberate oil.

Methods of Biodiesel Production

Mainly there are four methods of Biodiesel production i.e. Pyrolysis Process, Micro-emusification, Dilution and Trans esterification (catalytic and super critical methanol transesterification). The catalytic can be acid, alkaline or lipase catalyzed transesterification.

The transesterification reaction proceeds with catalyst or without catalyst using alcohol as follows :

Triglyceride + Alcohol = Esters + Glycerol
(Catalyst)

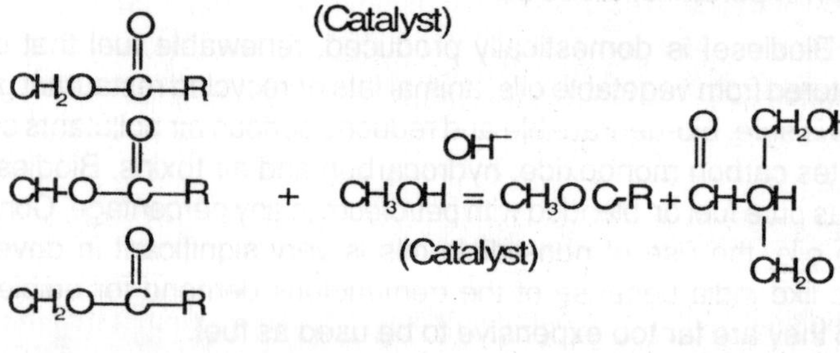

The product of the reaction are biodiesel itself and glycerine.

The final main product Biodiesel can be sold approx. @Rs. 26/ - per kg, by product glycerine approx. @Rs. 40/- litre and seed cake approx. @ Rs. 4000 per tone approximately.

BLENDING OF BIODIESEL WITH PETRO-DIESEL (FOSSILDIESEL)

Biodiesel can be used as a pure fuel or blended with petroleum in any percentage. B5 (i.e. 5% biodiesel and 95% fossil diesel by volume) has shown imporvements in performance enhanced libricity and some reduction in emission.

BENEFITS OF BIODIESEL

- The main benefits of using Biodiesel is that consumer can ensure that their fuel money stays in India rather than going overseas.
- Use of vegetable oil as biodiesel fuel for motor vehicle is in effect running them on solar energy. All bio–fuels are derived from conversion of sun light and CO_2 to energy (carbohydrates) in green leaves of plant.
- The Ozone-Forming Potential of biodiesel emission is nearly 50% less than fossile diesel fuel.
- Biodiesel NOx emissions can be efficiently eliminated as concern.
- Substantial reduction in unburned hydrocarbons carbon monoxide particulate matter, cancer causing PAH and Nitrited PAH comprents.
- Biodiesel reduces carbon dioxide exhaust emission by upto 80%.
- Biodiesel produces 100% less sulfur dioxide than petroleum diesel, Sulfur diooxide is the component of acid.
- Biodiesel reduces exhaust smoke (particulates) emission upto 75% Therefore usual black cloud associated with diesel engine can be eliminated.
- Biodiesel gives more pleasant small than petroleum diesel. It also gives pleasant experience while refuelling vehicle tank.
- Biodiesel is much easier to handle as the mechanic does not require any cream application to protect the skin from cracking or redness.
- The flash point of biodiesel is ±150°C as opposed to petroleum diesel is at ± 70°C. Therefore biodiesel is much less combustible and safe to handle, store and transport.
- Biodiesel degrades about four times faster than petroleum diesel after spillage.
- Biodiesel provides significant lubricity improvement our petroleum diesel.
- Biodiesel exhaust is not offensive and does not cause eye irritation (it smells like French fries).

- Biodiesel reduces the classic diesel engine "knocking" noise.Biodiesel does not require any change with the existing storage infrastructure.

COST ANALYSIS (INDUSTRY POINT OF VIEW)

Assuming that :

(i) Oil will be extracted from Jatropha seed.

(ii) Biodiesel will be produced through trans–esterification

(iii) Plant will work eight hours per shift.

(iv) Plant capacity is 300 tones.

(v) Jatropha seeds will give 30% oil.

TABLE 11.1

Product Sales Cost (Yearly)

S.No.	Product Name	Qty.	Selling Rate Rs.	Total Sales Rs.
1.	Biodiesel	300 T	25 Per kg.	75,00,000
2.	Glycerol	3T	40 per kg	1,20,000
3.	Seed Cake	750T	4000 per T	30,00,000
			(A) Grand Total Sale	1,06,20,000

Yearly production expenses :

(i)	Working capital	Rs.75,00,000
(ii)	Depreciation cost on Machinery (10% per year)	Rs. 4,50,000
(iii)	Interest on proposed bank loan (12 % per year)	Rs. 5,31,000
	Total Expenses	Rs. 81,81,000... (B)
	Yearly profit = A - B	= Rs. 1,06,20,000 - 81,81,000
		= Rs. 24,39,000

PROPOSAL FOR SUCCESS OF MISSION

The mission is proposed to be implemented in two phases. In first phase (during 2006-07) demonstration project is to be done in full swing. During this period each and every village farmer to be practically educated and influenced for : (i) Production of Jatropha seeds on unfertilized/ less fertilized lands and also as fencing around fertilized lands; (ii) Plantation and production of tendrill seasonal vegetable plants (e.g. bitter guord, bottle guord etc.) for additional financial income. Simultaneously other activities like setup of seed procurement centre, oil extraction, mobilization of funds from financial institutions, sale of Jatropha seed oil for trans–esterification. In second phase Research and Development, Progress audit and follow up to be made yearly at district and state level.

The NGOs, Gram Panchayat, college youth can play vital role in making the mission success. Government should provide proper incentive/award to the deserving candidate.

"Let us pledge together to make our mission success withing stipulated period.

12

Biomass Energy Technology

The need for energy and fuels is one of the most important topics in the past and present, since energy is the basic element, which influences our standard of living and technological progress. The demand for energy will increase at least by 50% over current levels during the next 50 years, raising grave concerns over how much energy can be produced without enormous damage to the environment. The two key factors that affect the new millennium is human population growth and human energy consumption. If energy policies remain as they are today, by the year 2020 world energy demand would grow by 65% and carbon dioxide emissions by as much as 70%. It is now believed by United Nations demographers that, barring unforeseen catastrophic events, there will be approximately 9 billion people on earth at close of year 2050. At that time population will still be growing though much more slowly than at present. It will probably level out around 9.5 billion late in the century. Mean while however, all those humans will be consuming energy at least as voraciously as humans today. With fully 50% more people in 2050 than - 2000 energy consumption will be at least 50% greater than today. The increase in human population will occur in today's developing nations, where per capita consumption can only be expected to grow rapidly. There are chances of decline in per capita consumption in energy in most developed nations because of greater energy efficiency. In the absence of technological breakthrough, it is reasonable to estimate that global per capita energy consumption might be as much as 10% greater in 2050 than it is now. According to the world watch institute, there are growing signs that the world may be nearing an environmental revolution comparable to the political revolution that swept Eastern Europe two decades ago.

Biomass a material of recent biological origin (non-fossil) is an important resource for sustainable energy supply for the future as the energy carrier biomass can be converted into power, heat and bio–fuels e.g. ethanol, hydrogen and biogas. Unlike electricity based sustainable resources, such as wind and solar energy, biomass can be stored and thereby used at times which suit the energy system. Biomass is also an important raw material for the environmentally friendly production of a large number of materials, which are presently petroleum based. Biomass energy is a form of solar energy. In fact solar energy is captured via photosynthesis as carbon dioxide and is incorporated as fixed carbon during the growth stage of all biomass. Fig. 12.1 shows the main features of biomass energy technology.

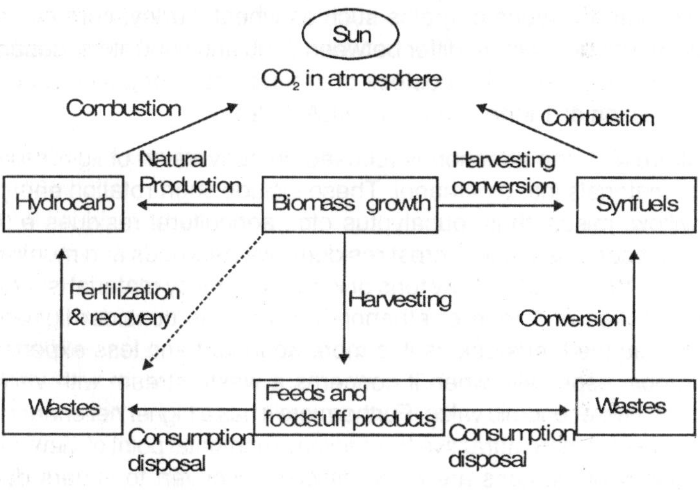

Fig. 12.1 : Main features of Biomass Energy Technology.

For the conversion of biomass into bio–fuels, various conversion routes are available tllat follow from different types of biomass feed stocks i.e. woody biomass, sugar rich crops, oil crops and wet biomass etc. Following is the data on conversion technologies for the production of biofuels, bioethanol and biodiesel in particular. The fuel characteristics of the bio–fuels in comparison with the fossil fuel it can replace are tabulated.

Bioconversion : The term bioconversion is used in several ways. One definition limits the term to the conversion of organic wastes to methane by micro–organisms, viz-anaerobic digestion. Further refining of methane may yield hydrogen, from which few other products are easily and economically produced.

The bioconversion of lignocellulosic biomass involves the use of enzymes, microbes, other biological agents and chemicals, alone or in combination. For example: the conversion of corn kernels into glucose syrup involves, steeping the corn kernels (a biological process), followed by grinding and separation, then conversion of corn starch by thermo stable ∝-Amylase at 100°C a combination of biological and thermal process), followed by treatment with a second enzyme to produce a 95% glucose syrup.

(A) Bioethanol : Ethanol has been used on a large scale, pure as well as in the blended form (gasohol) as a transportation fuel. Currently bioethanol is mainly produced from agricultural crops. Suitable raw materials for the production of ethanol are, sugar beet, sugar cane, molasses, sweet sorghum, potatoes various types of grains such as wheat, barley, corn etc. average ethanol yields per hectare differ between 2100 and 5600 liters, depending on the kind of crop used. A feedstock of around 3 tons of grains is needed for the production of 1 tone of ethanol. (IEA, 1996a).

At present, the attention is focused on conversion of lignocellulosic or woody materials into bioethanol. These include short rotation energy crops e.g. willow, miscanthus, eucalyptus etc., agricultural residues e.g. straw, and sugar cane bagasse, Forest residues, waste woods and municipal solid waste (MSW). About 2–4 dry tons of woody or grassy material is required for the production of 1 tone of ethanol. It is wiser to consider lignocellulosic biomass as the feedstock as it is more abundant and less expensive than food crops, especially when it concerns a waste stream with very little or even negative economic value. Furthermore it has a higher net energy balance, which makes it more attractive from an environmental point of view. However, these kinds of biomass are more difficult to convert to sugars due to the complex structure.

Lignocellulose consists of cellulose, hemi cellulose and lignin.

Cellulose : It is the most abundant biopolymer on earth constituting up to 50% mass in trees. It is a linear crystalline polymer composed of D-glucose residues joined by ß-1, 4-glucosidic bonds. In fact the repetitive units are cellobiose, a dimer of glucose. It is strong and resistant to hydrolysis.

Hemi cellulose : It is a heterogeneous mixture of different polysaccharides and the composition varies with the plant type. It is highly branched and amorphous with little inherent strength. Apart from glucose it may contain mannose, xylose, arabilnose etc.

Lignin : It is highly branched random polymer of coniferyl, sinapyl and p-coumaryl alcohols. In wood, lignin is bound covalently to the side groups of different hemi celluloses by ester- or ether bonds and forms a matrix surrounding the cellulose micro fibril. Table 12.1 shows the composition of different typps of lignocellulosic residues.

TABLE 12.1
Lignocellulose contents of common agricultural residues and wastes

Lignocell ulosic materials	Cellulose (%)	Hemi cellulose (%)	Lignin (%)
Hardwood stems	40–55	24–40	18–25
Softwood stems	45–50	25–35	25–35
Corn cobs	45	35	15
Paper	85–99	0	0–15
Wheat straw	30	50	15
Rice straw	32	24	18
News paper	40–55	25–40	18–30

The production of ethanol from sugar and starch impacts negatively on the economics of the process, thus making ethanol more expensive compared to fossil fuels. Hence the technological development focus for the production of ethanol has shifted towards the utilization of residual lignocellulosic materials to lower production costs. Of the three constituents of lignocellulose, lignin is the most recalcitrant to degradation whereas cellulose, because of highly ordered crystalline structure, is more resistant to hydrolysis than hemi cellulose. Alkaline (Chahal, 1992) and acid hydrolysis (Nguyen, 1993; Grethelin and Converse, 1991) have been used to degrade lignocellulose. Weak acids tend to remove lignin but result in poor hydrolysis of cellulose. Use of strong acids require use of costly equipments. Also, the side reactions leading to the formation of byproducts degrades glucose and reduces the yield. Some of the byproducts affect the fermentation reactions and hence should be removed. There is need to dispose off spent acids and alkalis. On the other hand using various enzymes for biodegradation may not be economically attractive since enzymes are very costly.

Bioconversion of lignocellulosic materials to useful products require multistep processes, which include,

(i) Pretreatment (mechanical, chemical and biological).

(ii) Hydrolysis of polymers (pentoses and hexoses).

(iii) Bioutilization of these molecules to support microbial growth.

(iv) The separation and purification.

Extensive research work has been done the production of cellulose and lignocellulosic enzymes in submerged and solid state fermentation methods. In a recent review,(Malherbe and Cloete, 2003) it is opined that a combination of solid state fermentation technology with a suitable fungus to selectively degrade lignin will make the process industrially viable.

TABLE 12.2
Fuel properties of ethanol, compared to petrol (IEA, 1996b; personal communication P. Kroon, ECN)

Fuel properties	Ethanol	ETBE	Petrol
Chemical formula	C_2H_5OH	C_4H_9-OC_2H_5	C_8H_{15}
Molecular wt. (kg/kmol)	46	102	111
Octane number	109	118	97
Density (kg/l) at 15°C	0.80	0.74	0.75
Stoichiometric air/fuel ratio (kg air/kg fuel)	9.0		14.7
Boiling temperature	78	72	30–190
Lower calorific value (MJ/kg) at 15°C	26.4	36	41.3

(B) Biodiesel (RME) : Biodiesel is obtained from vegetable oils, which can be extracted from seeds or the pulp of several oil crops. For the production of 1 tone of RME, about 2.5 tones rapeseed is needed, which requires a land area of 0.77 hectares. (IEA, 1996a).

Since oils obtained from crops as such have high viscosity and low cetane value, which requires engine modifications, are modified through esterification. Trans–esterification converts the large branched molecular structure of oils (triglycerides) into smaller straight chained methyl esters that are similar to fossil diesel component.

Biofuels can be either wholly or partially substituted for petrol or diesel. Bioethanol can be used as a blend (5%) with petrol under the appropriate EU quality standard (EN14214). This blend requires no engine modification and is covered by vehicle warranties. Higher proportions of ethanol can be used but engine modifications are needed. In Brazil, 18 million vehicles run on fuel blends of between 20–100% ethanol. Cars are currently produced in Sweden, France and UD that can run on up to 85% ethanol.

Biodiesel can be used as a direct substitute for conventional diesel with no need for engine modifications although it is more likely to be blended with fossil-based diesel.

Table 12.3 gives the comparison of fuel properties of diesel and biodiesel.

TABLE 12.3

Fuel properties of biodiesel (RME), compared to diesel (IEA, 1996b)

Fuel Properties	Biodiesel (RME)	Diesel
Chemical Formula	Methyl ester	$C_{12}H_{26}$
Molecular weight (kg/kmol)	296	170-200
Cetane Number	54	50
Density	0.88	0.84
Stoichiometric air/fuel ratio	12.3	14.53
Oxygen contnet (wt%)	9.2-11	0-0.6
Kinematic viscosity (mm^2/s) at 20°C	7.4	4
Flash Point (°C)	91–135	77
Lower calorific value (MJ/Kg) at 15°C	37.3	42.7

Interest in bio–fuels is increasing for a number of reasons :

- Reductions in green house gases.
- Reduced reliance on fossil fuels.
- Increased security of fuel supply.
- Applicability in environmentally sensitive areas.
- Employment and economic benefits through the development of a new form of fuel production.

(C) Hydro Thermal Oil Derived Diesel Equivalent: Here the biomass is decomposed in water to produce a crude oil like liquid called bio-crude. This process can be used for the conversion of a range of biomass feed stocks, like municipal solid wastes and agricultural wastes. The bio-crude obtained is a transportable energy carrier similar to fossil fuel.

(D) Gasification Routes: Gasification denotes the partial oxidation of biomass by treating it with limited supply of oxygen or air. The syngas consists of mainly, CO, CO_2, CH_4, H_2O and N_2 along with contaminants like, char particles, tars etc. For this, any type of biomass can be used. Gasification of biomass results in a mixture of combustible gasses. This is called synthesis gas or syngas. The syngas can be converted into a variety of value added products.

The predicted consumption of bio–fuels in future and thereby reduction in green house gas emissions is summarized in Table 12.4.

Table 12.4
Goals for bioenergy (biofuels) and potential GHG reduction (5)

	2001	2010	2020	2030
Projected transportation fuel (quads)		32.5	40	47.5
Projected gasoline (billion gallons)	130	387	476	565
Biomass share of demand for transportation fuel	<1%	4%	10%	20%
Quads/year	0.147	1.3	4.0	9.
Billon gallons of ethanol/year	1.76	15	48	
Reduction of GHG emission CO_2 eq Pg/year for E100	0.018	0.160	0.493	1.170
Reduction of GHG emission C eq Pg/year for E100 Reduction of	0.005	0.044	0.134	0.319
Reduction of GHG emission C eq Pg/100 years for E100	0.497	4.368	13.439	31.917

13

Jatropha Based Biodiesel

INTRODUCTION

The concept of using bio-fuels is not new. As early as 1900, Rudolf Diesel had used vegetable oils for running engines. Biofuels have been made from different seed-bearing trees such as castor, rapeseed, palm, soyabean, sunflower, safflower, etc. to jatropha, pongamia, etc. in the recent times. The oil extracted from these plants needs to be treated chemically (trans-esterification) in order to be used as a motor fuel.

Of all the oil-bearing plants, Jatropha has been found to be quite satisfactory, both cultivation-wise and performance-wise. In addition, it has several other advantages. Jatropha (*Jatropha curcas*) belongs to Euphorbiaceae family and has been known for its medicinal value in treating a variety of diseases, including cancer. Being inedible, it serves as a fence material; its leaves shedded during winter can make the soil fertile; its cake can be used as manure and as a substrate for production of biogas; its detoxified cake can be used as animal feed.

In India, use of bio–fuels is all the more important because of our high dependence on imported crude oil (being the sixth in the world in energy demand). Even a marginal decrease in imports can lead to reasonable savings. Besides this, large areas of wastelands can be put to use, preventing soil erosion and shifting of sand dunes. Further, we can provide unlimited job opportunities in the rural sector. Jatropha has been planned for plantation under the poverty-alleviation programme. The World Bank has recommended Jatropha from the perspective of erosion control, soil improvement, promotion of gender equality, poverty reduction, and renewable energy.

JATROPHA CULTIVATION

Jatropha can grow on almost any type of soil-gravelly, sandy, and saline soils. It is drought-resistant (surviving even upto 2 years of drought), has extremely low water requirement (needing only 600 mm of rainfall), does not resist water-logging, and adapts well to arid and semi-arid conditions. It can easily be propagated through seeds as well as stem cuttings and shoot tips. Hot and humid weather give better germination of the seed. Irrigation and use of fertilizer improve the yield of seeds, which can take place from the 3rd year onwards. The seed-bearing capacity is around 40 years. Average seed production is around 5 tones per ha and a yield of 0.75-2 tones of biodiesel is expected per year from the 5th year onwards. Although Jatropha can grow under adverse conditions, it is found that right amount of water, nutrients, heat, and the age of the plant determine the crop yield. It can grow upto a height of 3 metres making harvesting an easy task. Jatropha also does not show any intolerance towards other crops and hence this can be exploited by planting shade-loving herbs such as red and green peppers, tomatoes, etc.

India has only 19% land area under forest while National Forest Policy (1952, 1988) wants 33% to be covered under forest and plantations. The remaining land area, categorized as uncultivable wastes, can prove to be useful for Jatropha plantation, thus meeting the required target. If properly implemented, this would prove to be of value in the long run. Jatropha plantation can also be outside forests, such as roadsides, along railway lines (Northeast frontier Railways has already planted 4.47 lac plants along the railway tracks and in vacant railway spaces in 2005), home gardens and orchards.

Calculations show that an initial investment of Rs. 20,000/ - per ha can fetch an amount of Rs. 30,000/- per ha after the 3rd year and even in the first 3 years the farmer can go in for intercropping. Many financial institutions, including NABARD, have come up with loans at concessional rate of interest.

EXTRACTION AND TRANS-ESTERIFICATION

Jatropha oil can be extracted by hydraulic press method after grinding and steaming of the seed. The hard press method gives around 20% lesser oil than the modern industrial expellers. This oil consisting mainly of triglycerides has extremely high viscosity and tends to form undesirable resins. Hence to reduce the viscosity it has to be subjected to trans-esterification, in which the glycerol part is replaced by methanol. The oil is chemically reacted with methanol and a catalyst (NaOH) to give ester (biodiesel) and glycerol. Due to difference in densities between the two products, separation is easy. The filtered fuel is then subjected to a series of washing processes to finally become biodiesel. A comparison of some of the properties of petrodiesel, and biodiesel is given in Table 1. The following is an illustration of the trans-esterification:

H_2C-O-CO-R	H_3C-OH	H_2C-OH	
|		|	
HC-O-CO-R	H_3C-OH	H_2C-OH +	3 H_3C-O-CO-R
|	|	|	
H_2C-O-CO-R	H_3C-OH	H_2C-OH	
Jatropha Oil	Methanol	Glycerol	Biodiesel (Jatropha methyl) Ester

Trans-esterified oil is close to diesel in properties but also has several advantages over petro–diesel complying better with European Union (EU) standards for biodiesel. Further we have a lot of advantages over petrodiesel, as seen in the following:

(i) Superior lubricating properties, increasing functional engine efficiency.

(ii) Higher flash point, making storage safer.

(iii) Higher oxygen content, making combustion complete.

(iv) Complete elimination of lifecycle CO_2 emissions. Also reduction in unburned hydrocarbons, CO, carcinogenic polycyclic aromatic hydrocarbons, carcinogenic nitrated polycyclic aromatic hydrocarbons, particulate matter (black soot), etc.

(v) Low greenhouse gas emissions, reducing global warming. It is sustainable and environment-friendly.

(vi) Biodegradable and providing' cheaper and renewable source of energy for transport and power to effect savings on foreign exchange.

Jatropha crop can also be utilized for other purposes. The following benefits can be expected:

(a) The oil cake is rich in N, P, & K and can be used as organic manure.

(b) Detoxified cake can be used as animal feed.

(c) Barren lands can be made fertile and soil erosion controlled.

(d) The oil can be converted into soap, lubricants, varnish, etc.

(e) High medicinal value, through its various parts.

TABLE 13.1

Property	Biodiesel	Petrodiesel	EU Standards
Kinematic Viscosity	4.84	2-8	5
Cetane number	52	47.5	> 48
Sulphur %	0	< 0.5	< 0.55
Carbon residue %	0.024	< 0.35	< 0.1
Ester content %	> 99	0	> 99
Density (30° C)	0.88	0.85	> 0.8
Combustion point (OC)	192	55	> 55

In India, lots of projects involving jatropha have been taken up-these include massive cultivation in the rural sector covering barren lands as well as roadsides and along railway tracks, providing income generation potential for the downtrodden (collection of seeds etc.), making of biodiesel by setting up pilot plants, testing of biodiesel in railway engines, cars, and RTC buses.

CONCLUSIONS

Despite all the advantages that we have presented in favour of Jatropha, there are some problems at the present which can also be sorted out.

- Most emission tests have pointed towards an increased output of NO, from biodiesel, though this can be eliminated by adjusting the engine's injection timing.
- Making biodiesel involves certain risks–methanol is known to ignite spontaneously in the air while NaOH is caustic. Hence biodiesel plants require well-ventilated area and are to be explosion-proof. Biodiesel is also known to be a good solvent, dissolving rubber and some plastics, removing paint, oxidizing aluminum, destroying asphalt, etc. Hence care should be exercised while using biodiesel.
- Trans-esterification is a costly process and requires trained manpower. An alternative solution has been sought by proposing use of unesterified jatropha oil in the rural sector for decentralized electricity generation required in domestic lighting, street-lighting and lighting of public buildings, irrigation pumps, flour mill, etc.
- The yield of seeds and extraction of oil needs to be improved in order to be commercially viable. Hence newer varieties have to be developed to yield more amount of oil. Different genotypes were evaluated and the new genotype SDAUJ 1 (Chatrapati), developed

by Sardarkru Shinagar Dantiwada Agricultural University, showed 49.2 % oil with an average yield of 1000–1100 kg per ha under rainfed conditions. In the 9 species evaluated in India, Jatropha curcas has been found to be of more economic value.

The entire world is now gearing up towards use of the renewable biodiesel involving *Jatropha Curcas.* Egypt had imported jatropha seeds from India five years ago to successfully cultivate the crop using sewage water. Why not we in India get inspired by this and also start our own plans? The national leadership, planners and the people should get serious about this biofuel revolution. The involvement of several organizations in this biodiesel programme calls for proper collaboration, coordination, and cooperation–all for a single goal: making India self-sufficient, fertile, pollution-free, and a jobless-free nation.

The following are the few institutes are engaged in biodiesel work:

(1) CSMCRI, Bhavnagar, Gujarat,

(2) IISc, Bangalore,

(3) IICT, Hyderabad,

(4) Indian Institute of Technology (Delhi, Madras),

(5) Punjab Agricultural University,

(6) Indian Institute of Petroleum, Dehradun,

(7) Coimbatore Horticultural University, Coimbatore,

(8) Indian Oil Corporation, Faridabad,

(9) NBRI, Lucknow,

(10) NCL, Pune,

(11) UDCT, Mumbai

(12) Mahindra & Mahindra,

(13) Daimler Chrysler, India

14

Production of Biodiesel

Production of Biodiesel: Many developed countries have active biodiesel programme. Currently biodiesel is produced mainly from field crop oils like rapeseed, sunflower etc., in Europe and soybean in U.S, Malaysia utilizes palm oil for biodiesel production while in Tropical countries, it is *Jatropha curcas* oil.

Production of Vegetable Oil : The global and Indian production figures of vegetable oils are given in Tables 14.1 that follow :

TABLE 14.1

Global Production of the Major Vegetable Oils (2001)

Oil	Production (Million Tons)
Soya bean	27.8
Rape seed	13.7
Cottonseed	4.0
Sunflower	8.2
Peanut	5.1
Coconut	3.5
Linseed	0.6
Palm	23.4
Palm kernel	2.9
Olive	2.7
Corn	2.0
Castor	0.5
Sesame	0.8
Total	**95.2**

Source: Oilworld Weekly, (2002).

TABLE 14.2

Vegetable Oil Production in India (2001)

Oil	Production (Million Tons)
Groundnut	1.40
Soya	0.82
Rape/mustard	1.55
Sunflower	0.30
Sesame	0.26
Castor	0.25
Niger	0.03
Safflower	0.09
Linseed ,	0.10
Cottonseed	0.44
Coconut	0.55
Rice bran	0.55
Oil from expelled cake	0.28
Minor oilseeds	0.05
Total	**6.67**

•*Source: Solvent Extractors' Association of India.*

Derivatives of triglycerides (vegetable oils) as diesel fuels: The alternative diesel fuels must be technically and environmentally acceptable, and economically competitive. From the viewpoint of these requirements, triglycerides (vegetable oils/animal fats) and their derivatives may be considered as viable alternatives for diesel fuels. The problems with substituting triglycerides for diesel fuels are mostly associated with their high viscosity, low volatility and polyunsaturated character. The problems have been mitigated by developing vegetable oil derivatives that approximate the properties and performance and make them compatible with the hydrocarbon-based diesel fuels through:

- pyrolysis,
- micro emulsification,
- dilution,
- trans-esterification.

Pyrolysis : It refers to a chemical change caused by the application of thermal energy in the absence of air or nitrogen. The liquid fractions of the thermally decomposed vegetable oil are likely to approach diesel fuels. These cracked product has lower viscosity, flash point, and pour point than diesel fuel and equivalent calorific values. The cetane number of the cracked product is lower. These cracked vegetable oils contain acceptable amounts of sulphur, water and sediment and give acceptable copper corrosion values but unacceptable ash, carbon residue and pour point.

Micro-emulsification : The formation of micro-emulsions (co-solvency) is one of the potential solutions for solving the problem of vegetable oil viscosity. Micro-emulsions are defined as transparent, thermodynamically stable colloidal dispersions. The droplet diameters in micro-emulsions range from 100 to 1000 Å. A micro-emulsion can be made of vegetable oils with an ester and dispersant (co-solvent), or of vegetable oils, an alcohol and a surfactant and a cetane improver, with or without diesel fuels. Water (from aqueous ethanol) may also be present in order to use lower-proof ethanol, thus increasing water tolerance of the micro-emulsions.

Dilution : Dilution of vegetable oils can be accomplished with such materials as diesel fuels, solvent or ethanol.

Trans-esterification : Trans-esterification, also called alcoholysis, is the displacement of alcohol from an ester by another alcohol in a process similar to hydrolysis. This process has been widely used to reduce the viscosity of triglycerides. The trans-esterification reaction is represented by the general equation. RCOOR' + R"→RCOOR" + R'OH. If methanol is used in the above reaction, it is termed methanolysis. The reaction of triglycerides with methanol is represented by the general equation. Triglycerides are readily trans-esterified in the presence of alkaline catalyst at atmospheric pressure and at a temperature of approximately 60 to 70°C with an excess of methanol. The mixture at the end of reaction is allowed to settle. The lower Glycerine layer is drawn off while the upper methyl ester layer is washed to remove entrained glycerine and is then processed further. The excess methanol is recovered by distillation and sent to a rectifying column for purification and recycled. The trans-esterification works well when the starting oil is of high quality. However, quite often low quality oils are used as raw materials for biodiesel manufacture. In cases where the free fatty acid (FFA) content of the oil is above 1%, difficulties arise due to the formation of soap which promote emulsification during the water washing stage and at an FFA content above 2% the process becomes unworkable.

Biodiesel fuel can be made from new or used vegetable oils and animal fats, which are non-toxic, biodegradable, renewable resources. Fats and oils are chemically reacted with an alcohol (methanol is the usual choice) to produce chemical compounds known as fatty acid methyl esters. Biodiesel is the name given to these esters when they're intended for use as fuel. Glycerine (used in pharmaceuticals and cosmetics, among other markets) is produced as a co-product.

Biodiesel can be produced by a variety of esterification technologies. The oils and fats are filtered and preprocessed to remove water and contaminants. If free fatty acids are present, they can be removed or transformed into biodiesel using special pre-treatment technologies. The pre-treated oils and fats are then mixed with an alcohol (methanol) and a catalyst (sodium or potassium hydroxide). The oil molecules (triglycerides) are broken apart and reformed into esters and Glycerine, which are then separated from each other and purified.

Approximately 55% of the biodiesel industry can use any fat or oil feedstock, including recycled cooking oils. The other half of the industry is limited to vegetable oils, the least expensive of which is *Jatropha* oil. The *Jatropha* oil industry has been the driving force behind biodiesel commercialization because of large production capacity, product surpluses, and declining prices. Similar issues apply to the recycled oils and animal fats industry, even though these feed stocks are less expensive than *Jatropha* oils.

Process Variables in Trans-esterification : The most important variables that influence trans-esterification reaction time and conversion are :

- Oil temperature.
- Reaction temperature.
- Ratio of alcohol to oil.
- Type and concentration of Catalyst.
- Intensity of mixing.
- Purity of reactants.

Oil Temperature : The temperature to which oil is heated before mixing with catalyst and methanol, affects the reaction. It was observed that increase in oil temperature marginally increases the percentage oil to biodiesel conversion as well as the biodiesel recovery. However, the tests were conducted upto 60°C only, as higher temperatures may result in methanol loss in the batch process.

Reaction Temperature : The rate of reaction is strongly influenced by the reaction temperature. Generally, the reaction is conducted close to the boiling point of methanol (60 to 70°C) at atmospheric pressure. The maximum yield of esters occurs at temperatures ranging from 60 to 80°C at a molar ratio (alcohol to oil) of 6:1. Further increase in temperature is reported to have a negative effect on the conversion. Studies have indicated that given enough time, trans-esterification can proceed satisfactorily at ambient temperatures in the case of the alkaline catalyst.

It was observed that biodiesel recovery was affected at very low temperatures (just like low ambient temperatures in cold weather) but conversion was almost unaffected.

Ratio of Alcohol to Oil : Another important variable affecting the yield of ester is the molar ratio of alcohol to vegetable oil. A molar ratio of 6 :1 is normally used in industrial processes to obtain methyl ester yields higher than 98% by weight. Higher molar ratio of alcohol to vegetable oil interferes in the separation of Glycerine. It was observed that lower molar ratios required more reaction time. With higher molar ratios, conversion increased but recovery decreased due to poor separation of Glycerine. It was found that optimum molar ratios depend upon type and quality of oil.

Type and Concentration of Catalyst : Alkali metal alkoxides are the most effective trans-esterification catalyst compared to the acidic catalyst. Sodium alkoxides are among the most efficient catalysts used for this purpose, although potassium hydroxide and sodium hydroxide can also be used. Trans-methylation occurs many folds faster in the presence of an alkaline catalyst than those catalyzed by the same amount of acidic catalyst. Most commercial trans-esterification is conducted with alkaline catalysts. The alkaline catalyst concentration in the range of 0.5 to 1% by weight, yields 94 to 99% conversion of vegetable oil into esters. Further, increase in catalyst concentration does not increase the conversion and it adds to extra costs because it is necessary to remove it from the reaction medium at the end. It was observed that higher amounts of sodium hydroxide catalyst were required for higher FFA oil. Otherwise higher amount of sodium hydroxide resulted in reduced recovery.

Mixing Intensity : The mixing effect is most significant during the slow rate region of the trans-esterification reaction. As the single phase is established, mixing becomes insignificant. The understanding of the mixing effects on the kinetics of the trans-esterification process is a valuable tool in the process scale-up and design. It was observed that after adding methanol and catalyst to the oil, 5—10 minutes stirring helps in higher rate of conversion and recovery.

Purity of Reactants : Impurities present in the oil also affect conversion levels. Under the same conditions, 67 to 84% conversion into esters can be obtained, using crude vegetable oils, compared with 94 to 97% when using refined oils. The free fatty acids in the original oils interfere with the catalyst. However, under conditions of high temperature and pressure this problem can be overcome. It was observed that crude oils were equally good compared to refined oils for production of biodiesel. However, the oils should be properly filtered. Oil quality is very important in this regard. The oil settled at the bottom during storage may give lesser biodiesel recovery because of accumulation of impurities like wax etc.

Raw Material and its Quality for the Production of Biodiesel

Vegetable Oil.—Any sediment would collect at the bottom of the reaction vessel during settling of Glycerine and at the liquid interface during washing. This would interfere with the separation of the phases and may tend to promote emulsion formation. The oil must be free of moisture because every molecule of water destroys a molecule of the catalyst thus decreasing its concentration. The free fatty acid content should be less than 1%. It was observed that lesser the FFA in oil better is the biodiesel recovery. Higher FFA oil can also be used but the biodiesel recovery will depend upon type of oil and amount of sodium hydroxide used.

Alcohol : Methanol or ethanol, as near to absolute as possible, can be used. As with the oil, the water affects the extent of conversion enough to prevent the separation of Glycerine from the reaction mixture.

Catalyst : Sodium or Potassium Hydroxide, preferably the latter. The corresponding alkoxides also can be used, but it is prohibitively expensive. Best results are obtained, if the catalyst is z 85% potassium hydroxide. Best grades of potassium hydroxide have 14-15% water, which can not be removed. It should be low in carbonate, because the carbonate is not an efficient catalyst and may cause cloudiness in the final ester. Sodium hydroxide pellets have given very good results. Because quantity of catalyst used is quite less, good quality catalyst (in-spite of high cost) can be used.

Animal Fats : The most prominent animal fat to be studied for potential biodiesel use is tallow. Tallow contains a high amount of saturated fatty acids, and it has therefore a melting point above ambient temperature.

Waste Vegetable Oils : Every year many millions of tons of waste cooking oils are collected and used in a variety of ways throughout the world. This is a virtually inexhaustible source of energy, which might also prove an additional line of production for "green" companies. These oils contain some degradation products of vegetable oils and foreign material. However, analyses of used vegetable oils indicate that the differences between used and unused fats are not very great and in most cases simple heating and removal by filtration of solid particles suffices for subsequent trans-esterification. The cetane number of a used frying oil methyl ester was given as 49, thus comparing well with other materials.

Esters of Vegetable Oil : They make good biomass fuels as diesel substitutes, provided the following factors receive special attention :

- The yield of trans-esterified product should be >90%.
- The fuel should be as neutral as possible (pH 6.5—8.0)
- The fuel should be centrifuged at a temperature below the expected ambient operating temperature. Winterization has been suggested as the ideal solution.
- The neutralizing agent should form fuel low in soluble salts, free from carbonate groups.
- Ash content should be 0.01%. The fuel should be free from alcohol.

Storability of Biodiesel : It was observed that when the biodiesel manufactured using different oils were stored, their FFA as well as viscosity increased. However, FFA remained below 1% even after one and a half years of storage. Minimum increase was observed in ***Jatropha curcas*** oil biodiesel, followed by rice bran, sunflower and linseed oil biodiesel. During storage, the biodiesel also gained some weight. It may be mainly due to reaction with oxygen in the air.

Plants in Operation/under Construction : Different technologies are currently available and used in the industrial production of biodiesel, which is sold under different trademarks. For example, there are the Italian process of Novamont, and the French IFP as given in Table below. A number of units are manufacturing biodiesel worldwide. These units are using sunflower oil, soyabean oil, rapeseed oil, used-frying oil, *Jatropha* oil, etc. as a source of triglycerides as given in Tables below :

More than 85 plants were identified including a few pilot plants, over 30 small capacity plants (500—3000 tons) mostly with farmers' co-operative as owner and several big plants in the capacity range of 10,000 to 1,20,000 tons. Of these, 44 plants were in Western Europe with Italy as the leading country with 11 plants, 29 plants in Eastern Europe with Czech being the leading country with 16 plants, 8 plants in North America and 4 plants in the rest of the world. Overall capacity grew from 1,11,000 tons per year in 1991 to 1,286,000 tons per year in 1997. USA is the fastest growing newcomer and a number of companies are emerging there. Additional capacities are expected in Japan and the palm oil producing countries like, Indonesia and Malaysia. Actual production grew from 10,000 tons in 1991 to 6,61,000 tons in 1997. France is the leading producer with 227,000 tons (in 1996). The Table gives country wise number of plants, production capacity and feedstock oil used.

Work done in India

In India, attempts are being made for using non-edible and under-exploited oils for production of esters. The non-traditional seed oils available in the country, which can be exploited for this purpose, are *Madhuca indica, Shorea robusta, Pongamia glabra, Mesua ferra* (Linn), *Mallotus Philippines, Garcinia indica, Jatropha curcas* and *Salvadora.*

Lab Scale Projects

Punjab Agricultural University (PAU) is actively involved in Research and Development work on plant oils and their esters (biodiesel) as alternate fuel for diesel engines since early eighties. Firstly a number

TABLE 14.3
Available Biodiesel Production Technologies

Company	Reaction Conditions			
	P (atm)	Temp. (°C)	Catalyst	Mode of peration
Trans-esterification				
Comprimo/Vogel and Noot	1	Ambient	KOH	Batch
Idaho University	1	Ambient	KOH	Batch
Novamont/Technimont	1	> Ambient	Organic	Batch
Conemann/Cold and Hann	1	60—70	NaOH	Continuous
Lurgi	1	60—70	Alkaline	Continuous
IFP/Sofiproteal	1	50—130	Alkaline/ Acid	Batch
Gratech	3.5	95		Continuous
Desmet	50	200	Non Alkaline	Continuous
Others: Oleofina, Proctor and Gamble, MEKFT				
IICT, Hyderabad			Catalyst free	Batch

IIP Dehradun			Base Catalyst Acid Catalyst	Batcfa
Punjab University	1	55—6o	NaOH pellets	Batch

Source: Tadashi Murayama.

Table 14.4 : Countrywise Capacity of the Biodiesel Plants

Country	Number of plants	Total annual capacity '000 tones	Oils used
Austria	11	56.2 to 60	Used frying oil
Belgium	3	241	
Canada	1		
Czech Republic	17	42.5 to 45	Used frying oil
Denmark	3	32	
France	7	38.1	
Germany	8	207	
Hungary	17	18.8	
Ireland	9	5	Used frying oil
Italy	9	779	Sunflower oil
Nicaragua	1		*Jatropha*
Slovakia	10	50.5 to 51.5	
Spain	1	0.5	
Sweden	3	75	
Switzerland	1	2	
U.K.	1		
U.S.A.	40	190	Used frying oil
Yugoslavia	2	5	

Source: Anjana Srivastava and Ramprasad.

of plant oils were used in blend with HSD (high speed diesel) fuel and kerosene oil in the existing diesel engine. Then a simple biodiesel production process was standardized in the laboratory. Based on that a 12 liter batch reactor was developed and used for bulk production of biodiesel which was later scaled up to 60 liters. Biodiesel has been prepared from a number of plant oils (edible as well as non-edible) and used successfully in existing diesel engines.

Indian Institute of Petroleum (IIP) is actively pursuing the utilization of non-edible oils for the production of biodiesel, additives for lubricating oils, saturated and unsaturated alcohol and fatty acids and many other value added products. The results obtained so far are encouraging and need further investigations for commercial exploitation of these products. Some of the products used as lube additives are being produced commercially from non-edible oils based on IIP's technologies. IIP is pursuing programme sponsored by DBT on "Liquid fuels form Renewable Resources". The project has two parts :

1. **Part - A** deals with the indigenous technology development for biodiesel production using *Jatropha curcas,* Karanj Oil, Mahua Oil and *Salvadora* Oil, as a networking project along with Central Salt and Marine Chemical Research Institute, Bhavnagar and National Botanical Research Institute Lucknow.
2. **Part - B** deals with the recovery of Hydrocarbons from biomass and their conversion to liquid fuel with Rajasthan University Jaipur as a networking partner. Rajasthan University will be supplying the biomass to IIP for its extraction and conversion to liquid fuels. Under this programme bulk sample of biodiesel will be prepared using the 30 liter capacity batch pilot plant available at IIP.

Indian Institute of Chemical Technology (IICT) extracted oil from *Jatropha curcas.* The oil extraction was based on cooking of *Jatropha* seeds with water followed by drying and expelling of oil. A catalyst-free process (Indian patent filed, US Patent being filed) that is insensitive to moisture or high FFA content has been developed at IICT, and an oil of any FFA content can be converted to the alkyl ester. Active work is also going on at IICT for the preparation of fatty acid esters from low and high FFA vegetable oils using enzymes and solid catalysts.

Besides, preliminary studies on the utilization of non-edible oils such as Neem, Mahua, Linseed etc. as fuel, are being carried out at Indian Institute of Technology, Delhi and Indian Institute of Technology, Madras. Indian Oil Corporation's Research and Development Center at Faridabad, is also doing some work on the trans-esterification of vegetable oils. Indian Oil Corporation's Research and Development Center at Faridabad has already set-up a biodiesel production facility of 60 kg/day. Mahindra and Mahindra Ltd. has a pilot plant utilizing Karanj for biodiesel production in Mumbai. This plant has carried out successful trails on tractors using this fuel. Parameters such as power, torque, fuel consumption, emissions, etc., have been found quite satisfactory on tractors operating on this biodiesel. Field trials for about 30,000 kilometers have also been carried out on the tractors. In India most of the trials were done using biodiesel from feedstock like Karanj and *Jatropha.* Biodiesel manufactured from different feedstocks may vary in composition, lubricity, oxidation stability, etc., even after meeting American Standards for Testing Materials (ASTM) standards. It is desirable to carry out tests on biodiesel from all possible feed stocks available in India and generate comparative data on fuel composition.

PLANT FOR TRANS-ESTERIFICATION OF VEGETABLE OILS

1000 Liters per day Pilot Plant

A. **Background :** Alcohol trans-esterification of vegetable oils results in Glycerine, and Fatty Acid Alcohol Ester, commonly known as Bio-Diesel.

B. **Description :** The plant is a single stainless steel vessel, pressurized, electrically heated and isolated batch unit, capable of either base, or base/base processes for trans-esterifying vegetable oil. The plant is skid mounted, self-contained, and can be powered by either 240 or 440 Volts AC. Compressed air 0.75 bar must be provided. The vessel has a 1500 liter capacity; it normally processes 1200 liters of vegetable oil/alcohol mix, delivering on average 1000 liters of Biodiesel and 180 liters of Glycerine, per batch, in approximately 18 hours.

   Vegetable oil and alcohol are pumped through ball valves and visual level gauges. The alkali catalyst is pre-measured and then added to the alcohol. Proportions can be modified by the operator to suit different. feedstock. Operator pre-set temperature and pressure values are kept automatically.

   Instruments, fail-safe visual and sound alarms are incorporated into the control panel. A pressure relief valve and vent manifold allow outside venting to a service line, complying with both ambient and work safety requirements. Metal bodied, spherical valves, are used throughout.

C. **Brief Process Description.**—The alcohol is pumped into the vessel and mixing starts with vent open. The catalyst is pre-measured first testing the feedstock, and then poured into vessel. Finally the vegetable oil is pumped into, heaters turned on and vent closed. The mixing continues under selected conditions of temperature and pressure during a stated period.

Fig. 14.1

Once finished, the mixture settles under pressure, until stratification of the Glycerine and liquid alcohol ester occurs.

The resulting Glycerine is first extracted under pressure, and the remaining biodiesel is pushed through a 5 microns filter before being stored.

Dimensions

- Length x breadth x height 1730 x 1360 x 2500 mm.
- Weight 1200 kg.
- Volume 1500 Liters total volume.
- Production 1000 Liters of Biodiesel.
- Glycerine production 180 kg.
- 1.5 HP motor centrifugal mixer pump.
- ½ HP motor centrifugal oil pump.
- 9 KW. Heaters.
- 10 kwh energy consumption per batch.

HOW THE TRANS-ESTERIFICATION PROCESS WORKS

What is meant by completion and equilibrium? The trans-esterification process converts triglycerides (in other words vegetable or animal fats and oils) into alkyl esters (biodiesel) by means of an alcohol reagent (usually methanol) and a catalyst NaOH. It happens in three stages (this has nothing to do with the single-stage or two-stage processes): first the Ttri-Glycerides (TGs) are converted to Di-Glycerides (DGs), then the Di-Glycerides are converted to Mono-Glycerides (MGs), and finally the Mono-Glycerides are converted to esters, with glycerine as the by-product on completion. The problem is that it can run out of reagent or catalyst before it gets that far, or agitation, temperature or processing time may be inadequate.

The result is unconverted or partly converted material. So what if the process isn't completed? SVO (Straight Vegetable Oil) is a good fuel anyway, so what's it matter if some of it is unreacted? But it's not just unreacted material that's the problem so much as the partly-reacted stuff. Di-Glycerides and Mono-Glycerides are bad things to put in your diesel. Di-Glycerides don't burn well and lead to coking problems, Mono-Glycerides can lead to corrosion and other problems like bad fuel. The level of Glycerine, mono and Di-Glycerides at levels of 0.1% (a factor of 1/1000 or less of the main ester components) or lower appears necessary for optimum engine performance.

In fact the process never reaches 100% completion, it always reaches equilibrium first, so there will always be some unreacted glycerides left. The various biodiesel standards stipulate just how much is allowable, and it's not very much at all : Di-Glycerides range from less than 0.4% to less than 0.1% by mass, Mono-Glycerides less than 0.8% by mass.

The first part of the process happens rapidly, which is why some people think it only needs a thorough mixing and that's it. Not so. If it takes X minutes to convert half the TGs to DGs, it takes almost as long, another X minutes, to convert half the remaining TGs, then a further X minutes for the remaining half, and so on. So the process goes more and more slowly, and end never quite arrives, there's always half left. Finally comes a point when the remaining half is insignificant, and, indeed, within the limitations set by the various quality standards.

What are Free Fatty Acids : Vegetable or animal oils and fats, are tri-glycerides, composed of three chains of Fatty Acids (FAs) bound by a glycerine molecule. Free Fatty Acids (FFAs) are FAs that have been separated from the tri-glycerides by hydrolysis, via water in the foods cooked in the oil. Oxidation also plays a role, especially at high temperatures and with continued use of the fry oil. The hotter the oil gets and the longer it's cooked, the more FFAs it will contain.

As glycerine is an alcohol, a FA attached to it (a glyceride) forms an ester. A trans-esterification is the conversion (switching) of one ester into another, a glyceride into an alkyl ester in the case of biodiesel, where methanol (or ethanol) replaces the glycerine.

An esterification is the conversion of a non-ester into an ester. A FFA is not an ester. FFAs are converted into esters by acid esterification in the first stage of the two-stage acid-base process, but can not be converted by the usual single-stage trans-esterification biodiesel process. Here the FFAs must be removed from the process, or they will dissolve in the alkyl-ester biodiesel being formed, yielding an acidic, poor-quality fuel that will not meet quality standards.

In trans-esterification, extra NaOH is used to neutralize the FFA content of the oil, turning it into soaps. These soaps drop out of the process as a by-product, joining the so-called glycerine layer at the bottom, more often a soap layer as it may contain more soap than glycerine.

The basic NaOH quantity used in trans-esterification acts as a catalyst, not a neutralizer. NaOH attacks ester bonds, breaking the bond, and the alcohol drops off. With tri-glycerides the alcohol that drops off is glycerine. The affinity of the replacement methyl or ethyl alcohol for the resulting open bond is strong enough to prevent the Glycerine reattaching to the open FA.

This is also why it is critical that a minimal amount of NaOH is used, as NaOH will continue to attack ester bonds, even those of biodiesel. Too much NaOH will break the biodiesel ester bonds; some of the broken bonds will mate with the NaOH and form excess soap, and others will match up with a water molecule to form FFAs, which dissolve back into the biodiesel. It is this excessive formation of FFAs that the acid number reflects. While it is unavoidable that some FFAs are formed by biodiesel ester bonds being broken, excess NaOH increases the proportion.

The single-stage process produces more and more uncertain results with higher FFAs. The two-stage base—base method avoids the need for titration and produces good results even with higher FFA levels. It's the method-of-choice for animal fats. Growing numbers of biodiesel manufacturers are now turning to the two-stage acid-base method, especially with high-FFA oils.

Here are some of the Reasons : Less base catalyst needed. Less soap production. Higher conversion rates as a result of less soap formation. Less emulsion formation in the wash. Less loss of fuel in the wash as a result of emulsion formation. Less wash water as a result of less soap formation. Less neutralizing acid needed for the wash. Less acid needed to neutralize base during glycerine recovery. High quality product.

The Negatives : A little extra processing time. Even with higher-FFA oils, the production rate should be 100% or more by volume (biodiesel has a lower density than the original oil). In fact the same advantages apply to new oil, although to a lesser extent. Many biodiesel manufacturers use the two stage method for high FFA oils and this can be used for all oils.

CATALYST

The catalyst used in trans-esterification of vegetable or animal fats and oils is either sodium hydroxide (NaOH, caustic soda), or potassium hydroxide (KOH, caustic potash). It is hygroscopic, it absorbs water from the atmosphere. So make sure you get fresh material, and keep the container tightly sealed. When weighing it out, don't leave it exposed to the air too long. In humid weather, weigh it out into plastic bags, one on either side of the scale to equalize the extra weight of the bag. As soon as it's weighed out, close the container, close the bag, and add the catalyst to the methanol as quickly as possible.

It also absorbs carbon dioxide from the atmosphere and becomes carbonated if not stored properly. Carbonated material is white, fresh material is almost translucent. You can still use carbonated material, but you'll have to use a bit more (add about 25%). Sodium hydroxide (NaOH) is more readily available than potassium hydroxide (KOH) and cheaper. It usually comes in three grades: flakes and 5 mm pearls or half-pearls are 96-97%, small pearls (1-2 mm) are 99%+, but more expensive. Either will do.

KOH is not as strong as NaOH, you have to use 1.4 times as much KOH (actually 1.4025 times). Titration is the same, just use a 0.1% KOH solution instead of NaOH solution, and use 1 gm of KOH for every milliliter of 0.1% solution used in the titration. But instead of the basic 3.5 grams of NaOH per liter of oil, use 3.5 x 1.4 = 4.9 grams of KOH. So, if your titration was 5 ml, use 5 + 4.9 = 9.9 gm KOH per liter of oil. One more complication, check the purity of your KOH, it's generally not as pure as NaOH. Anhydrous grade KOH flake is usually about 92%, sometimes less, check the label. Common one is half-pearls assayed at 85%. Adjust the basic quantity accordingly: the basic 4.9 grams would be 5–8 (5-775) grams for 85% KOH, or 5.3 (5.33) grams for 92% KOH. KOH dissolves in methanol much more easily than NaOH does, and doesn't clump together as NaOH can do.

First Titration : An electronic pH meter is best, but you can also use pH test strips (or litmus paper), or phenolphthalein solution. Dissolve 1 gram of KOH in 1 liter of distilled or de-ionized water (0.1% lye solution). In a smaller beaker, dissolve 1 ml of WVO oil from which moisture is removed in 10 ml of pure isopropyl alcohol. Warm the beaker gently by standing it in some hot water, stir until all the oil dissolves in the alcohol and the mixture turns clear. Add 2 drops of phenolphthalein solution.

Using a graduated burette, add 0.1% lye solution drop by drop to the oil-alcohol-phenolphthalein solution, stirring all the time, until the solution stays pink (actually magenta) for 10 seconds. Take the number of milliliters of 0.1% lye solution you used and add 3.5. This is the number of grams of lye you'll need per liter of oil. With a pH meter or test strips, use the same procedure without adding the phenolphthalein. Add the 0.1% lye solution drop by drop as before until the pH reaches 8.5.

Second Titration : Unless you have a very accurate scale, it's not easy to Measure exactly 1 gram of sodium hydroxide. It's much easier to measure 5 gm than 1 gm, so mix 5 gm of sodium hydroxide with 500 milliliters of . distilled or de-ionized water. Before titration measure out 5 ml of the stock solution, add 45 ml of distilled or de-ionized water. This makes a 0.1% solution. It's also not easy to measure exactly 1 milliliter of oil. Instead of the usual 1 ml of oil and 10 ml of isopropyl alcohol, mix 4 ml of oil in 40 ml of isopropyl alcohol in a glass beaker. Warm the mixture gently by standing the beaker in hot water, stir until all the oil disperses and it becomes a clear mixture. Then titrate as usual, measuring milliliters of stock solution used. When it reaches pH 8.5 count up the number of milliliters used as normal and divide by 4. This will give a much more precise measurement. To save on isopropyl alcohol, use 2 ml of oil in 20 ml of isopropyl and divide the results by two, still twice as accurate.

High FFA Levels : Most people find their used cooking oil generally gives a titration of 2-3 ml, but some used oils can have much higher FFA levels than this. Titration levels of 9.6 ml. This is not good because FFAs are not good for reaction. It is difficult to succeed in making biodiesel with our 96 ml of titration level. It's not easy to process oil like this with the usual single-stage base process. You're likely to end up with about 50% production half the time, and maybe not a very good product, and lump, the rest of the time. If you're really precise with everything you can do it, you can manage to get a consistent 75% production with the single-stage base process, good product, easy wash.

The oil has to be thoroughly dried first, traces of water make a big difference with high FFA levels, because there is more catalyst for the water to react with. And the reaction itself releases traces of water, especially with high levels of lye. The better way is to use the two-stage acid-base method, which effectively handles high FFA levels and still produces high production rates with low levels of reactants and easy washing.

Removing Fatty Acids from Waste Vegetable Oils : In commercial oil refining, this is done with NaOH. Use the titration amount of NaOH, 1 gram for 1 ml WVO, and mix it with 40 ml of water per liter of oil. It gets hot. Using a stainless steel container, it is mixed by stirring. Add the dissolved NaOH to the oil (room temperature), stir gently by hand until thoroughly mixed. Settle overnight. This leaves soap stock at the bottom. The water is apparently in the soap stock. Filter to remove the soap stock, no need for fine filtering, fine steel mesh will do like a fine tea strainer). Now process as usual for virgin oil, 3.5 grams NaOH per liter of oil, but use 25% methanol, 55^0 C, good and prolonged agitation as usual.

Production rate is around 80%. With oil like this, it's much easier process than the normal single-stage, and it's nice not to have to make such strong methoxide as a straight single-stage process would require with this oil, 13.1 grams of NaOH per liter of oil, or more like 13.6 grams (needs a bit of excess NaOH). You can add the soap stock to the glycerine layer after separation and neutralize as usual to separate catalyst, glycerine and FFAs. It's an alternative, better than straight single-stage base for oil like this, and while it won't get as a high a production rate as the acid-base method, and it uses more catalyst and gives you more co-products, it's very quick and simple. This is also useful if you're making ethyl esters biodiesel, using ethanol rather than methanol, the ethyl esters process doesn't work well with oils with more than about 2 ml titration.

The basic lye quantity, 3.5 grams : This is the amount of NaOH, (sodium hydroxide) required as catalyst to trans-esterify 1 liter of virgin, uncooked oil. For used oils, titration determines the amount of lye needed to neutralize the Free Fatty Acid (FFA) content, and this quantity is added to the basic figure of 3.5 grams per liter. In fact 3.5 grams is an empirical measure, an average. Different oils have slightly different requirements, and even the same type of oil varies according to how and where it's grown. Other estimates are 3.1 gm, 3.4 gm.

Different oils also require different amounts of methanol. For oils and fats requiring more methanol, coconut, palm kernel, as well as tallow, lard, butter, use more NaOH, up to 4.5 gm, even with new oils, and especially when it's used. Once again, do small test batches first.

How much methanol should you use? : The stoichiometric quantity of methanol is the amount needed to convert triglycerides (fats and oils) into esters (biodiesel), the methyl portion of methyl esters. Excess of methanol is required to push the conversion process towards completion, without the excess the process runs out (reaches equilibrium) before all the triglycerides are converted to esters, resulting in poor fuel that doesn't combust well and can be corrosive. The excess methanol acts more like a catalyst, it encourages the process but does not become a part of the final product and can be recovered afterwards.

Stoichiometric Quantity : The stoichiometric quantity is usually said to be 12.5% methanol by volume, that is, 125 milliliters of methanol per liter of oil. Some manufacturers use it at 13%, or 13.5%, or even as low as 8%. In fact it depends on the amounts of the various fatty acids in the oil, and varies from one oil to another.

Excess Methanol : How much excess is needed, to achieve 98% conversion? It depends on several different factors like the type of oil, its condition, the type, size and shape of the processor, the type and duration of agitation, the temperature of the process. However, excess is usually between 60% and 100% of the stoichiometric amount. So if the stoichiometric ratio of the oil you're using is 12.5%, that is 125 ml of methanol per liter of oil, the excess would range between 75 ml and 125 ml, for a total amount of methanol of 200—250 ml per liter of oil.

Oils with higher stoichiometric ratios seem to need higher excesses. So, for fresh oils, you can try 60%, though 67% or more would be better. For palm kernel or coconut, closer to 100% excess would be better. For tallow and lard, use higher excesses. For used oil, WVO, waste vegetable oil, often contains animal fats from the cooking, use *67%* minimum excess. For heavily used oils with high titration levels, use higher excesses, up to 100%.

If you don't know what kind of oil your WVO is, try using 25% methanol, 250 ml methanol to 1 liter of oil. If you've taken care with the titration, used accurate measurements and followed the instructions carefully, you should get a good, clean split, with esters on top and the glycerine and free fatty acids cleanly separated at the bottom. If you have trouble washing it, with a lot of frothing, that could be because the process didn't go far enough and unconverted material is forming emulsions, try using more methanol next time. If everything works well, try using less methanol. You'll soon figure out what's best for you. With the acid-base two-stage method, don't worry about it.

Ethyl Esters : The same principles apply for making ethyl esters instead of methyl esters, using ethanol rather than methanol, with some differences. Use 1.4 times more ethanol than methanol. It won't work if there's any water in the ethanol or the oil. It works much better with some methanol added, up to 3 : 1 ethanol : methanol. Virgin oil is better, with waste oil (WVO) it won't work with FFA content much more than 1ml by titration.

RECLAIMING EXCESS METHANOL

Depending on the kind of oil you use, it takes from 110—160 milliliters of methanol per liter of oil to form the methyl esters molecule. But you also need to use an excess of methanol to push the conversion process towards completion, the total used is usually 20% and more of the volume of oil used, 200 ml per liter or more. Much of the excess methanol can be recovered after the process for reuse, simply by boiling it off in a closed container with an outlet leading to a simple condenser. Methanol boils at 64.7^{0}C, though of course it starts vapourizing well before it reaches boiling point. Unlike ethanol, methanol does not form an azeotrope with water and relatively pure methanol can be recovered, pure enough to reuse in the next batch.

Methanol can be recovered at the end of the process, or just from the glycerine by-product layer, since most of the excess methanol collects in the by-product and it's that much less material to heat. Start at 65 to 70^{0}C, as the proportion of methanol left in the by-product mixture decreases, the boiling point will increase, so you'll have to raise the temperature to keep the methanol vaporizing, perhaps to as high as 100^{0}C or more, though the bulk of it should have been recovered by then. If you're planning to separate the glycerine from the soaps (FFAs) and catalyst it's best to leave methanol recovery to later as the glycerine probably won't separate without the methanol. The excess methanol can then be recovered from the separated glycerine layer. To keep costs down, biodiesel producers try to salvage the unreacted methanol. There are two major methods to do this: heat extraction and vacuum/heat extraction.

Heat Extraction : Heat the second-stage product to 70^{0}C in a sealed boiler or vessel and lead the fumes into a condenser. Intercept the condensed methanol in a liquid trap. Take great care because methanol is highly flammable and the fumes are explosive.

Vacuum/Heat Extraction : This is basically the same as heat extraction, but it requires less energy. The drawback of this method is that you need a special vessel and equipment to do this when building your reactor it may be a good idea to take one step at a time. Build the reactor, get confident with the process and eventually upgrade to methanol recovery. At least a quarter of the methanol used can be recovered, that is, 50+ ml per liter of oil/fat. Mix it with fresh methanol for preparing the next batch of methoxide.

Glycerine : There is no set amount of by-product, such as 200 ml per liter, and there is no rule that the by-product must be solid at room temperature. What is much more important is that in each of the cases above, the test batch produced a good split, the glycerine separated and settled to the bottom, and, if the directions are followed carefully, the rest would have been good biodiesel, needing no more than settling and washing. The rule of thumb is 79 milliliters of glycerine for every liter of oil used (7.9%). And crude glycerine is not solid at room temperature. But the so-called glycerine layer is not just glycerine, it's a variable mixture of glycerine, soaps, excess methanol, and the catalyst NaOH. The quantity varies according to the oil used (more with heavily-used oil), the process used (less with the acid-base two-stage method), the amount of excess methanol used (most of the excess methanol ends up in the by-product layer).

It's mainly the soaps combined with the glycerine that can cause it to solidify. Soaps made from saturated fats such as stearin are harder than those made from unsaturated fats such as olein, so the type of oil used makes a difference. More important is how much soap there is, the more soap, the more likely the by-product layer will solidify, no matter what oil you used.

Other factors are Excess methanol which makes the by-product layer thinner, Too much NaOH creates excess soap, Potassium hydroxide (KOH) makes the by-product slightly thinner than sodium hydroxide (NaOH).

MANUFACTURING PROCESS FOR BIODIESEL

1. Filter the used cooking oil first as usual.
2. For a successful reaction the oil must be free of water. Here are two methods of removing the water content :
   (a) **Settling the water out :** This method saves energy. Heat the oil to 60°C, maintain the temperature for 15 minutes and then pour the oil into a settling tank. Let it settle for at least 24 hours. Make sure you never empty the settling vessel more than 90%.
   (b) **Boiling the water off.**—Less-preferred method as it uses more energy and helps to form more FFAs in the oil. Heat the oil to 100°C. As the heat rises water separates out and

falls to the bottom, drain it off to avoid steam explosions. Maintain the temperature until no more steam bubbles rise.

First Stage

3. Measure the volume of oil/fats to be processed (preferably in liters).
4. Heat the oil to 35°C, make sure that all solid fats are melted.
5. **Methanol :** Use only 99%+ pure methanol. Measure out the methanol, 0.08 liters of methanol for each liter of oil/fats (8% by volume). Add the methanol to the heated oil.
6. Mix for five minutes, the mixture will become murky because of solvent change (methanol is a polar compound, oil is strongly non-polar; a suspension will form).
7. For each liter of oil/fats add 1 milliliter of 95% sulfuric acid (H_2SO_4). Use a graduated pipette. Take care when handling the concentrated sulfuric acid.
8. Mix gently at LOW rpm (don't splash!) while keeping the temperature at 35°C. The rotation of your stirrer should not exceed 500 to 600 rpm, speed is not crucial and splashed oil is a mess to clean.
9. Maintain the temperature at 35°C for one hour then stop heating. Continue stirring.
10. Stir the unheated mixture for another hour, a total of two hours, then stop mixing. Let the mixture sit for at least eight hours, overnight is better.
11. In the meantime prepare the sodium methoxide: measure 0.12 liter of methanol for each liter of oil/fat (12% by volume) and weigh 3.1 grams (up to 3.5 grams if purity is in doubt) of sodium hydroxide, NaOH, per liter of oil/fat. Mix the NaOH into the methanol until the lye is completely dissolved. This process uses only about half the usual amount of NaOH as there is less fat left to trans-esterify. Use 99%+ pure sodium hydroxide. After opening the container, close it again as quickly as possible to prevent moisture getting in. Weigh NaOH carefully, using too much will complicate the washing process later.

    Methoxide : Mixing NaOH with methanol creates an exothermic reaction, generating Heat. It is nasty stuff and it is not easy to mix, and it must be thoroughly mixed before you use it, with all the NaOH dissolved. This is a safe and easy way to do it. The disadvantage is that you have to do it in advance, but that is easily arranged. Add the required amount of NaOH, if you are doing large quantities, add it bit by bit rather than all at once, agitate the container in between. Once it is all added, replace the lid, and agitate the mixture about for a few seconds. Then let it stand. Do that a few more times, every few hours or so (at least 4 to 6 times in all). It will be thoroughly dissolved in 24 hours, or maybe a bit longer. The proportion of NaOH to methanol used in making biodiesel is low.

12. After settling for eight hours, or the next morning, pour half of the prepared methoxide into the unheated mixture and mix for five minutes. This will neutralize the sulfuric acid and boost the base catalysis. If you have used solid fat, it probably solidified during settling, gently melt the mixture first. Now you can continue with the normal procedure with the lye as the second stage.

Second Stage: This is the Base-catalyzed Stage

13. Heat the mixture to 55°C and maintain for the whole reaction.
14. Add the second half of the prepared sodium methoxide to the heated mixture and start mixing at the same low speed of not more than 500 to 600 rpm. Take care when handling the sodium methoxide with full safety precautions.
15. If your reactor allows for it, Start draining glycerine from the bottom, 20—25 minutes after the start of the base stage. (Pump-mixing works best for this.) Repeat every 10 minutes. Take care, the glycerine is quite hot and caustic.
16. Take regular samples in a 25 to 40 mm diameter glass container. Watch for a straw yellow colour of the ester portion. Glycerine (brown and sticky) will settle at the bottom of the jar. When this colour is reached (usually in 1.5 to 2.5 hours) turn the heat and mixer off. Instead of taking out samples to check the colour you could use translucent braided tubing for the pump.
17. Allow to settle for one hour.
18. For easier washing drain off the glycerine. Measure off 25% of the total glycerine (including previously drained glycerine) and mix with 10 milliliters of 10%, phosphoric acid (HPO_4) per each liter of oil/fat processed. The mixing can be done with a wooden spoon in a plastic container. Pour the acidified glycerine back into the reactor and stir for 20 minutes, unheated. Allow to settle for at least six hours and then drain the glycerine fraction completely. During the first stage, free fatty acids were esterified and some triglyeerides were trans-esterifled. The base-catalyzed stage does only trans-esterification, but it's much quicker and more complete.

Washing

19. Use the bubble wash method, but no need to monitor pH anymore. Just add a little 10% phosphoric acid (H_3PO_4) to the washing water first, 2.5 milliliters per liter. If you are curious about the results of your wash, use ordinary litmus paper, it will tell you the rough pH level (acidity/alkalinity). The end result should be neutral (pH 7) or just below neutral.
20. Use one-third the volume of water as the amount of biodiesel to be washed. Make sure both the water and biodiesel are roughly at the same (room) temperature. Pour your biodiesel into the vessel with the water, and start pumping air through a perforated stone assembly at the bottom. Let it bubble for 24 hours minimum. Turn the pump off and let the mixture settle for half an hour. The water will fall to the bottom, turning completely white, and the fuel will be much lighter in color now. Drain the water, repeat the procedure two more times. Remove the biodiesel from the vessel, taking care not to get any water with it.
21. Let the biodiesel stand for about a weeks and use only when it becomes crystal clear; take a sample and wait until it is completely cleared.

Acid-Stage Questions : A question will probably arise : why not mix the methanol with the sulfuric acid before adding them to the oil/fats? There are two major reasons : *(a)* the reaction between methanol and concentrated H_2SO_4 is quite violent and it could splash, which does not happen if you mix it as described; and *(b)* dimethyl ether can form. Mixing alcohols with concentrated H_2SO_4 is a way to dry the alcohols (which is good) and also a way to make di-alcohol ethers. It is not good for dimethyl ether, since it is a gas, colourless and highly explosive.

Base-stage Questions : The second-stage product should be quite murky. This is no problem, as it will wash out. After the processed oil/fat has turned straw-yellow (step 16), you have let it settle for an hour and . drained the glycerine, you should have a total of about 120 ml of glycerine per liter of oil/fat used. If it's less than about 100 ml per liter of oil, something's wrong, even if the colour is right, the process hasn't gone far enough.

This will almost certainly be due to carbonated NaOH. NaOH has a really limited shelf life. CO_2 from the air neutralizes it and forms sodium carbonate. Carbonated NaOH is much whiter than pure NaOH, which is almost translucent. The carbonate in the NaOH will not harm the reaction, but you will have to use more NaOH.

The solution is to repeat the procedure from step 13. Prepare a fresh batch of methoxide with 0.03 liters of methanol and 0–75 grams of lye for each liter of oil/fat. Reheat the biodiesel to 55°C, add the fresh monoxide and mix as before. No need this time to remove glycerine during the processing as in step 15, and don't worry about the colour. Mix lor one hour, settle, drain off the extra glycerine, and proceed from step 18. If you plan to continue using the carbonated NaOH, make sure to increase the amount by 25% next time you make biodiesel. Store NaOH at room temperature, in dry conditions if possible, with the container lid really tightly closed.

OTHER USES OF BIODIESEL

Wood Treatment : Biodiesel is very useful to treat wood, floors included. The smell soon goes away (and it's a pleasant enough smell anyway).

Lubricant : It is an excellent lubricant, very slippery indeed. It is better than household lubricating oils, and it is non-obnoxious and non-toxic. It doesn't matter much if the kids swallow some by mistake. Great for gardeners, especially organic gardeners, nothing better for lubricating your tools and keeping them clean and rust-free, and non-toxic. And great in the workshop.

You can also use biodiesel as a lubricating additive for low-sulphur fuels. With diesels, engine parts are lubricated by the fuel itself. There are already indications that diesel motors are not lasting as long as they did because of the lack of lubrication with low-sulphur fuel (500 ppm), let alone the new ultra-low-sulphur fuel (15 ppm), and biodiesel can change that. Adding just 1% biodiesel improves the lubricity up to 65%. Research suggests that just 0.4% to 0.5% is enough.

Biodiesel can be used as two-stroke oil in two wheelers, at a mix of 20 to 1 with petrol. It works fine. Biodiesel does not travel up a wick very well, like kerosene oil will, so it can not be used for ordinary wick lamps or stoves. However, tests have found that it will travel about 7 cm up a wick but not more than that and the wick should preferably be thick (about 1 cm) and loosely wound, tightly-woven commercial wicks will not work well. Biodiesel also might not work in some heating furnaces or stoves, though some models work just fine, and others can be adjusted. Petromax multi-fuel lantern works just fine on biodiesel. You need not have to re-pressurize the lantern as often as you would using other fuel-types. The performance is great, and the lantern is just as bright, and there is no smell.

Better than Detergent.—The soap/water suspension pulls a good bit of the surface oil off first, with the biodiesel removing the balance of the oil embedded and soaked into the fibers. The suspension also seems to keep the oily effect of the biodiesel from getting locked into the fiber, which can give the look of wet spots (oil soaked spots) even when the garment is dry.

15

Blending of Esters and Diesel

Blending conventional High Speed Diesel Fuel (HSD) with esters (usually methyl esters) of vegetable oils is presently the most common form of biodiesel. The most common ratio is 80% conventional diesel fuel and 20% vegetable oil ester, also termed B-20, indicating the 20% level of biodiesel. There have been numerous reports that significant emission reductions are achieved with these blends.

No engine problems were reported in larger-scale tests with, for example, urban bus fleets running on B-20. Fuel economy was comparable to HSD, with the consumption of biodiesel blend being only 2 to *5%* higher than that of conventional HSD. Another advantage of biodiesel blends is the simplicity of fuel preparation, which only requires mixing of the components. Ester blends have been reported to be stable, for example, a blend of 20% peanut oil with 80% HSD did not separate at room temperature over a period of 3 months. A 50:50 blends of peanut oil with HSD was also found quite stable. Several studies have shown that diesel/biodiesel blends reduce smoke opacity, particulate, un-burnt hydrocarbons, carbon dioxide and carbon monoxide emissions, but nitrous monoxide emissions are slightly increased. One limitation to the use of biodiesel is its tendency to crystallize at temperatures below 0°C. Methyl and ethyl esters of vegetable oils will crystallize and separate from diesel at temperatures often experienced in winter time operation. Such crystals can plug fuel lines and filters, causing problems in fuel pumping and engine operation. One solution to this problem may be the use of branched-chain esters, such as isopropyl esters. The isopropyl esters of soyabean oil crystallize 7 to 11°C lower than the corresponding methyl esters. Another method to improve the cold flow properties of vegetable oil esters is to remove high melting saturated esters by inducing crystallization with cooling, a process known as winterization.

16

Storage of Biodiesel

Pure vegetable oils are completely harmless to the environment, especially the groundwater. However, esterification of vegetable oil increases its water hazard. German EPA classifies waste vegetable oil as a toxic waste. As a general rule blends of biodiesel and petroleum diesel should be treated like petroleum diesel. It is recommended to store biodiesel in clean, dry and approved tanks. Though the flash point of biodiesel is high, storage precautions somewhat like that in storing the diesel fuel still need to be taken biodiesel can be stored for long periods in closed containers with little head room but the container must be protected from direct sunlight, low temperature and weather. Underground storage is preferred in cold climates but it can be stored in open with proper insulation, heating and other equipment should be installed. B-20 fuel can be stored in tanks, above ground depending on the pour point and cloud points of the blend. Low temperature can cause biodiesel to gel. Additives can be used for low temperature storage and pumping. The biodiesel / its blends should be stored at temperatures at least 15°C higher than the pour point of the fuel. While splash blending the biodiesel, care should be taken to avoid very low fuel temperatures, as the saturated, compounds can crystallize and separate out to cause plugging of fuel lines and filters, Condensation of water in the tank should be avoided as hydrocarbon degrading bacteria and mould can grow and these use biodiesel as food.

Biodiesel and its blends are susceptible to growing microbes when water is present in fuel biocides, chemicals that kill bacteria and moulds growing in fuel tank, can be added in small concentration. Biocides. do not remove sediments. Moreover, storage of biodiesel in old tanks can release accumulated deposits and slime and can cause very severe filter and pump blockage problem. For long term storage stability of biodiesel and blends adequate data are not available. Based on experience so far it is recommended that biodiesel can be stored up to a maximum period of 6 months. Some anti-oxidant additives are also used for longer periods of storage. Similar periods are applicable for storage of biodiesel and its blends in vehicle fuel tank. Due to being a mild solvent, biodiesel has a tendency to dissolve the sediments normally encountered in old tanks, used for diesel fuel and these cause filter blockage, injector failures in addition to clogging of fuel lines. Brass, copper, zinc etc. oxidizes diesel and biodiesel fuels and create sediments. The fuel and fittings will start changing colour as the sediments are formed. Storage tanks made of aluminum, steel etc. should be used.

17

Handling of Biodiesel

As a general rule blends of biodiesel and petroleum diesel should be treated like petroleum Diesel. Biodiesel, vegetable oil methyl easters, contain no volatile organic compounds that can give rise to poisonous or noxious fumes. There are no aromatic hydrocarbon (benzen, toluene, xylene) or chlorinated hydrocarbons. There is no lead or sulfur to react and release any harmful or corrosive gases. However, in case of biodiesel blends significatn fumes released by benzene and other aromatic chemicals present in the petroleum diesel fuel can continue. On contact with eye, biodiesel may cause irritation to eye. Safety glasses or face shields should be used to avoid mist or splash on face and eyes. Fire fighting measures to be followed as per its fire hazard classification. Hot fuel may cause burn. Biodiesel should be handled with gloves as it may cause soft skin. Mild irritation on skin can occur.

India Explosive Regulations classify the product as C Class (similar to heavy oils due to its high flash point). The glycerine also falls under same classification. There is no risk of explosions from vapours of biodiesel as the flash point is high and the vapour pressure is less than 1 mm Hg. Large biodiesel spills can be harmful. Biodiesel, while not completely harmless to the larvae and fish, is less harmful than petroleum diesel fuel.

Biodiesel methyl esters have very low solubility in water (saturation concentration of 7 ppm in sea water and 14 ppm in fresh water at 17°C) compared to petroleum diesel that contain benzene, toluene, xylene and other more water soluble, highly toxic compounds. However, when the biodiesel is vigorously blended into water, the methyl esters form a temporary emulsion of tiny droplets that appear to be harmful to the swimming larvae. The half life for biodegradation of vegetable methyl ester is about 4 days at 17°C, about twice fast as petroleum diesel. In the laboratory tests, rapeseed methyl eater degraded by 95% while the diesel fuel degraded only 40% at the end of 23 days.

Any accidental discharge/spill of small amounts of biodiesel should have little impact on the environment compared to petroleum diesel, which contains more toxic and more water-soluble aromatics. Nonetheless, the methyl esters could still cause harm. Environmental Protection Agency still considers spills of vegetable oils and animal fats as harmful to the environment. Spilling biodiesel in water is as illegal as spilling petroleum. Biodiesel need to be handled like any other petroleum fuels and laws should be reviewed to ensure that biodiesel is covered in the same class, if not included already. When bioddes are used in the fuel tank to kill bacteria, suitable handling precautions like use of gloves and eye protection is must. One must check if the laws on disposal of petroleum products are applicable to biodiesel also. Similarly check if Laws for spill prevention and containment action for those who produce or store biodiesel exists. Discharge of animal fats and vegetable oil are order of magnitude less toxic than petroleum discharge, do not create carcinogenic compounds and, are really biodegradable by bacteria thus minimizing physical impact on environment.

Nevertheless, extreme discharges of animal fats, vegetable oils and biodiesel can cause negative impact on aquatic life. Biodiesel spills compare more favourably to petroleum oil spills. Moreover, likelihood of a vegetable oil or biodiesel oil spill being comparable in magnitude to a petroleum spill is also very small due to differences in volumes in the two industries. Petroleum tankers exceed 2,50,000 tone capacity whereas vegetable oils are carried in tankers with 3,500 to 5,000 tones capacity.

. There is a need to differentiate between the vegetable oils and petroleum oil through the creation of separate classes for animal fats and vegetable oils from petroleum oils, and apply separate standards based on the differences in physical characteristics between the classes. Biodiesel is currently controlled in the same manner as animal fats, vegetable oils and petroleum oils are controlled under oil spill laws and regulations, biodiesel facilities and tanker vessels transporting biodiesel remain controlled in the same manner as if they were petroleum oil facilities or tanker vessels transporting petroleum oil.

18

Analysis of Technologies with Reference to Indian Resources and Requirements

India has rich and abundant forest resources with a wide range of plants and oilseeds. The production of these oilseeds can be stepped up many folds if the government takes the decision to use them for producing biodiesel fuels. Economical feasibility of biodiesel depends on the price of the crude petroleum and the cost of transporting diesel to long distances to remote markets in India. Further, the strict regulations on the aromatics and sulphur contents in diesel fuels will result in higher cost of production of conventional diesel fuels.

The production of ethyl esters from edible oils is currently much more expensive than hydrocarbon based diesel fuels due to the relatively high costs of vegetable oils. The rising prices of crude petroleum, has now caused concern, and the cost of petroleum diesel is quite comparable to that of biodiesel, if the price of crude petroleum oil remains higher than US$ 60 per barrel. The cost of biodiesel can be reduced by using non-edible oils, and used frying oils instead of edible oils. Non- edible oils such as rice bran, sal, neem, mahua, karanj, *Jatropha,* etc. are easily available in many parts of the world including India, and are very cheap compared to edible oils. The potential availability of some non-edible oils in India is given in Table18.1 that follows.

TABLE 18.1 : Non-edible Oil Sources of India

Oil	Botanical Name	Potential (Tons)	Utilized (Tons)	% Utilization
Rice bran	*Oryza sativa*	474,000	101,000	21
Sal	*Shorea robusta*	720,000	23,000	3
Neem	*Melia azadirachta*	400,000	20,000	6
Karanj	*Pongamia glabra*	135,000	8,000	6

Source: Anjana Srivastava and Ramprasad.

The processing of oilseeds for the production of edible vegetable oils generates by-product streams, containing triglycerides, phospholipids and free fatty acids. In many cases these streams are of considerably lower value than the finished oil. Successful development of a scheme for ester synthesis from low-value lipids could address the economic barriers to a wider adoption of biodiesel.

Fatty acid methyl ester could be produced from tall oil, a by-product in the manufacture of pulp by the Kraft process. Tall oil consists of free C_{18} unsaturated fatty acids, resin acids and relatively small amounts of unsaponifiables. The fatty acid fraction of tall oil contains mainly oleic acid, linoleic acid and its isomers.

With the mushrooming of fast food centers and restaurants in India, it is expected that considerable amounts of used-frying oils will be discarded into the drains. These can be used for making biodiesel, thus helping to reduce the cost of water treatment in the sewerage system and assisting in the recycling of resources. Acid oil, which is cheaper than both raw and refined oils, is a major by-product of the alkali refining industries and is a potential raw material for making biodiesel.

It is also possible to use vegetable oils directly blended with diesel oil. With about 25% diesel oil mixed with vegetable oil, it is possible to achieve improved thermal efficiency and lower smoke emissions. Heating the fuel to lower the viscosity and then using vegetable oils directly as fuels is also an option.

Thermal and catalytic decomposition of vegetable oils to produce gasoline and diesel fuel has been studied by a number of scientists using various methods with the objective of finding a gasoline replacement, but the fuel obtained possessed an inferior octane number. At the present, a hydrocarbon fuel with a similar volatility and molecular weight as diesel fuel can be produced with an approximate volume yield of 50% from the decomposition of vegetable oils. The method that appears most promising is pre-hydrogenation followed by thermal or catalytic decomposition of vegetable oils.

Biodiesel can be used as a pure fuel or blend with petroleum diesel depending on the economics and emissions. The Indian Scenario is different from Europe and USA where refined vegetable oils, waste frying oils and tallow are used to produce biodiesel. In India, non-edible oils are likely the preferred feed stock. The trans-esteriflcation of non-edible oils has been studied extensively with a view to produce biodiesel. Data on oil characteristics, their behaviour in trans-esteriflcation and quality of biodiesel produced from each oil is available for application of this process such as: catalysts (basic, acidic, homogeneous/heterogeneous); continuous/batch operation; scale of operation; by products valuation and utilization.

TABLE 18.2
Available Biodiesel Production Technologies.

Company	Reaction Conditions			
	P (atm)	**Temp. (°C)**	**Catalyst**	**Mode of Operation**
Trans-esterification				
Comprimo / Vogel and Noot	1	Ambient	KOH	Batch
Idaho University	1	Ambient	KOH	Batch
Novamont/ Technimont	1	> Ambient	Organic	Batch
Conemann / Cold and Hann	1	60—70	NaOH	Continuous
Lurgi	1	60—70	Alkaline	Continuous
IFP / Sofiproteal	1	50—130	Alkaline/ Acid	Batch
Gratech	3.5	95		Continuous
Desmet	50	200	Non-alkaline	Continuous
Others: Oleofina, Proctor and Gamble, MEKFT				
IICT, Hyderabad			Catalyst free	Batch
IIP Dehradun			Alkaline/ Acid	Batch
Punjab University	1	55—60	NaOH	Batch

The cheapest oils are *Jatropha* and Karanj. The *Jatropha* oil industry will be the driving force behind biodiesel commercialization when large production capacity is set up and product is in surplus, which will lead to declining prices. Similar issues apply to the recycled oils and animal fats industry, even though feedstock are less expensive than *Jatropha* oils.

TABLE 18.2 : BIODIESEL PLANT SUPPLIERS

- **ENERGEA :** The next generation of biodiesel technology, Continuous Trans esterification Reactor (CTER) technology opens a new chapter in biodiesel production. It has up to 50% lower cost of investment, turn-key modules are of size of a container, multiple feedstock is possible, production capacity can be 5,000 to 1,00,000 metric tones/year or more, and can produce high quality fuel according to DIN 51,606, future CEN-standard.
  Web Site: http://www.energea.at
  e-mail : mail@energea.at,

- **Bio-fuel Systems** provides state-of-the-art biodiesel process equipment which meets all recognised international safety standards (eg. ATEX) and will produce biodiesel from a range of feedstocks to meet recognised standards, including ASTM 6751-03, EN 14214:2003, DIN V 51606. Company currently offers systems from 900 litres per week upwards. Available in Europe through Euro-biodiesel Ltd. (http://www.eurobiodiesel.com), in Australasia through New Zealand Biofuels Limited, and in the rest of world direct from:

  Bio–fuel Systems
  58 Church Street, Ormskirk, Lancashire
  ENGLAND L39 3AW
  Fax: +44 1695 571222
  Web Site: http://biofuelsystems.com
  e-mail : info@biofuelsystems.com.

- **Biodiesel Technologies,** Vienna, has Compact biodiesel manufacturing plants installed in a 20-ft container frame, ready to operate, multi–feedstock re-esterification and final conditioning of biodieseL Optional module offered is feed stock oil purifier, dryer. Production capacity 500 to 1,000 liters per hour of biodiesel (depending on model). Member of the Biodiesel Austria Group,

  Contact: **Dr. L. Kortdor**
  Managing Director
  Tel: + 43 1 877 0553
  Fax: + 43 1877 8446
  Web Site: http://www.biodieselaustria.com
  e-mail : dr-kondor@eunet.at,

- **NOPEC Corporation** (Ocean Air Environmental Fuels) Lakeland, Florida has a plant that is a world showcase of the latest processing technology, with a 10 million gallons/year capacity. Company provides contract manufacturing services and biodiesel production technology and Flexible, multi-feed stock technology.

  Jim Davis, Wes Berry or Mahesh Talwar
  Phone (863) 683-7199
  Fax (863) 683-1058
  Web Site: http://www.oceanairenvironmental.com
  e-mail :sales@oceanairenvironmenta1.com, oroceanair1@att.net.

- **Pacific Biodiesel** offers plant installations in two configurations: 2,00,000 gallons / year (7,50,000 liters / year), expandable in 2,00,000 gallons / year increments to maximum 8,00,000 gallons/ year (30,00,000 liters / year); or 4,00,000 gallons / year (15,00,000 liters / year) expandable in 4,00,000 gallons / year increments to maximum 16,00,000 gallons / year (60,00,000 liters/ year).

  Contact: **Bob King,** President,
  Telephone: (808) 877-3144
  Fax: (808) 871-5631
  e-mail: bking@biodiesel.com or info@biodiesel.com
  Web Site: http://www.biodiesel.com.

- **Bio–Diesel International** of Austria uses re-esterification in its multi-feedstock production system to handle fresh vegetable oils and/ or waste cooking oils and/or animal fats and/or fatty acids (as much as 20%), with no loss of free fatty acids, 0% wastes, 0% waste water and no disposal costs, resulting in pure biodiesel plus glycerine (for use in the chemical and pharmaceutical industries) plus a solid fertilizer for agricultural use (potassium phosphate). Yield is 100%: 1 kg of raw material makes 1 kg of high-quality biodiesel.

  Web Site: http://www.biodiesel-intl.com.

- **Superior Process Technologies,** USA, offers Multi-feedstock biodiesel processing technology, turn-key engineering and design services. Superior's biodiesel technology offers the highest efficiency and is scalable from the largest continuous processing facilities in the world to small-scale alternative feedstock facilities.

Web Site: http://www.SuperiorProcessTech.com
e-mail : sales@SuperiorProcessTech.com.

- **Crown Iron Works Company,** USA offers enhanced continuous and batch methyl ester production processes. The continuous process is a two-stage reaction system followed by ester washing, drying and methanol recovery; batch process is designed for smaller scale and/or multi-feed stock capability, several reactor options. Glycerine recovery equipment capable of producing 99.7% USP glycerine is also offered. Technology and design assistance to enhance existing ester plants.

  P-O. Box 1364, Minneapolis
  MN 55440-1364 USA
  Tel: 1/651/639-8900
  Fax: 1/651/639-8051
  Web Site: http://www.crowniron.com/index.html
  e-mail : sales@crowniron.com.

  Also in Europe, Australia, Honduras, China.

- **The Austrian Bio–fuels Institute,** an international center of competence for liquid biofuels offers production feasibility studies, process technologies for biofuels, project management. It also offers feed stock supply of oil seed plant production and oil-mill technologies, waste oil recycling, logistic systems for waste oil collection.

  Web Site: http://www.biodiesel.at/index2.html

19

Properties of Biodiesel

A general understanding of the various properties of biodiesel is essential to study their implications in engine use, storage, handling and safety.

Density/Specific Gravity

Biodiesel is slightly heavier than conventional diesel fuel (specific gravity 0.88 compared to 0.84 for diesel fuel). This allows use of splash blending by adding biodiesel on top of diesel fuel for making biodiesel blends. Biodiesel should always be blended at top of diesel fuel. If biodiesel is first put at the bottom and then diesel fuel is added, it will not mix. Density control is specified in European specifications but not in ASTM specification. But for India it is proposed to keep density specifications to check for contamination/adulteration.

Cetane Number

Cetane number of a diesel engine fuel is indicative of its ignition characteristics. Higher the cetane number better it is in its ignition properties. Cetane number affects a number of engine performance parameters like combustion, stability, drive ability, white smoke, noise and emissions of carbon monoxide and hydro carbons. Biodiesel has higher cetane number than conventional diesel fuel. This results in higher combustion efficiency and smoother combustion. No correlation was found between the specific gravity and the cetane number of various biodiesel. It is important to note that Cetane Index, commonly used to indicate the ignition characteristics of diesel fuels, does not give correct results for biodiesel. Hence Cetane Index is not specified and a cetane number test is necessary. Even for a biodiesel blend, cetane index is not applicable as it does give a correct approximation of cetane number of the blend.

Viscosity

In addition of lubrication of fuel injection system components, fuel viscosity controls the characteristics of the injection from the diesel injector (droplet size, spray characteristics etc.). The viscosity of methyl esters can go to very high levels and hence, it is important to control it within an acceptable level to avoid negative impact on fuel injection system performance. Therefore, the viscosity specifications proposed are same as that of the diesel fuel.

Distillation Characteristics

The distillation characteristics of biodiesel are quite different from that of diesel fuel. Biodiesel does not contain any highly volatile components, the fuel evaporates only at higher temperature. This is the reason that sometimes sump lubrication oil dilution observed in many tests. The methyl esters present in biodiesel generally have molecular chains of 16 to 18 carbons which have very close boiling points. In other words, rather than showing a distillation characteristics, biodiesel exhibits a boiling point. Boiling point of biodiesel generally ranges between 330°C to 357°C. The limit of 360°C is specified mainly to ensure that high boiling point components are not present in biodiesel as adulterants/contaminants.

Flash Point

Flash point of a fuel is defined as the temperature at which it will ignite when exposed to a flame or spark. The flash point of biodiesel is higher than the petroleum based diesel fuel. Flash point of biodiesel blends is dependent on the flash point of the base diesel fuel used, and increase with percentage of biodiesel in the blend. Thus in storage, biodiesel and its blends are safer than conventional diesel. The flash point of biodiesel is around 160°C, but it can reduce drastically if the alcohol used in manufacture of biodiesel is not removed properly. Residual alcohol in the biodiesel reduces its flash point drastically and is harmful to fuel pump, seals, elastomers etc. It also reduces the combustion quality.

A minimum flash point for biodiesel is specified more from the point of view of restricting the alcohol content rather than a fire hazard. A minimum flash point of 100°C is specified to ensure that excess methanol used for the esterification is removed. Another important consideration is that the test method used to find out flash point (ASTM D-93) gives high scatter in results at the flash point nears 100°C. Due to this reason, the ASTM D-6751 standard issued in Feb. 2002 calls for a flash point of min. 130°C though the intent is to get a min. value of 100°C (as specified in 1999 Draft standard PS-121).

Cold Filter Plugging Point (CFPP)

At low operating temperature fuel may thicken and not flow properly affecting the performance of fuel lines, fuel pumps and injectors. Cold filter plugging point of biodiesel reflects its cold weather performance. It defines the fuels limit of filterability. CFPP has better correlation than cloud point for biodiesel as well as diesel fuel. Biodiesel thicken at low temperatures so need cold flow improver additives to have acceptable CFPP.

Pour Point

Normally either pour point or CFPP are specified. French and Italian biodiesel specifications specify pour point whereas others specify CFFP. Since CFFP reflects more accurately the cold weather operation of fuel, it is proposed not to specify pour point for biodiesel. Pour point depressants commonly used for diesel fuel do not work for biodiesel.

Cloud Point

Cloud point is the temperature at which a cloud or haze of crystals appear in the fuel under test conditions and thus becomes important for low temperature operations. Biodiesel generally has higher cloud point than diesel fuel. Cloud point limit is not specified but ASTM D-6751 calls for reporting of the cloud point to alert the user of possible problem under cold climatic-conditions.

Aromatics

Biodiesel does not contain any aromatics, so aromatic limits are not specified. It may be noted that conventional aromatic determination tests used for petroleum fuels does not give correct results for biodiesel, hence aromatics in a biodiesel blend can be determined only by testing the base diesel fuel before blending.

Stability

Biodiesel ages more quickly than fossil diesel fuel due to the chemical structure of fatty acids and methyl esters present in biodiesel. Typically there are up to 14 types of fatty acid methyl esters in the biodiesel. The individual proportion of presence of these esters in the fuel affects the final properties of biodiesel. Saturated fatty acid methyl esters (C-14 : O,

C-16 : 0, C-16 : O) increase cloud point, cetane number and improve stability whereas more poly-unsaturates (C-18 : 2, C-18 : 3) reduce cloud point, cetane number and stability. There are three types of stability criteria :

- Oxidation stability - more related to engine operation as engine components attain high temperatures during operation.
- Storage stability.
- Thermal stability.

Oxidation Stability

Poor oxidation stability can cause fuel thickening, formation of gums and sediments, which, in turn, can cause filter clogging and injector fouling. Iodine number indicates the tendency of a fuel to be unstable as it measures the presence of C = C bonds that are prone to oxidation. Generally instability increase by a factor of 1 for every C = C bond on the fatty acid chain. Thus, .C-18 : 3 are three times more unstable than C-18 : O fatty acids. Oxidation stability of biodiesel varies greatly depending upon the feedstock used. In one study of 22 biodiesel samples taken from 7 European production sites, the induction period was found to vary from 1 hrs to 10 hrs.

Thermal Stability

Current knowledge and database is still inadequate. More information is needed in this area.

Storage Stability

Very little data is available on the long-term storage stability of biodiesel. Effect of presence of water, sediments, and additives on storage stability need to be investigated more. Based on the data available so far it is recommended that biodiesel and its blends should not be stored in a storage tank or vehicle tank for more than 6 months. Depending upon the storage temperature and other conditions use of appropriate antioxidants (e.g. Tenox 21, t-butylhydroquinone etc.) is suggested. The anti–oxidants must be properly mixed with the fuel for good effectiveness. To avoid growth of algae in fuel, water contamination need to be minimized and if necessary some biocide should be used.

Currently not all of the biodiesel standards issued, mention oxidation stability. Iodine number, viscosity and neutralization number indirectly assesses it. Higher values are indicative of poor oxidation stability. Iodine number test does not pick up the stability additives if used. There is need to develop appropriate test methods for oxidation and storage stability of biodiesel. ASTM D-2274 is a good candidate test method.

Iodine Number and Polyunsaturated Methyl Ester (C-18:3+)

In diesel engines, Methyl esters have been known to cause engine oil dilution by the fuel. A high content of unsaturated fatty acids in the ester (indicated by high Iodine number) increases the danger of polymerization in the engine oil. Oil dilution decreases oil viscosity. Sudden increase in oil viscosity, as encountered in several engine tests, is attributed to oxidation and polymerization of unsaturated fuel parts entering into oil through dilution. In saturated fatty acids all the carbon is bound to two hydrogen atoms by double bonds. More the double bonds the lower is the cloud point of oil. The tendency of the fuel to be unstable can be predicted by Iodine number. Different biodiesel have different stability performance. When iodine is introduced in the oil, the iodine attaches itself over a double bond to form a single bond. Thus iodine number refer to the amount of iodine required to convert unsaturated oil into saturated oil. It does not refer to the amount of iodine in the oil but to the presence of unsaturated fatty acids in the fuel. ASTM D-1520 method for measurement of Iodine number does not recognize the presence of stability additive.

Iodine number is not well suited to indicate the influence of methyl ester on engine. One value of iodine number can be obtained by using several grades of unsaturated acids. So an additional parameter, linolenic acid (C-18 : 3) content is specified and limited to 15% in Austrian Standard ON C-1191.

Free and Total Glycerol

The degree of conversion completeness of the vegetable oil is indicated by the amount of free and total glycerol present in the biodiesel. If the actual number is higher than the specified values, engine fouling, filter-clogging etc. can occur. Manufacturing process controls are necessary to ensure low free and total glycerin. Free glycerol if present can build up at the bottom of the storage and vehicle fuel tanks.

Mono-, Di-, and Triglycerides

Most of the biodiesel standards, except Austrian and ASTM, specify a max. limit of 0,08 for Mono-glyceride. Draft EU standard calls for same limit. Di- and Triglycerides are also controlled in most of the standards. High levels of these glycerides can cause injector fouling, filter clogging etc.

Ester Content

France (96.5%), Italy (98%) and Sweden (98%) specify a minimum eater content whereas Austrian and ASTM Standards do not specify any limit.

Alkaline Matter CNa, K)

Alkaline matter is controlled mainly to ensure that the catalysts used in the esterification process are properly removed.

Total Contamination

Left over impurities at the time of manufacture (such as free proteins) may form solid particles and clog the fuel lines. Filtration and washing treatments at manufacturing level need to be robust.

Sulfur Content

Biodiesel generally contain less than 15 ppm sulfur. ASTM D-5453 test is a suitable test for such low level of sulfur. ASTM D-2622 used for sulfur determination of diesel fuels gives falsely high results when used for biodiesel. More work need to done to assess suitability of ASTM D-2622 application to B-20 biodiesel blend. The increase in oxygen content of the fuel affects precision of this test method.

Lubricity

Wear due to excessive friction resulting in shortened life of diesel fuel pumps and injectors, has sometimes ascribed to lack of lubricity in the fuel. Numerous premature breakdown and in some cases, catastrophic failures, have occurred failures. All diesel fuel injection equipment (fuel pump and injector) of the diesel engine have reliance on diesel fuels for its lubrication, especially the Rotary (Distributor) and Common Rail type systems. The lubrication of the pump is not provided by viscosity alone but also by the lubricity property of the fuel. Even when the viscosity of the fuel is correct, several parts of the pump can wear out due to lack of lubricity. The lubricity of the fuel depends on the crude source, refining process to reduce sulfur content and the type of additives used. BOCLE (Ball on Cylinder Lubricity Evaluator) and HFFR (High Frequency Reciprocating Rig) are commonly used for evaluating the lubricity of the fuel. BOCLE is normally used for finding the lubricity fuel without additive, as it does not properly characterize the lubricity of fuels with lubricity additives. HFFR method has been adopted by Fuel Injection.

Manufactures for lubricity evaluation of diesel fuels and they recommend a limit of 460 microns wear scar diameter (WSD). Lower the WSD better is the lubricity of fuel. In case of BOCLE method a higher value is better. Even with 2% biodiesel mixed in diesel fuel, the WSD values comes down to around 325 micron and is sufficient to meet the lubricity requirements of the fuel injection pump (460 micron max). B100 performs still better, with a WSD of about 314 micron. With further reduction of sulfur content is diesel for Euro II and Euro IV fuels, the lubricity loss due to sulfur removal can easily be compensated by the addition of appropriate amount of biodiesel in diesel fuel.

2% addition into any conventional diesel fuel is sufficient to address the lubricity problem. It also eliminates the inherent variability associated with use of other additives to make fuel fully lubricious. Second the biodiesel is a fuel component itself - any addition of it does cause any adverse consequences. Since pure biodiesel has high lubricity, it is not specified in the specification. When biodiesel is used as lubricity blend (B-2) or diesel fuel extender (B-20), its lubricity characteristics has to meet the specification for the base fuel.

Sulfated Ash

Sulfated ash is controlled to ensure that all the catalysts used in the trans-esterification process are removed. Presence of ash can cause filter plugging and or injector deposits. Soluble metallic soap, un-removed catalysts and other solids are possible sources of sulfated ash in the fuel.

Acid Number/Neutralization Number

Acid number/Neutralization number is specified to ensure proper aging properties of the fuel and/or a good manufacturing process. Acid number reflects the presence of free fatty acids or acids used in manufacture of biodiesel. It also reflects the degradation of biodiesel due to thermal effects. For example, during the injection process several times more fuel returns from the injector than that injected into the combustion chamber of the engine. The temperature of this return fuel can, sometimes, be as high as 90°C and thus accelerate the degradation of biodiesel. The resultant high acid number can cause damage to injector and also result in deposits in fuel system and affect life of pumps and filters. Sodium hydro peroxide and sulfuric acids are highly corrosive and can cause serious, many times permanent, injuries.

Water Content

Biodiesel and its blends are susceptible to growing microbes when water is present in fuel. The solvency properties of the biodiesel can cause microbial slime to detach and clog fuel filters.

Phosphorous Content

Phosphorous can come as impurity and can affect oxidation catalyst and cause injector fouling. As more and more OEMs are going to use catalytic converters in diesel engines, it is necessary to keep the level of phosphorous in fuel low. Usually biodiesel have <1ppm phosphorus. The specification of minimum 10 ppm phosphorous content is intended to ensure compatibility with catalytic converters irrespective of the source of biodiesel.

Methanol/Ethanol Content

High levels of free alcohol in biodiesel cause accelerated deterioration of natural rubber seals and gaskets. Damage to fuel pumps and injectors which have natural rubber diaphragms has been very common type of failure Methanol is membrane-permeable and can cause nerve damage. Therefore control of alcohol content is required.

Conradson Carbon Residue (CCR)

Carbon residue of the fuel is indicative of carbon depositing tendencies of the fuel. Conradson Carbon Residue (CCR) for biodiesel is more important than that in diesel fuel because it show a high correlation with presence of free fatty acids, glycerides, soaps, polymers, higher unsaturated fatty acids, inorganic impurities and even on the additives used for pour point depression. Two methods are used to measure carbon residue :

- 100 % residual.
- 10% residual.

Since most of the biodiesel boils at almost the same temperature it is difficult to get a 10% residual upon distillation. Though the 10 % CCR test is easier to do, more work need to be done before we use it in Indian specifications for biodiesel.

20

Biodiesel Project Report

PRODUCT DESCRIPTION AND USES

Biodiesel is a domestically produced, renewable fuel that can be manufactured from vegetable oils, or recycled restaurant oils. Biodiesel is safe, biodegradable, and reduces serious air pollutants such as participate, carbon monoxide, hydrocarbons, and air toxic. Blends of 20% biodiesel with 80% petroleum diesel (B-20) can generally be used in unmodified diesel engines. Biodiesel can also be used in its pure form (B-100), but it too may require certain engine modifications to avoid maintenance and performance problems.

Biodiesel (fatty acid alkyl esters) is a cleaner-burning diesel replacement fuel made from natural, renewable sources such as new and used vegetable oils and animal fats. Just like petroleum diesel, biodiesel operates in compression-ignition engines. Blends of up to 20% biodiesel (mixed with petroleum diesel fuels) can be used in nearly all diesel equipment and are compatible with most storage and distribution equipment. These low level blends (20% and less) generally do not require any engine modifications. Biodiesel can provide the same payload capacity and as diesel.

Using biodiesel in a conventional diesel engine substantially reduces emissions of unburned hydrocarbons, carbon monoxide, sulfates, polycyclic aromatic hydrocarbons, nitrated polycyclic aromatic hydrocarbons, and particulate matter. These reductions increase as the amount of biodiesel blended into diesel fuel increases. The test emissions reductions are seen with B-100.

The use of biodiesel decreases the solid carbon fraction of particulate matter (since the oxygen in biodiesel enables more complete combustion to CO_2) and reduces the sulfate fraction (biodiesel contains less than 24 ppm sulfur), while the soluble, or hydrocarbon, fraction stays the same or increases. Therefore, biodiesel works well with new technologies such as diesel oxidation catalysts (which reduce the soluble fraction of diesel particulate but not the solid carbon fraction).

Emissions of nitrogen oxides increase with the concentration of biodiesel in the fuel. Some biodiesel produces more nitrogen oxides than others, and some additives have shown promise in modifying the increases. More R & D is needed to resolve this issue.

TABLE 21.1

Biodiesel has physical properties very similar to conventional diesel. Biodiesel's Physical Characteristics.

Specific gravity	0.87 to 0.89
Kinematic viscosity @ 40°C	3.7 to 5.8
Cetane number	46 to 70
Higher heating value (btu/lb)	16,928 to 17,996
Sulfur, wt %	0.0 to 0.0024
Cloud point °C	-11 to 16
Pour point °C	-15 to 13
Iodine number	60 to 135
Lower heating value (btu/lb)	15,700 to 16,735

Biodiesel is packed in 35 kg carboys, 225 kg MS Barrels and Bulk in Tankers.

How is Biodiesel Made : Biodiesel fuel can be made from new or used vegetable oils, which are non-toxic, biodegradable, renewable resources. Fats and oils are chemically reacted with an alcohol (methanol is the usual choice) to produce chemical compounds known as fatty acid methyl esters. Biodiesel is the name given to these esters when they are intended for use as fuel. Glycerol (used in Pharmaceuticals and cosmetics, among other markets) is produced as a co-product.

Biodiesel can be produced by a variety of esterification technologies. The oils and fats are filtered and pre–processed to remove water and contaminants. If free fatty acids are present, they can be removed or transformed into biodiesel using special pretreatment technologies. The pre–treated oils and fats are then mixed with an alcohol (usually methanol) and a catalyst (usually sodium or potassium hydroxide). The oil molecules (triglycerides) are broken apart and reformed into esters and glycerol, which are then separated from each other and purified. Approximately 55% of the biodiesel industry can use any fat or oil feedstock, including recycled cooking oils. The other half of the industry is limited to vegetable oils, the least expensive of which is *Jatropha* oil. The *Jatropha* oil industry has been the driving force behind biodiesel commercialization because of large production capacity, product surpluses, and declining prices. Similar issues apply to the recycled oils and animal fats industry, even though these feedstock are less expensive than *Jatropha* oils.

Biodiesel Benefits : Biodiesel is a substitute or extender for traditional petroleum diesel and you don't need special pumps or high pressure equipment for fueling. In addition, it can be used in conventional diesel engines, so you don't need to buy special vehicles or engines to run biodiesel.

Scientists believe carbon dioxide is one of the main greenhouse gases contributing to global warming. Neat biodiesel (100 per cent biodiesel) reduces carbon dioxide emissions by more than 75 per cent over petroleum diesel. Using a blend of 20 per cent biodiesel reduces carbon dioxide emissions by 15 per cent.

Biodiesel also produces fewer particulate, carbon monoxide, and sulfur dioxide emissions, all targeted as public health risks by the Environmental Protection Agency.

Since biodiesel can be used in conventional diesel engines, the renewable fuel can directly replace petroleum products; reducing the country's dependence on imported oil.

Biodiesel offers safety benefits over petroleum diesel because it is much less combustible, with a flash point greater than 150°C, compared to 77°C for petroleum diesel. It is safe to handle, store, and transport.

Biodiesel can help reduce our dependence on foreign oil and help us leverage our fossil fuel supplies. It can also help reduce greenhouse gas emissions, as well as public health risks associated with air pollution. It is non–toxic and biodegradable. Biodiesel contains only trace amounts of sulfur, typically less than the new EPA standards that will go into effect in 2006 for diesel fuel. It is safe to handle, transport, and store, and has a higher flash point than petroleum diesel. It can also be stored in diesel tanks and pumped with regular equipment except in colder weather, where tank heaters or agitators may be required. Biodiesel mixes readily with petroleum diesel at any blend level, making it a very flexible fuel additive.

Biodiesel is an oxygenated fuel, so it contributes to a more complete fuel burn and a greatly improved emissions profile. The more biodiesel used in a blend, the higher the emission reductions. One of the unique benefits of biodiesel is that it significantly reduces air toxic that are associated with petroleum diesel exhaust and are suspected of causing cancer and other human health problems. NO_x emissions are an exception to the rule, since biodiesel tends to increase NO_x emissions. Recent research has shown a number of ways to mitigate this problem. You can use pure biodiesel in most engines made after 1994 with some limitations. Engine performance (fuel economy, torque, and power) can be less than that of diesel by 8% to 15%, because of the lower energy content of the biodiesel (about 93%). Consumers should be aware of potential cold weather problems during vehicle operation and fuel storage. Consumers should also watch for obvious signs of damage around seals and gaskets. You can use pure biodiesel in older engines, but the seals and gaskets are more likely to be damaged by biodiesel. Also, it helps to start out with a clean storage tank if pure biodiesel is used.

Most people use a blend of 20% biodiesel with petroleum diesel (B-20) to avoid the problems listed above. Engine performance with B-20 is virtually the same as with petroleum diesel. Problems associated with storage, seals and gaskets, and cold weather are minimal. Even very low amounts of biodiesel (1% to 2%) can provide substantial lubricity benefits to premium diesel fuels.

Every liter of biodiesel displaces 0.95 liter of petroleum-based diesel over its life cycle. It is also very energy efficient. For every unit of fossil energy used to produce biodiesel, 3.37 units of biodiesel energy are created. Additionally, biodiesel reduces the amount of carbon dioxide (CO_2) being released into the atmosphere. It releases less fossil CO_2 than does conventional diesel, and the crops used to produce biodiesel absorb large amounts of CO_2 as they grow. And because biodiesel is non–toxic and biodegradable, it is an excellent fuel for use in fragile environments such as estuaries, lakes, rivers, and national parks.

Description : Biodiesel is a manufactured product, slightly yellow in colour, oily liquid with a slight aromatic odour and a bitter taste.

Applications : It is commonly used as fuel for stationary diesel engine like pump sets and other agricultural implements and also in Diesel cars.

Standards.—Specifications for Biodiesel (B-100): provided by the National Biodiesel Board.

- Standard Specification for Biodiesel Fuel (B100) Blend Stock for Distillate Fuels — provided by ASTM International.
- *Biodiesel Production and Quality:* Provided by the National Biodiesel Board.
- Biodiesel Handling and Use Guidelines.
- Biodiesel Handling and Use Guidelines - Japanese version.
- Pure biodiesel (B-100 needs to meet the requirements of ASTM D-6751 to avoid engine operational problems. To obtain a copy of ASTM's Standard Specification for Biodiesel Fuel (B-100) Blend Stock for Distillate Fuels, visit the ASTM International Web site. This table summarizes the requirements for B-100.

Keep up with the latest biodiesel activities by reading the National Biodiesel Board's newsletter, Biodiesel Bulletin.

Transport Information : Hazardous for air, sea and road freight.

Personal Protection : Safety glasses, adequate ventilation.

Consumer Safety : Biodiesel is used as substitute for Diesel and all safety precautions are same as that of petroleum diesel.

MARKET SURVEY AND DEMAND SUPPLY POSITION

Recent trends are indicative of tremendous increase in the production of Commercial Vehicles and the consumption of Diesel. The import bill is mounting and the availability is going down. New sources will have to be developed and new units have to be put up in the next decade to manufacture Biodiesel which will substitute imported diesel in large quantities to meet the domestic demand where by causing smaller drain of our limited sources of foreign exchange.

The growth of Automotive Industry, particularly in the last 15 years, has been spectacular. It is not the magnitude of volume only, but also the diversity of products (commercial vehicle, cars, two/three wheelers), which have been impressive. The proposed product, i.e. Biodiesel also shows a good potential growth for demand.

Existing Manufacturers : Presently there are no manufacturers and a number of small scale units manufacturing this product will be set up, all over the country in next few years.

Installed Capacity and Production : This product is manufactured depending on availability of local raw material supply and local demand to substitute petroleum diesel. The production of last few years is given below :

Year	Production Kilo liters/year
2002-2003	Nil*
2003-2004	500*

* Estimated.

So the present total production in India, of Biodiesel is estimated to be 500 Kilo liters per year.

Future Demand : The major user of Biodiesel will be small farmers as well as for blending with diesel in petroleum refinery. The demand for the product will grow with the increase in production of Oil Engines. Due to shortage and irregular supply of electrical power, the growth rate for oil engines, is expected to be very high in coming years for states where electrical power is not easily available. Looking at the tremendous growth in Automotive and Stationary Oil Engines, which is projected to be 10% pa in terms of number of new engines, large quantities of diesel oil will be required. Taking into account the potential for Biodiesel units, the total capacity of these Biodiesel plants will substitute only a tiny fraction of the total diesel requirement.

Conclusion : From the demand and supply position, it appears that there should be a good scope for a number of new venture with a capacity of 1 to 30 Kilo liters per day.

MANUFACTURING PROCESS DESCRIPTION

Raw Materials : To manufacture 1 Kilo liters of Biodiesel, consumption of raw materials is as follows:

Methyl Alcohol (98 %)	150	liters
Vegetable Oil	1,050	liters
Caustic Potash	3.8	Kgs.

Input Materials Preparation : *Jatropha* or Physic Nut Oil is the input material oil can be crude but should be filtered first if recently obtained from oil press. The feedstock should be free of water and other foreign materials. In case the temperature causes the vegetable oil to gel up or become solid, the material should be liquefied by heating up to 40°C in the reactor tank. (Oilseed Crushing Plant is an Optional Activities for input requirements).

Methanol, MeOH - Anhydrous and at least 98% pure, and container grounded to protect from sparks.

Potassium Hydroxide, KOH - At least 85% in purity in flakes, powder or pellets. It is very sensitive to atmospheric moisture and must be stored in air-tight containers. It can be purchased in 20 kg plastic bags.

First, an acid value test is run then a bench-scale batch (50 ml to 200 ml input oil) should be conducted to determine optimum amount of MeOH and KOH for successful operation for every batch of incoming vegetable oil or animal fat (30 minutes esterification or mixing).

Chemical Reaction : The chemical reaction involved in the manufacture is as follows :

$$(C_nH_{n+2})COOH + CH_3OH \overset{\text{Catalyst}}{=} H_3C\text{-}OOC(C_nH_{n+2}) + H_2O.$$

Brief Process Description

Trans-esterification (for a series of batches or semi-continuous process) : Required amount of MeOH and KOH are mixed in catalyst reactor (takes about 10 minutes), until KOH has completely dissolved, (the solution becomes potassium methoxide). Vegetable oil is then poured or transferred to main reactor having desired amount of vegetable oil or animal fat. (Reactor tank is calibrated to allow faster determination of volume).

The methoxide is then poured into the reactor and mixing is started immediately. It is mixed for 60 minutes (esterrfication process). The ester material is then transferred (by pump or gravity) into the settling tank(s). In semi-continuous process, mixing of MeOH and KOH can be simultaneously done during the esterification step.

Settling/Phase Separation : The mixture is settled for 6—18 hours. Two phases or layers will be observed. (Settling tank has a viewing mechanism, either a clear hose, sight glass or window strip). The bottom phase (crude glycerin) is drained, or pumped out into the glycerin container for purification or removal of excess MeOH. The upper phase (Biodiesel) is transferred into a washing tank for washing.

Biodiesel Sweetening/Refining : Excess MeOH in the Biodiesel is removed using either vacuum or by heating. The Biodiesel may be washed with acidified water. This can be accomplished by mixing acetic acid (tannic or acetic acid) with water. Volume of water is about 40% that of Biodiesel. The acidified water is stirred into the Biodiesel as aeration stones near the bottom of the tank bubble water and air up through the fuel. After settling overnight the water is drained off the bottom. If necessary the fuel is then dried with heat, stirring and aeration. This step toay me omitted if settling time is over 18 hours, or KOH in the Biodiesel is below 50 ppm or 0.005% and filtered using at least 2 microns. The Biodiesel is pumped into the storage or packaging container. The pump should be equipped with at least 2 microns filter.

Optional Activities : Methanol Recovery: Methanol recovered from Biodiesel and crude glycerin may be used back in the esterification process. Recovered methanol must be anhydrous and 98% pure, for effective use.

Crude Glycerin Purification/Disposal : MeOH is removed from crude glycerin by vacuum or heating. Glycerin may be purified using ion-exchange method (Bulgarian Process) or tower distillation method (High heat traditional method). Glycerin may be shipped to a glycerin purification plant nearby.

Oilseed Crushing Plant.—For a 500 liter per day Biodiesel plant (with 21 days per month or 250 days operation per year), the crushing plant should be able to provide at least 125,000 liter per year. This requires at least 72 hectares of area planted with *Jatropha.* For *Jatropha* at 80% oil expelling efficiency and 30% oil content, the crushing plant needs 1150 kg of *Jatropha* seeds per day (200 kg/hr expeller is needed), at 8 hours/day operation. For semi-continuous 4 batch/day these amounts will increase by four times.

BIODIESEL PROCESS IN DETAIL

Ingredients

Reaction Raw Materials : *Jatropha* Oil, Methanol (CH_3OH) 99%+ pure, Potassium hydroxide (must be dry).

Titration : Isopropyl alcohol 99%+ pure, Distilled water, Phenolphthalein solution (not more than a year old, kept protected from strong light).

Washing : Vinegar, Water.

Procedure

Filter oil to remove any solid particles. Heat oil to remove any water content (optional). Perform titration to determine how much catalyst is needed. Prepare potassium methoxide. Heat oil if required, mix in the potassium methoxide while stirring. Allow to settle, remove the glycerine. Wash and dry. Check quality.

This procedure is called trans-esterification, similar to soap making. (To make soap you take a transfatty acid or triglyceride oil and blend it with a solution of potassium hydroxide and water. This reaction causes the ester chains to separate from the glycerine. These ester chains are what becomes the soap. They are also called lipids. Their unique characteristic of being attracted to polar molecules such as water on one end and to non-polar molecules like oil on the other end is what makes them effective as soap).

In trans-esterification, KOH and methanol are mixed to create potassium methoxide ($K^+ CH_3O^-$). When mixed in with the oil this strong polar-bonded chemical breaks the trans–fatty acid into glycerine and also ester chains (biodiesel), along with some soap if you are not careful. The esters become methyl esters. They would be ethyl esters if reacted with ethanol instead of methanol.

1. **Filtering :** Filter the oil to remove solid particles. You may have to warm it up a bit first to get it to run freely, 35°C should be enough. Use a double layer of cheesecloth in a funnel, or a restaurant or canteen-type coffee filter.
2. **Removing the Water :** Heat the oil first to remove any water content. Waste oil will probably contain water, which can slow down the reaction and cause saponification (soap formation). The less water in the oil the better. Raise the temperature to 100°C, hold it there and allow any water to boil off. Use a mixer to avoid steam pockets forming below the oil and exploding, splashing hot oil out of the container. Or drain water puddles out from the bottom as they form, you can save any oil that comes out with the water later. When boiling slows, raise the temperature to 130°C

for 10 minutes. Remove heat and allow to cool. Regular source of oil does not need to have the water boiled off, in which case do not do it, boiling means extra energy and time.

3. **Basic Titration :** Dissolve 1 gram of KOH in 1 liter of distilled or de-ionized water (0.1% KOH solution). An electronic pH meter is best, but you can also use pH test strips (or litmus paper), or phenolphthalein solution to get end point. In a smaller beaker, dissolve 1 ml of dewatered oil in 10 ml of pure isopropyl alcohol. Warm the beaker gently by standing it in some hot water, stir until all the oil dissolves in the alcohol and the mixture turns clear. Add 2 drops of phenolphthalein solution.

   Using a burette, add 0.1% KOH solution drop by drop to the oil alcohol phenolphthalein solution, stirring all the time, until the solution stays pink (magenta) for 10 seconds. Take the number of mis of 0.1% KOH solution you used and add 5.0. This is the number of grams of KOH you will need per liter of oil.

   With a pH meter or test strips, use the same procedure without adding the phenolphthalein. Add the 0.1% KOH solution drop by drop as before until the pH reaches 8.5.

4. **Test Batches :** The first few times you do this process, it is a good practice to first try out your KOH amounts on a 1 liter batch. This works really well and you do not need to heat up the oil too much, just enough so it will spin well. Start by mixing up the KOH and methanol. First make sure that vessels used are dry. Forming the exothermal potassium methoxide polar molecule will heat up the vessel a bit. Keep mixing until all the KOH has been dissolved.

   Once the potassium methoxide is prepared, add to 1 liter of oil. Make certain all your weights and volumes are precise. If you are unsure of the titration result then use 5.0 grams of KOH per liter of oil. Smaller batches need only be run for about 15—20 minutes for separation to be completed before switching off. The settling takes sometime to complete. The solution can be poured from the vessel into another container right after switching off the agitator. It is good to do a few batches with varying amounts of KOH recorded, so later when checking results one can choose the KOH quantity that did the best job. When too much KOH is used the result can be a troublesome gel that is tough to do anything with. When not enough KOH is used the reaction does not go far enough so some unreacted oil will be mixed with the biodiesel and glycerine. This will form three levels with biodiesel on top above unreacted oil with glycerine on the bottom. If there is too much water in the oil it will form soaps and settle right above the glycerine forming a fourth level in the container. This layer is not too easy to separate from the unreacted oil and glycerine layers.

5. **Preparing the Potassium Methoxide :** Generally the amount of methanol needed is 20% of the oil by mass. The densities of these two liquids are fairly close, so 20% of methanol by volume should be about right. To be completely sure, measure out a half-liter of both fluids, weigh, and calculate exactly what 20% by mass is. Different oils can have different densities depending on what type of oil it originally was.

   Example : When trans-esterifying 100 liters of oil, use 20 liters of methanol. The methanol is mixed into a solution with the KOH, creating potassium methoxide in an exothermic reaction (it gets warm from bonds forming). Keep all utensils the KOH comes in contact with as dry as possible.

   CAUTION : Treat potassium methoxide with extreme caution! Do not inhale any vapours! If any potassium methoxide gets splashed on your skin, it will burn you without your feeling it (killing the nerves). Wash immediately with lots of water. Always have a hose running when working with potassium methoxide. Potassium methoxide is also very corrosive to paints. KOH reacts with aluminum, tin and zinc. Use glass, enamel or stainless steel containers, stainless steel is best.

6. **Heating and Mixing :** Pre-heat waste vegetable oil 48—54 °C. A propeller coupled to a electric motor works fine as a mixer. Too much agitation causes splashing and bubbles through vortexing and reduces mix efficiency. There should be a vortex just appearing on the surface. Adjust the speed, or the pitch or size of the stirrer to get the right effect. Alternately an electric pump plumbed to form a mixing loop for stirring the oil would do a nice job. Mount the pump above the level that glycerine will gel at, to prevent clogging up the pump.

   Add the potassium methoxide to the oil while stirring, stir the mixture for 50 minutes to an hour. The reaction is often complete in 30 minutes, but longer is better. The trans-esterification process separates the methyl esters from the glycerine. The CH_3O of the methanol then caps off the ester chains and OH from the KOH stabilizes the glycerine.

7. **Settling and Separation :** Allow the solution to settle and cool for at least eight hours, preferably longer. The methyl esters (biodiesel) will be floating on top while the denser glycerine will have congealed on the bottom of the container forming a hard gelatinous mass (the mixing pump must be mounted above this level). An alternative method is to allow the reactants to settle for at least an hour after mixing while keeping the mixture above 38°C, which keeps the glycerine semi-liquid (it solidifies below 38°C). Then carefully decant the biodiesel. This can be done by draining the reactants out of the bottom of the container through a transparent hose. The semi-liquid glycerine has a dark brown colour and the biodiesel is honey-coloured. Keep a watch on what flows through the sight tube. When the lighter-coloured biodiesel appears divert it to a separate container. If any biodiesel stays with the glycerine it is easy to retrieve it later once the glycerine has solidified. If you left the mixture in the tank until the glycerine gelled, reheat the tank just enough to liquify the glycerine again. Do not stir it! Then decant it out as above.

8. **Glycerine :** The glycerine from oil is brown and usually turns to a solid below about 38°C. Glycerine from fresh oil often stays a liquid at lower temperatures. Reclaimed glycerine is composted after being vented for three weeks to allow residual methanol to evaporate off or after heating it to 66°C to boil off any methanol content (the boiling point of methanol is 64.7°C). The excess methanol can be recovered for re-use when boiled off if you run the vapours through a condenser. Another way of disposing of the glycerine, though a great bit more complicated, would be to separate its components, mostly methanol, pure glycerine (a valuable product for medicines, tinctures, hand lotions, dried plant arrangements and many other uses) and wax. This is often accomplished by distilling it, but glycerine has a high boiling point even under high vacuum so this method is difficult. Other idea for disposing of the glycerine is breaking it down to usable methane gas, with a Bio Gas methane digester.

9. **Soap Residue :** Suspended in the biodiesel will also be some soapy residues. These are the result of K^+ ions from the KOH reacting with water created when the methanol bonds with the ester chains along with any other water that was suspended in the oil. If the reaction produces more than the usual amount of soap, this happens when KOH comes into contact with water before it has a chance to react with the oil. In this case the excess water should have been boiled off first.

   The part of the process where it is vital to keep all water out of the reaction is when making the potassium methoxide. Keep the vessels KOH comes in contact with as dry as possible. The chances of a good clean splitting of ester from glycerine with little soap by-product are much better on a warm dry summer day than on a damp winter day.

10. **Washing and Drying :** The biodiesel from this stage can be used to the fuel tanks of vehicles. It is to let it settle for a while (about 2 days), allowing the majority of the soap residues to settle before running the biodiesel through a filtration system then into the vehicle fuel tank. Another method is to wash the soaps out of the fuel with water, one or more times. When washing biodiesel the first time it is best to add a small amount of dilute acetic acid before adding the water. The acetic acid brings the pH of the solution closer to neutral because it neutralizes and drops out any KOH suspended in the biodiesel.

    A simple way of washing is using a PVC container with a valve 3-4 inches from bottom. Fill with water until it is halfway between the container's bottom and the valve, then fill up with the biodiesel to be washed. After a gentle stirring (keep it gentle, do not agitate up soaps) followed by 12—24 hours of settling, the oil and water will separate, the cleaned oil can be decanted out the valve, leaving the denser soapy water to be drained out the bottom. This process might have to be repeated two or three times to remove close to 100% of soaps. The second and third washings can be done with water alone. After the third washing any remaining water gets removed by reheating the oil slowly, the water and other impurities sink to bottom. The finished product should have a pH of 7, checked with litmus paper or with a digital pH tester.

    The water from the third wash can be used for the first or

second washes for the next batch. The impurities can be left in the re-heater for the next batch and removed when it accumulates. Transesterified and washed biodiesel will become clearer over time as any remaining soaps drop out of the solution.

QUANTITY OF METHANOL TO BE USED

The stoichiometric quantity of methanol is the amount needed to convert triclycerides (oils) into esters (biodiesel), the methyl portion of methyl esters. You also need an excess of methanol to push the conversion process towards completion, without the excess the process runs out (reaches equilibrium) before all the triglycerides are converted to esters, resulting in poor fuel that does not combust well and can be corrosive. The excess methanol acts more like a catalyst. It encourages the process but does not become a part of the final product and can be recovered afterwards.

1. **Stoichiometric Quantity :** The stoichiometric quantity is usually said to be 12.5% methanol by volume, that is, 125 ml of methanol per litre of oil. In fact it depends on the amounts of the various fatty acids in the oil, and varies from one oil to another. Calculate the average proportions of the different fatty acids in each of the more common oils, calculate their total molecular weights, and from this calculate the stoichiometric amount cf methanol required to convert them. The amount varies from 11.3% for rapeseed oil (canola) to 16.3% for coconut oil. These figures are averages, fatty acid quantities vary somewhat when oil crops are grown in different conditions in different parts of the world. But they are close enough for our purposes, and a lot more accurate than the general figure of 12.5%. If you have an analysis of the fatty acid content of your oil, you can calculate the correct stoichiometric ratio.
2. **Excess :** How much excess is needed depends on several different factors: the type of oil, its condition, the type, size and shape of the processor, the type and duration of agitation, the temperature of the process, and it does not make much sense anyway if the stoichiometric ratio is wrong in the first place. However, excess is usually between 60% and 100% of the stoichiometric amount.

The stoichiometric ratio of *Jatropha* oil is 12.5%, that is 125 ml of

Table 20.1 : Production of Biodiesel using Jatropha as Feedstock.

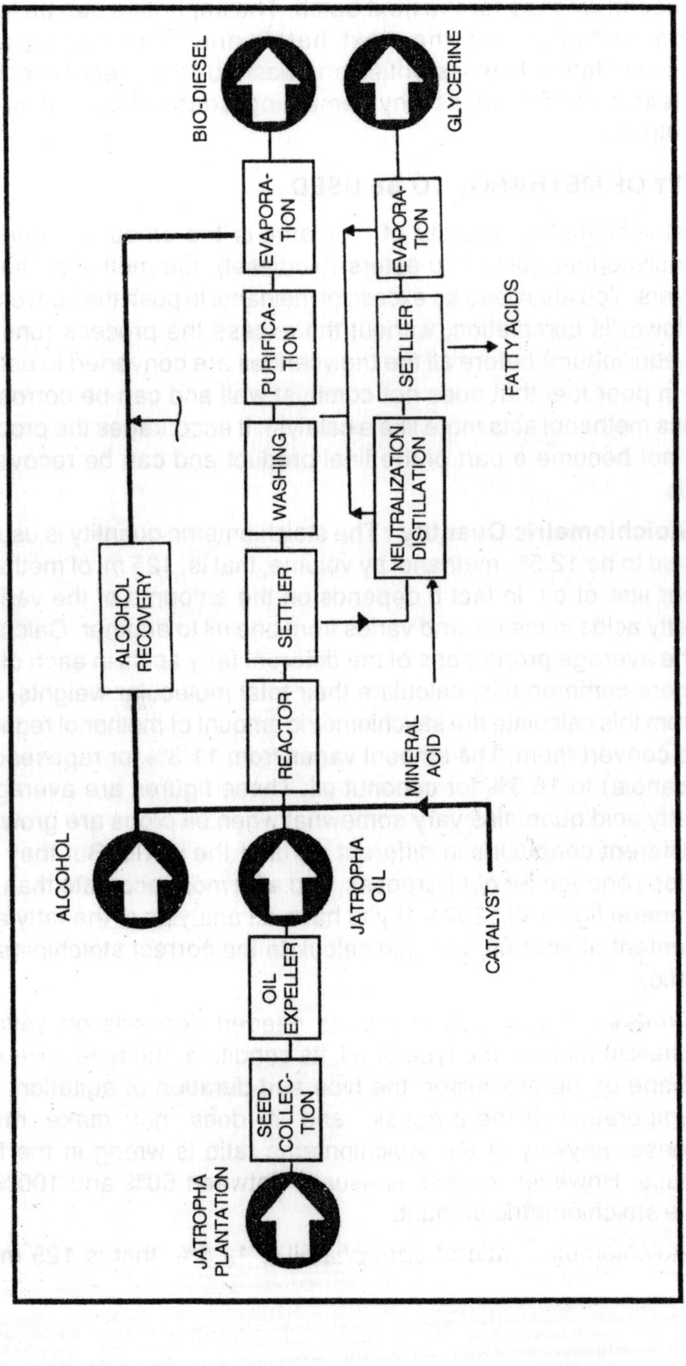

Table 20.2

Biodiesel Specifications and Testing Results.

Property (units)	ASTM D-6751	Limits	Methyl Esters of oils			
			Sunflower Oil	Palm Oil	Jatropha Oil	*Pongamia pinnata*
Flash point (°C)	D-93	Min. 130	73	127	163	92
Phosphorus (% mass)	D-4951	Max.0.001	<0.001	<0.001	<0.001	0.001
Water *and* sediment (% vol)	D-2709	Max. 0.050	0.04	0.01	0.05	0.03
CCR100% (% mass)	D-4530	Max. 0.050	0.01	<o.o1	<o.o1	<o.o1
Sulphated ash (% mass)	D-874	Max. 0.020	0.001	n.d	n.d.	0.002
Viscosity at 40° C (cst)	D-445	1.9—6.0	4.103	4.506	4.440	4.16
Sulphur (% mass)	D-5453	Max. 0.05	0.04	0.038	O.020	0.003
Cetane number	D-613	Min. 47	55.6	54.6	57.1	55.1
Copper corrosion	D-130	Max. 3	1	1b	1b	1b
Neutralization value	D-664	Max. 0.80	0.20	0.24	0.48	0.10
Free glycerin (% mass)	D-6584	Max. 0.020	0.02	0.01	0.01	0.01
Total glycerin (% mass)	D-6584	Max. 0.240	0.02	0.01	0.02	0.01
Distillation temp. (360°C)	D-1160	90%	90%	90%	90%	90%

methanol per liter of oil, the excess would range between 75 ml and 125 ml, for a total amount of methanol of 200—250 ml per litre of oil. Oils with higher stoichiometric ratios seem to need higher excesses. So, for fresh soya or canola, you can try 60%, though 67% or more would be better. For palm kernel or coconut, closer to 100% excess would be better. If you do not know what kind of oil it is, try using 25% methanol, 250 ml methanol to 1 liter of oil. If you've taken care with the titration, used accurate measurements and followed the instructions carefully, you should get a good, clean split, with esters on top and the glycerine and free fatty acids cleanly separated at the bottom. If you have trouble washing it, with a lot of frothing, that could be because the process did not go far enough and unconverted material is forming emulsions, try using more methanol next time. If everything works well, try using less methanol. You will soon figure out what's best for you.

TREATMENT OF LIQUID EFFLUENTS

There is only one point from where the effluent is discharged with traces of catalyst. The methanol will be recovered and will be absent in effluent. It is lead to collection tank. It is then allowed to settle. The clear treated water which will be within limits for BOD and COD will be used for gardening purposes.

POWER REQUIREMENT

The requirement of electrical power will be 20.5 KW of connected load, which is available from local electrical supply agency.

TABLE : 20.3

Details of power requirement for the equipments is given below :

Sl. No.	Equipments	Quantity	Power HP
1.	Catalyst Reactor Pump	1	1.00
2.	Main Reactor Pump	1	1.00
3.	Washing Vessel Pump	1	2.00
4.	Settling Tank Pump	1	2.00
5.	Heaters	1	15.00

6.	Lighting		0.50
7.	Miscellaneous		2.00
8.	Air Compressor	1	2.00
9.	Cooling Water Pump	1	2.00
		TOTAL H.P.	27-50

Requirement of connected load	=	27.50	x 0.75 KW
	=	20.63	KW
Requirement of Fuel Oil	=	0.2	KL.
Requirement of Water	=	50	cu.m.

UTILITIES SPECIFICATIONS

Process Water : Process water should be free of mud and suspended particles. It should be available at a pressure of 3 Kg/sq.cm.

Electricity : It shall be available at 440 volts, A/C supply at 50 Hz. frequency and 3 phase supply.

Cooling Water : It should be available at 30°C and a return temperature of 37°C at a pressure of $4/cm^2$.

Steam : It should be available at 10 Kg/sq. cm pressure.

MARKET AND SELLING ARRANGEMENTS

The item will be manufactured by a few units. This will help in selling product, taking advantage for schemes in remote area. The entrepreneur is well connected with consuming industry. The product will be mostly sold in local area.

The product will be sold directly to bulk customers and in certain cases through agents and suppliers allowing some commission. Competition is proposed to be met by aggressive marketing, maintaining good quality and cheaper rates.

Negotiations are being made with various prospective customers and they are found interested in purchasing the product for their annual requirements.

TABLE 20.4

Production Capacity and Target.

Year	I	II	III	IV	V	VI	VII
Capacity	70	80	90	100	100	100	100
	Utilization % BIODIESEL						
Production KL/year	175	200	225	250	250	250	250
	Crude GLYCERINE						
Production tones/year	41	46	52	58	58	58	58

Cost of Project and Means of Finance

A.	**Cost of Finance**	**Rs.**
1.	Land and site	5300
2.	Building and Civil Work	98400
3.	Plant And Machinery	978652
4.	Utilities	340000
5.	Knowhow and Engineering Fees	50000
6.	Misc. Fixed Assets	171673
7.	Prelim, and Pre–operative Expences	46980
8.	Contingencies, and Escalation	97700
9.	Margin Money for working Capital	348206
	Total	**2136911**

Land

(a)	Cost of 100 sq. mt. Land @Rs. 40/sq.m.	4000
(b)	Cost of Leveling and Land Development @Rs. 2.0 per sq. m.	200
(c)	Cost of Construction of Roads	500
(d)	Cost of Fencing	500
(e)	Cost of Gate	100
	Total Rs.	5300

Building

		Area sq. m.	Rate Rs/sq. m.	Total Rs.
(a)	Factory Building with Staircase and Water Tank Office Building	30	2500	75000
(b)	Watchman's Cabin	5	2000	10000
(c)	Equipment Foundations, Sewers, Drains etc.			2500
(d)	Effluent Tanks			5000
(e)	Misc. Civil Work			5000
(f)	Architect and Structural Engineers' fee			900
			Sub Total	**98400**
	Total of Land and Building			**103700**

Cost of Utilities

Sl.. No.	Description	Capacity	Rate Rs.	Cost Rs.
1.	Boiler 100 Kg/hr		5000	300000
2.	Air Compressor		10000	10000
3.	Cooling Tower for Cooling Water	20 USGPM	20000	30000
			Total	**340000**
	Add: Transport, Erection, Fitting, Insurance etc. @5%			17000
			Total	**357000**

TABLE 20.5
PLANT AND MACHINERY

Sl. No.	Equipment Specifications	Capacity Liters	Qty Nos.	Price Rs.
A. MAIN PLANT				
1.	Catalyst Reactor made of SS-304	340	1	50000
2.	Main Reactor made of SS-304	1500	1	100000
3.	Vapour Condenser of area 1 sq.m. of MS		1	50000
4.	Settling Tank made of SS-304	1500	1	150000
5.	Settling Tank made of SS-304	2000	1	200000
6.	Micron Filters made of SS-304			20000
		Total		**570000**
B. STORAGE TANKS				
1.	Methyl Alcohol Storage Tank	5000	1	30000
2.	Product Storage Tank	5000	1	30000
3.	Vegetable Oil Storage Tank	5000	1	30000
		Total		**90000**
C. PUMPS				
1.	Catalyst Reactor Pump		1	5000

Sl. No.	Equipment	Specifications	Capacity Liters	Qty Nos.	Price Rs.
2.	Main Reactor Pump			1	5000
3.	Washing Vessel Pump			1	10000
4.	Settling Tank Pump			1	10000
			Total		**30000**
	Total P lantco st (A+ B + C)				690000
	Add:C Excise@ 15.75 %'				108675
					798675
	Add: M.Sales Tax @ 10 96				79868
					878543
	Add: Insurance @ 1%				8785
					887328
	Add: Transportation, Freight, Packing, Loading, Forwarding, Unloading Charges to Factory Site @ 4%				35493
					922821
	Add: Erection and Commissioning charges @ 5%				46141
					968962
	Add: Painting/Coating Charges				9690
			Grand Total		**978652**

21

GLYCERINE

GENERAL

Glycerine (glycerin, glycerol) is the main by-product of making biodiesel. The name comes from the Greek word glykys meaning sweet. It is a colourless, odourless, viscous, non–toxic liquid with a very sweet taste and has literally thousands of uses. That is, pure glycerine has thousands of uses — the biodiesel by-product is crude (and it's not colourless, and it's not only glycerine).

Lots of information, on glycerine, from a Japanese manufacturer (in English) — Sakamoto Yakuhin Kogyo Co., Ltd.

http: //www, sy-kogyo.co.jp/english/sei/ i_gry.html

Glycerin—King's American Dispensatory, by Harvey Wickes Felter, M.D., and John Uri Lloyd, Phr. M., Ph.D., 1898.

http://www.ibiblio.org/herbmed/eclectic/kings/glycerinum.html

BURNING GLYCERINE

The glycerine burns well,, but unless it's properly combusted at high temperatures it will release acrolein, which is toxic. Some waste oil burners are suitable. Some biodiesel manufacturers are burning the by product raw to provide heat for the biodiesel process. They use pot burners with a forced air supply piped in from an external fan. There are various designs being used, and a variety of ways of controlling the fuel supply and pre-heating the by-product so it flows evenly to the burner. The separated FFAs from the by-product also work well in such burners, and so does WVO.

SEPARATING THE GLYCERINE

What sinks to the bottom of the biodiesel processor during the settling stage is a mixture of glycerine, methanol, soaps and the lye catalyst. Most of the excess methanol and most of the catalyst remains in this layer. Once separated from the biodiesel, adding phosphoric acid to the glycerine layer precipitates the catalyst out and also converts the soaps back to free fatty acids (FFAs), which float on top. You're left with a light-coloured precipitate on the bottom, glycerine/methanol/water in the middle, and FFA on top. The glycerine will be approx. 95% pure, a much more attractive product to sell to refiners.

SEPARATING GLYCERINE/FFAS

A commonly asked question : How much glycerine do you get? A better question would be: How much of the glycerine layer is actually glycerine? The rule of thumb is 79 milliliters of glycerine per liter of oil used, 7.9%. In fact there's usually more soap and the glycerine layer is more of a soap layer than anything else, unless you use acid-base two-stage process.

PURIFYING GLYCERINE

Biodiesel can be made with ethanol, instead of methanol (which is toxic, fossil-fuel derived). But the ethanol has to be anhydrous (free of water) which can't be achieved by distillation. One way to dry it is to use the byproduct of making biodiesel, i.e, glycerine. See Absolute Alcohol Using Glycerine by Mariller-Granger Processes, from E. Boullanger: Distillerie Agricole *et* Industrielle (Paris: Ballire, 1924). Mariller's absolute alcohol production process by dehydration using glycerine, various systems examined and explained. Translation from the French by F. Marc de Piolenc.

But the glycerine has to be 99%+ pure. Purifying it is no simple matter, it's difficult to distill it because glycerine has a very high boiling point (290°C). Set the temperature and leave it alone. It'll purify the glycerine, at a price.

PAINTBRUSH CLEANER

There is another use for the by-product from biodiesel production, cleaning paint brushes which have been used with oil-based paints. It is superior to turpentine, and does not harden the brush from residual paint.

With the oily brush, dilute the paint in the brush (with biodiesel or turpentine) until it is runny when the brush is pushed onto a firm surface. Work the brush to ensure that the bristles are fully moistened. Remove from dilution liquid. Rinse brush under water until all milkiness is removed. If brush still shows signs of paint, repeat glycerin stage with fresh glycerin. Check that brush doesn't smell of paint and store brush as usual.

SOAP

The crude glycerine by-product from homemade biodiesel makes a powerful degreaser. Let it stand for 10 days or so to let any methanol residue evaporate, or (better) heat it to 65—70°C in a closed vessel and recover the methanol via a simple condenser. If you separate the glycerine by-product from the impurities, you'll be left with about 95% pure glycerine. You can add it to plain liquid soap to make a high-glycerine shower-soap or shampoo. It doesn't need much, 10 to 20 CC per 500 CC of liquid soap, and add some essential oils for fragrance.

Glycerine is a natural by-product of the soap making process. Glycerine moisturizes the skin, but commercial soap manufacturers remove the glycerine for use in lotions and creams, which are more profitable. Handcrafted soap retains the glycerine and is soft and kind to the skin.

GLOP SOAP

If you use too much NaOH when trying to make biodiesel it won't separate into biodiesel and glycerine but turn instead into a sort of gloppy Jelly, maybe with some soap solidified at the bottom. You can turn it into soap. Pour off the jelly and heat it to 65—70°C for 10—15 minutes to boil off any methanol residue. To turn the jelly into high-glycerine soap you need 135 grams of lye (caustic soda or sodium hydroxide, NaOH) per litre, minus the amount of NaOH you used in the first place. Soap making purists will object that the amount of NaOH needed depends on the saponification value of the type of oil or fat being used, but this is probably used oil anyway, and 135 grams per litre is about average and should work. You also need a third as much water as jelly. The water should be lukewarm. Slowly add the NaOH to the water, stirring until it dissolves (avoid fumes, take safety precautions). This heats the water: let it cool to lukewarm again. Heat the glop to about 45°C (no more) in a pot, and carefully add the water and NaOH, stirring constantly for 15—20 minutes, maintaining the heat, until the mixture starts to thicken.

High-Explosives

The most earth-shattering use of glycerine remains that discovered by Italian chemist Ascanio Sobrero 150 years ago when he subjected it to nitration to make the world's first real high-explosive, nitroglycerin, one of the most dangerous substances ever concocted. Sobrero's face was badly scarred in an explosion during an early experiment. He said nitroglycerin was so dangerous it was useless, and it had killed so many people he was ashamed to be its discoverer. But Swedish chemist Alfred Nobel set about mass-producing the stuff, in spite of several explosions, one of which killed his brother. Nobel discovered that nitroglycerin could be mixed with silica (diatomaceous earth) to form a stable high-explosive which he called dynamite. It made him one of the richest men of the age.

Nitroglycerin is extremely powerful. A mere 10 ml will expand 10,000 times into 100 liters of gas at an explosive velocity of 7,700 meters per second (17,224 miles per hour) more powerful than TNT.

HEART DISEASE DRUG

In one of the more curious coincidences of science, the first modern high explosive, nitroglycerin, also became one of the very first man-made drugs. To this day, it remains the most commonplace treatment for chronic angina, the chest pain of heart disease. Nitroglycerin is a vasodilator, it relaxes the blood vessels, reducing the pressure on the heart. There can be side-effects, some patients get killer headaches, others low blood-pressure and dizziness, and it can clash seriously with other drugs. It comes in the form of tablets for under the tongue, ointment and skin patches, and it cannot be turned into an explosive.

LOVE POTION

Nitroglycerin's action as an effective vasodilator led in 1998 to the release of RESTORE, the first ever fully tested, effective topical cream for the safe treatment of male erectile dysfunction (impotence). "Restore" contains 1% nitroglycerin and is effective within minutes of application of achieving an erection of up to 45 minutes duration. No significant side effects were reported.

SAFE SWEETENER

Glycerine is an alcohol (glycerol) and is used as a preservative in the food industry, as well as a sweetener: it is very sweet, yet it contains no sugar. This makes it an ideal sweetener for patients who cannot take sugar, such as the increasing number of Candida sufferers. Vegetable glycerine is said to be the only acceptable sweetener for Candida patients.

Health Supplement

Health supplement for sportsmen, Glycerine increases blood volume, enhances temperature regulation and improves exercise performance in the heat, or so it is claimed. It helps "hyperhydrate" the body by increasing blood volume levels and helping to delay dehydration. Following glycerol consumption, heart rate and body core temperature are lower during exercise in the heat, suggesting an performance enhancing effect. In long duration activities, a larger supply of stored water may lead to a delay in dehydration and exhaustion.

Other Uses

Glycerine is also a source of lecithin (used in foods as a fat emulsifier, and a vital component of all cell membranes in the body) and of tocopherols (vitamin E). It is used in skin moisturizers, lotions, deodorants, makeup, toothpaste, sweets and cakes, Pharmaceuticals and patent medicines, in paper manufacturing, printing ink, in textiles, plastics, and electronic components.

Disposal

Failing all else, you can compost excess glycerine, it is nontoxic and biodegrades quickly. It will need to be mixed thoroughly with other materials so that the air and bacteria can get at it, rather than a sticky mass. Composting should be "hot" compost, aerobic, thermophilic compost that reaches high temperatures.

PURIFICATION

Introduction

Plant is fit to purify raw glycerin, from saponification or splitting, which has been conveniently treated and concentrated during prior phases.

Description of the Plant

Concentrate total distillation is done (performed) during the first phase, in order to separate glycerol and other constituents which have a close, (similar), boiling point, from salt and those other organic constituents which confer glycerin its dark and unpleasant odour. In order to diminish glycerol partial pressure, during glycerol. liquid equilibrium phase, operations are carried out at high vacuums bubbling steam for striping process.

Following this procedure, it is possible to evaporate glycerol at low enough temperatures, to allow the use of heating steam at an intermediate pressure of (800 to 1200 kpa), so avoiding, at the same time, the polymerization and breaking down of the product, which would not only affect the distilled product quality, but also the operation satisfactory performance.

By working at reduced pressure (6 to 7 Torr.) at the still, it is always possible to distil at temperatures of approximately 155°C, using a very low proportion of striping steam. Such a proportion affects very remarkably the motive steam consumption of the vacuum system thermo-compressor. This operation requires the use of a still, with a heating coil and a bubble steam injection system through a well dimensioned nozzle, of the mixing ejector. The nozzle makes it possible to inject a well measured quantity of steam steadily, while the mixing ejector guarantees a perfect mixture. This greater mixture efficiency make smaller steam consumption than in traditional plants. The glycerine steam mixture goes to an efficient multi-layers separator which generates a large evaporation surface for glycerine and water vapours detaching. On the other hand the periodical elimination of salt, and organic impurities in the still, that are part of the distillation residue, also helps operating at a lower temperature, with consequently less risk for the Glycerin to get burned. The feeding of the load is performed in a steady way, regulated by a level control device, that keeps the still content constant.

Detaching vapours go through a low load loss drop separator of the demister type, which sends the impure entrained liquid particles, back into the boiling mass. There is a deposit connected to the lower side of the still, which can be set apart by means of valves, which facilitates the elimination of waste at regular periods of time.

The second phase process consists in fractionation up the vapour coming from the still. This operation is performed by means of a fractionation column with high efficiency and low loss of head filling. On the upper part of this column there appears a partial contact type condenser, operating at well regulated temperature so that undesirable impurities might not return with the reflux, but remain vapourized to be separated in the next equipment. The partial condenser circuit, where through concentrated glycerin runs, consists of a collecting plate, a receiver vessel, a circulation pump, a heat exchanger, an atomizing station and a packed bed. The condensed product flows on the plate, where from, the most of it goes back to the buffer vessel and the pump, and the rest of goes back to the fractionation column, as part of the reflux, by means of a distribution system that spreads it on the filling. Highly concentrated glycerin coming out from the bottom is gathered in the collector receiver, where from it is pumped to the bleaching set up.

90% of the still distilled products derive from the bottom layer, (from the tail) as pharmacopoeia suitable products, the remaining 10% approximately, are head products consisting in water, glycerin, and impurities, the boiling points of which come closer to that of the glycerin.

The above described system, that implies the incorporation of a fractionation phase guarantees greater purification, better pharmacopoeia type glycerin yielding performance, than with the traditional methods, which only operated with partial condensation resource, because, as it is widely known, it results in a greater differentiation between bottom and top products.

Vapours coming from the fractionation column go over to a second partial condenser passing first through a demister type drop separator, placed on the first condenser distributor. This second condenser operates in a similar way to the first one, by means of an industrial glycerin close circuit, made up of a collector tank, a circulation pump, and a heat exchanger. The circulating liquid, at low temperature, condenses practically all of the glycerin and the volatile impurities, having similar molecular weight, and part of the water. Some of the main distilled product, about the 10%, is extracted as industrial glycerin, the concentration of which ranges between 90 and 94%. Secondary partial condenser, is the same type as the first one, that is, it is made up of an atomizing station, for the good distribution of the liquid on the filling, a packed bed, and on the upper part, a high efficiency, low head loss, demister type drop separator.

Water vapour, containing some glycerol traces, coming out or the partial condenser, is eliminated by means of a thermo compressor, which, at this point sets an absolute pressure of 4 to 5 Torr. Vacuumed vapour, together with motive steam, is condensed at a barometric condenser, using water coming from the cooling tower, Non-condensable gas is eliminated, by means of a two phase ejector, with an inter-condenser, that keeps main condenser at a pressure of 40 to 60 Torr.

Bleaching Equipment

Elimination of colour and odour traces from the main distilled matter is done by adding activated carbon into a conical bottom tank, equipped with mixing eductor that keeps particles in suspension. A circulation pump makes glycerin steadily run through a heat exchanger to adjust temperature at 80/90°C, value that allows a fast an efficient discolouration. After half and hour treatment, the same pump sends the mixture to a press filter, where from pharmacopoeia quality glycerin comes as a finished product.

Since this plant may produce glycerin at a concentration which can reach up to 99%, we might consider incorporating an extra and last concentration adjusting tank to slightly dilute glycerin, if this proved convenient.

Performance and Consumption Indexes

- Every 100 kg of fed in raw glycerin consumes:
- Half pressure steam (8 to 12 bar) 230 kg., Cooling water (30°C) 17 m^3.
- Electric energy 2 kw/h.
- Performance: Greater than 97% glycerol contained in raw glycerin.

22

CULTIVATION OF JATROPHA CURCAS

INTRODUCTION

The "Greening" represents a huge challenge for the Indian Government. Afforestation has a very important role in meeting this challenge. Several initiatives have been taken in recent years in different parts of the country to promote afforestation. The Indian Administration is now taking up cultivation of *Jatropha curcas (VanaErand)* in many sites of the country, especially due to use of *Jatropha curcas (VanaErand)* oil for the fuel manufacture.

Botanical Features : It is a small tree or shrub with smooth gray bark, which exudes a whitish coloured, watery, latex when cut. Normally, it grows between three and five meters in height, but can attain a height of up to eight or ten meters under favourable conditions.

Leaves: It has large green to pale-green leaves, alternate to sub-opposite, three-to five-lobed with a spiral phyllotaxis.

Flowers : The petiole length ranges between 6–23 mm. The inflorescence is formed in the leaf axil. Flowers are formed terminally, individually, with female flowers usually slightly larger and occurs in the hot seasons. In conditions where continuous growth occurs, an unbalance of pistillate or staminate flower production results in a higher number of female flowers.

Fruits : Fruits are produced in winter when the shrub is leafless, or it may produce several crops during the year if soil moisture is good and temperatures are sufficiently high. Each inflorescence yields a bunch of approximately 10 or more ovoid fruits. A three, bi-valved cocci is formed after the seeds mature and the fleshy exocarp dries.

Seeds : The seeds become mature when the capsule changes from green to yellow, after two to four months from fertilization. The blackish, thin shelled seeds are oblong and resemble small castor seeds.

Ecological Requirements : *Jatropha curcas (VanaErand)* grows almost anywhere - even on gravelly, sandy and saline soils. It can thrive on the poorest stony soil. It can grow even in the crevices of rocks. The leaves shed during the winter months form mulch around the base of the plant. The organic matter from shed leaves enhance earth-worm activity in the soil around the root-zone of the plants, which improves the fertility of the soil. Climatically, *Jatropha curcas (VanaErand)* is found in the tropics and subtropics and likes heat, although it does well even in lower temperatures and can withstand a light frost. Its water requirement is extremely low and it can stand long periods of drought by shedding most of its leaves to reduce transpiration loss. *Jatropha curcas (VanaErand)* is also suitable for preventing soil erosion and shifting of sand dunes. Analysis of the *Jatropha curcas (VanaErand)* seed shows the following chemical composition:

- Moisture 6.20 %
- Protein 18.00 %
- Fat 38.00 %
- Carbohydrates 17.00 %
- Fiber 15.50 %
- Ash 5.30 %

The oil content is 35—40% in the seeds and 50—60% in the kernel. The oil contains 21% saturated fatty acids and 79% unsaturated fatty acids. There are some chemical elements in the seed which are poisonous and render the oil not appropriate for human consumption.

Oil as Raw Material : Oil has a very high saponification value and is being extensively used for making soap in some countries. Also, the oil is used as an illuminant as it burns without emitting smoke.

Medicinal Plant : The latex of *Jatropha curcas (VanaErand)* contains an alkaloid known as "jatrophine" which is believed to have anti-cancerous properties. It is also used as an external application for skin diseases and rheumatism and for sores on domestic livestock. In addition, the tender twigs of the plant are used for cleaning teeth, while the juice of the leaf is used as an external application for piles. Finally, the roots are reported to be used as an antidote for snake-bites.

Raw Material for Dye : The bark of *Jatropha curcas (VanaErand)* yields a dark blue dye which is used for colouring cloth, fishing nets and lines.

Soil Enrichment : *Jatropha curcas (VanaErand)* oil cake is rich in nitrogen, phosphorous and potassium and can be used as organic manure.

Feed : *Jatropha* leaves are used as food for the tusser silkworm.

Insecticide/pesticide : The seeds are considered anthelimintic in Brazil, and the leaves are used for fumigating houses against bed-bugs. Also, the ether extract shows antibiotic activity against *Styphylococcus aureus* and *Escherichia coli.*

Alternative to Diesel : It is significant to point out that, the non-edible vegetable oil of *Jatropha curcas (VanaErand)* has the requisite potential of providing a promising and commercially viable alternative to diesel oil since it has desirable physico-chemical and performance characteristics comparable to diesel. Cars could be run with *Jatropha curcas (VanaErand)* without requiring much change in design.

TABLE 22.1

The Chemical Analysis of Jatropha curcas (VanaErand) oil

Item	Value
Acid value	38.2
Saponification value	195.0
Iodine value	101.7
Viscosity (31°C) cp	40.4
Fatty acids composition	
Palmitic acid %	4.2
Stearic acid %	6.9
Oleic acid %	43.1
Linoleic acid %	34.3
Other acids %	1.4

TABLE 22.2

The Comparison of Properties of Jatropha curcas (VanaErand) Oil and Standard Specifications of Diesel Oil

Specification of *Jatropha curcas*	Standard Specification of Diesel *(VanaErand)* Oil	Standard Specification
Specific gravity	0.9186	0.82/0.84
Flash point	240/110°C	50°C
Carbon residue	0.64	0.15 or less
Cetane value	51.0	50.0 up
Distillation point	295°C	350°C
Kinematics Viscosity	50.73 cs	2.7cs up
Sulpher %	0.13%	1.2% or less
Calorific value	9,470 kcal/kg	10,170 kcal/kg
Pour point	8°C	10°C
Colour	4.0	4 or less

TABLE 22.3

Physical and Chemical Properties of Diesel Fuel and Jatropha curcas (VanaErand) Oil

Property	*Jatropha curcas* (VanaErand) Oil	Diesel Oil
Viscosity (cp) (30°C)	52.6 (5.51)	3.60
Specific gravity (15°C/4°C)	0.917/ 0.923(0.881)	0.841 / 0.85
Solidfying point (°C)	2.0	0.14
Cetane value	51.0 (38)	47.8 to 59
Flash point (°C)	110/340	80
Carbon residue *(%)*	0.64	< 0.05 to < 0.15

Distillation (°C)	284 to 295	< 350 to < 370
Sulfur (%)	0.13 to 0.16	< 1.0 to 1.2
Acid Value	1.0 to 38.2	
Saponification Value	188 to 198	
Iodine Value	90.8 to 112.5	
Refractive Index (30°C)	1.47	

Egypt imported some seeds from India five years ago, and were cultivated in the southern part of Egypt and irrigated by treated sewage water. It is worth mentioning that the cultivation has been very successful. It is now producing seeds, and the local people now making use and of its oil product.

As one of the most important oilseed grower, producer, importer and exporter, India is one of the four major players in the vegetable oil scenario of the world. Vegetable oil scenario is complex and is highly influenced by market sources, conflicting interests, policies of the government, income of the consumers, demands of industry, economies of production, correction and processing vagaries of weather, technology and various biotic and abiotic problems.

For mitigating climate change by reducing emission of green house gases, meeting rural energy needs, protecting the environment and generating gainful employment, *Jatropha curcas (VanaErand)* has multiple role to play. All attempts to increase its production and productivity, oil extraction by application of appropriate technology, product development and diversification and policies that will protect and promote national interest would be welcome.

Undertaking plantation of *Jatropha curcas (VanaErand)* and collection of seed, processing of seeds for producing oil will be a part of processing it to biodiesel. The oil cake is rich in nutrients and will give bio-gas and very good compost for our soils which are getting increasingly deficient in carbon and nutrients. Every component of the programme will generate massive employment for the poor belonging to the Scheduled Tribes, Scheduled Castes and other under privileged categories living mostly in backward areas which have experienced the adverse impact of forest degradation, and loss of natural resources.

Jatropha curcas* - Source of Biodiesel :** There are many tree species which bear seeds rich in oil. Of these some promising tree species have been evaluated and it has been found that there are a number of them such as *Jatropha curcas* and *Pongamia pinnata* ('Honge' or 'Karanja') which would be very suitable in our conditions. However, ***Jatropha curcas has been found the most suitable tree specie for the reasons summarized below :

- It can be grown as a quick yielding plant even in adverse land situations *viz.* Degraded and barren lands under forest and non-forest use, dry and drought prone areas, marginal lands and as agro forestry crop. It can be planted on fallow lands and along farmers field boundaries as hedge because it does not grow too tall as well as on vacant lands alongside railways, highways, irrigation canals and unused lands in townships etc. under Public/Private Sector Undertakings.
- The seeds of *Jatropha* are available during the non-rainy season, which facilitates better collection and processing. The cost of plantation is largely incurred in the first year and improved planting material can make a huge difference in yield.
- Raising *Jatropha* plant and its maintenance creates jobs for the rural poor, particularly the land less, in plantation and primary processing through expellers.
- It has multiple uses and after the extraction of oil from the seeds, the oil cake left behind is an excellent organic manure, the bio–mass of *Jatropha curcas* enriches the soil and it can also be put to other uses.
- Retains soil moisture and improve land capability and environment.
- *Jatropha* adds to the capital stock of the fanners and the community, for sustainable generation of income and employment.
- *Jatropha curcas* was the most neglected plant so far. It can grow wildly. Now it has acquired significance, because :
- It can provide raw material for the production of Bio-Fuels.
- Low demands in terms of cultivation, water and soil quality with resulting suitability for degraded, unused and drought prone lands.
- Leaves and fruits are non-edible, which stop stress passing (if

grown on hedges) and browsing by animals, but can be used as nutrient rich fertilizer and as windbreak, thus conserving soil humidity.

- A nut, whose oil can be used or processed for any energy purposes, such as, lighting, soap manufacture and for pharmaceuticals, varnish and plant protection.
- Wooden parts of the plant can be used for reforestation, home for bees and birds, and as firewood in rural areas.

Biodiesel is being manufactured in a number of developed countries, who depend on Developing Countries for supply of raw oil. Due to this, *Jatropha* plantation is suddenly in limelight. It is the widely talked about plant in the world today.

Reasons for past failures:

- Inconsistent approaches and exaggerated expectations concerning yields, input-output relations and resulting incomes.
- Lack of knowledge and wrong and misleading information about requirement of water, sunlight, nutrients and fertilizer, pruning of branches to get better fruit yield.

The main tree born seeds with potential for biodiesel manufacture are :

- *Jatropha curcas* or VanErand.
- Pongomia pinnata or Karanj.
- Mahuca indica or Mahua.
- Neem.

The advantage is clearly in favor of *Jatropha* due to the following reasonsur :

- Oil yield per hectare of plantation, is among the highest of tree borne oil seeds.
- It can be grown in areas of low rainfall (200 mm per year) and in problematical soils. In high rainfall and irrigated areas, it can be grown with much higher yields. Therefore, it can be grown in most parts of the country.
- *Jatropha* is easy to establish, grows relatively quickly and is hardy.
- *Jatropha* lends itself to plantation with advantage on lands developed on watershed basis and on low fertility marginal,

degraded, fallow, waste and other lands such as along the canals, roads, railway tracks, on borders of farmers' fields as a boundary fence or live hedge in the arid/semi-arid areas and even on alkaline soils. As such it can be used to reclaim waste lands in the forests and outside.

- *Jatropha* fruits are easy to collect as they are ready to be plucked after the winter season and as the plants are not very tall.
- *Jatropha* is not browsed by animals.
- Being rich in nitrogen, the seed cake is an excellent source for manufacture of Bio Fertilizer.
- Seed production ranges from about 0.4 tone/hector per year to over 12 tones/hector per year.
- The plant gives seeds in a maximum period of two years after planting.
- Raising plants in nurseries, planting and maintaining them and collection of seed are labour intensive activities. Except for the cost of seeds, plastic bags, fertilizer and transportation of the plants from the nursery, all the activities in the nurseries and in planting consist of labour.
- Various parts of the plant are of medicinal value, its bark contains tannin, the flowers attract bees and thus the plant has potential of production of honey.
- Like all trees, *Jatropha* removes carbon from the atmosphere, stores it in the woody tissues and assists in the build up of soil carbon. It is thus environment friendly.
- *Jatropha* can be established from seed, seedlings and vegetatively from cuttings. Use of branch cutting for propagation is easy and results in rapid growth.
- The plant is undemanding in soil type and does not require much tillage.

Most of the soils in India are favourable for *Jatropha* plantation. The plantation and down stream processing is going to provide large scale opportunities for poorer sections of society. In arid desert places like Rajasthan in India, there are large plantations of these, which proves that it can grow well in desert lands.

References are found in Ayurved (Indian Medicinal Practice) about *Jatropha*. Plenty of information is available in it, especially about its medicinal value. Now it is gaining popularity as a sturdy bush which can grow in scanty rainfall areas, and providing rich dividends.

Portuguese seamen brought some varieties of this plant to India from tropical countries of Central America in 16th century. Its origin lies in Central America and Africa. Portuguese imported and cultivated this plant in India for its medicinal values. It was propagated all over India only for its medicinal values. Today these grow wildly in all Tropical and sub-tropical regions.

There are a number of varieties *of Jatropha.* Some of them are :

- *Jatropha curcas* (non–toxic)
- *J. curcas* x *J. integrerrima*
- *Jatropha gossypifolia*
- *Jatropha glandulifera*
- *Jatropha tanjorensis*
- *Jatropha multifida*
- *Jatropha podagrica*
- *Jatropha integerrima*

It has 200 names in different languages and in different parts of the world. This shows how far and wide it has spread.

In India it is known by different names in Regional Languages :

1. *Sanskrit:* Kanan-Erand, Parvat-Erand,
2. *Hindi:* Bhagirend, Jangli-Erand, Safed-Erand,
3. *Marathi:* Van-Erand, Ran-Erand, Mogli-Erand, Chandra Jyot, Chandri,
4. *Gujrathi:* Ratan Jyot, Jamal Gota, Parshi Erand, Kala Erand,
5. *Telgu:* Nepalamu, Paddanepalamu, Adaviya Haralu,
6. *Tamil:* Kadala Manuku, Rat Manukku,
7. *Kannada:* Kadhala Vanakka, Bettada Haralu, Marahalu, Karnochi
8. *Odiya:* Katta Vanakka, Kadhala Vanakka, Jahangba
9. *Asami:* Bongoli Bhotora
10. *Punjabi:* Jamal Gota, Kala Erand

It is classified under a generic name of ERAND. It grows wildly as a big tree, or as a cluster of number of bushes, packed very closely, in wild.

Whether it is a tree or a bush, it is always green. Depending on local-climatic conditions, these can grow 7 to 10 meters tall, but in rain-fed areas these grow only 2 to 3 meters tall. In jungle, 3 or 4 plants grow together, as if it is one tree. In case of plantation, it is grown as 1 trunk and 2 branches at every node. In jungle its trunk can be 200 to 250 mm in perimeter, but in plantation it can be only 100 to 120 mm. On fully grown trunk and branches, there are layers of darker colour. These peel out if you rub on it. If trunk, branches or leaves are cut, an off-white latex flows down the tree. The leaves are 100 to 150 mm or 70 to 100 mm in size. These are broad, egg-shaped with a heart shape. Its ends are lobes of 3 to 5 fingers. The periphery of the leaves are cut like saw-teeth. The edges are sharper. The surface of the leaves is extremely soft and sticky. Since the leaves are bitter in taste, no cattle likes to eat it.

Bunches of flowers grow at the end of the branches. The central bunches generally have female flowers while the outer ones are male flowers. The fruits are 25 mm long and oblong. In the beginning these are green. As these ripen, these turn yellowish with golden tinge. On drying, these darken and when fully dry, these are black. When these dry fruits are peeled, 2 seeds each are found in 3 pockets. These fresh seeds are oblong, gray in colour and resemble castor seeds. But it is smaller than castor seed. The seeds are 10 to 20 mm long and weigh 0.5 to 0.7 grams. In India, number of flowers peak in July-August and these start ripening in September. Maximum seeds are available in the month of September.

23

Types of Lands where it can Grow with Advantage and Potential of Plantation

The list of advantages mentioned above make *Jatropha* plantation very attractive on the kinds of lands mentioned below. The potential for coverage of each kind of land in India, is as follows :

- Forests cover 69 million hectares of which 38 million hectare is dense forest and 31 million hectare is understocked. Of this 14 million hectares of forests are under the Joint Forestry Management. About 3.0 million hectare (notional) of land in forests should easily come under *Jatropha curcas (Vana Erand)* plantation.
- 142 million hectare of land is under agriculture. It will be reasonable to assume that farmers will like to put a hedge around 30 million hectare of their fields for protection of their crops. It will amount to 3.0 million hectare (notional) of *Jatropha curcas (Vana Erand)* plantation.
- The cultivators are expected to adopt it by way of agro-forestry. Considerable land is held by absentee land lords who will be attracted to *Jatropha curcas (Vana Erand)* as it does not require looking after and gives a net income of Rs. 15000 per hectare. Two million hectare of notional plantation is expected.
- Culturable fallow lands are reported to be 24 million hectare of which current fallow lands are 10 million hactare and other fallows are 14 million hectares. Ten per cent of such land (2.4 million hectare) is expected to come under *Jatropha curcas (Vana Erand)* plantation.
- On waste lands under Integrated Watershed Development and

other poverty alleviation programmes of Ministry of Rural Development a potential of 2 million hectare of plantation is assessed.

- On vast stretches of public lands along railway tracks, roads and canals. One million hectare of notional coverage with *Jatropha curcas (Vana Erand)* is a reasonable assessment.

On the basis of above analysis it should be reasonable to assume that with proper extension, research, availability of planting material and funds plantation of *Jatropha curcas (Vana Erand)* on 13.4 million hectares of land is feasible in the immediate future. Institutional finance for private plantation and governmental allocation for public lands will have to be provided. Once success is achieved on the lands described above it should be possible to include very low fertility soils which are classified unculturable in this programme. A significant proportion of such lands can also be brought under *Jatropha curcas (Vana Erand)* plantation in an economically feasible manner. It will result in their (degraded lands) rehabilitation also.

CLIMATIC CONDITIONS

Most parts of tropical and sub-tropical areas are ideal for *Jatropha* plantation. These can grow in areas where minimum rainfall is 500 to 750 mm. However these can grow in desert areas around towns, which can be watered by domestic waste water from towns around these plantations. It can also grow in drought prone areas and where rainfall is scanty. In such areas, the seed production is less. The plant germinates in hot and humid atmosphere. As temperature starts dropping it blooms with flowers and fruits grow in winter. It can not tolerate very harsh winter or fog. At the time of start of flowering, atmosphere should be dry with bright sunshine.

Jatropha can bear fruits for 25 years. It can withstand drought for 3 consecutive years. If the soil is bad and if rainfall is unreliable, these plants need to be watered for first 2 to 3 years. Later on it can survive.

SOIL

It can grow in soft, rocky, sloping soils along a mountain as well as medium fertile lands. These can be grown along canals, water streams, boundaries of crop fields, along the roads, along railway lines. In short, the least fertile lands are best for this plant. However, fertile lands in which water does not accumulate, can also be used for *Jatropha* plantations. Highly fertile black cotton soils, which hold water and alkaline soils are not good for *Jatropha* Plantations. Once the roots penetrate deeper, *Jatropha* can tolerate acidic or salty soils. The soil productivity and fertility is low in the initial stage. It needs to be improved by compost fertilizer, cow dung and other fertilizers. Some micro nutrients are also helpful in improving productivity.

Soils that should be avoided are those containing 10 to 40% sand, 60 to 90% normal soil. These are black in colour, hold water and cracks are found in these soils in summer. The roots of *Jatropha* plants are shallow in the beginning, hence these can grow in cracks of rocky mountain slopes. The pH of soil is an important consideration for the survival of the plant. Some soils are highly acidic due to accumulation of salts. Some soils are alkaline due to calcium and aluminum deposits in the soil. It should be ideally 5.5 to 6.5.

PRE-PLANTATION ACTIVITIES

The entire land should be fenced before plantation. Stones lying around can be used to create a wall around the plot. Considering the slope of land, flow of water streams, small walls should be erected along to the contours. On top of this dead fencing, a live fence is created by growing plants of cactus varieties. Though plantation can be done without any cleaning activities, but it is advisable to partly clean up the area. Tall trees can be left as it is. All small shrubs and bushes on the soil should be cut above the roots. It stops soil erosion. The left over roots eventually die and provide green manure or composting fertilizer.

The soil should be tilled and it should be porous. Inter–crops are planted in these lands for first 3 to 4 years. All weeds and fungus should be completed rooted out. In case of plantation, it is advisable to keep the plants short in height. This can be achieved by cutting branches from time to time. In this case the distance between 2 plants is less. Days in June and July, on the onset of monsoon rains in India, is the ideal period for *Jatropha* plantation. Land should be tilled in the months of April and May, and all dry vegetation should be burnt and destroyed before plantation.

GERMINATION AND PLANTING

Jatropha plantation can be done by sowing seeds or by planting branches of existing trees. The land is marked in squares of 2 meters x 2 meters all along. 2 seeds or one branch is inserted at each inter–

section. Plants grown from seeds or branches in plastic bags can also be planted. This method has advantage that, these can be cultivated throughout the year, and can be watered easily in a small area. Good quality seeds of attractive colour should be selected for germination. For this purpose, good quality fruits should be collected in the months of September or October and these should be dried in shade for 3 to 4 days, after de-pulping. It should then be soaked in water for 4 days.

A good seed is one which gives out oil if pressed by nail. Cracked, scratched or infected seed should not be used for germination. 5 to 6 kgs of seeds are enough for plantation in one hector of land.

Plantation from Branches : Half to one meter long branches can be used for plantation. These are planted on the onset of monsoon rains. Plants grown from such branches can yield 50 fruits in 8 months time.

Plantation in Plastic Bags : Good quality seeds are planted in black polythene bags having size of 70 x 100 mm. A good soil mix is prepared by mixing 2 kgs of compost, 1 kg of filtered sand. Some insecticide and weedicide is then sprayed on it.

While filling the bags, top 20 to 30 mm is not filled. That portion is folded, which gives a good strength to the bag. Each bag should be filled with soil enriched by 500 gms of cow dung, 100 gms of 7 : 10 : 5 NPK and 400 gms compost fertilizer. 2 seeds should be planted 50 to 60 mm deep in each bag. After a month, the weaker plant of the two is eliminated.

PLANTATION

Pits of standard sizes, are dug initially, based on the slope of land, availability of water and quality of soil. Pits of 300 mm long, 300 mm wide and 300 mm deep are dug in square formation. The distance between the two pits is 2 meters. It can be less in poor soils. A layer of dry leaves is spread at the bottom up to about 50 mm and insecticide is sprayed on it. Along with the compost fertilizer and cow dung, 20 gms of urea, 120 gms of single super phosphate and 16 gms of potassium nitrate is added in each pit.

In the initial phase of growth, roots grow very rapidly and try to penetrate in soil to suck nutrients from the soil. For this the pits should be filled with good, fertile soil. Initial growth is very important, and hence nutrients should be provided from time to time in initial years. If soil is poor in nutrients, the pit should be filled with excess compost fertilizer and cow dung.

The requirement of chemical fertilizers per hector per year is 50 kgs of urea + 300 kgs of single super phosphate + 40 kgs of potassium nitrate.

MAINTANANCE OF SOIL

All the weeds around the plant should be removed. Initially for 3 to 4 months, land should be tilled 2 or 3 times after 20 days, to remove weeds. 10 gms of urea should be mixed in the soil, for each plant, one month after plantation. Later, it should be repeated after one and half month.

The soil between two plants, should be tilled lightly, and should not be tilled deep. Branches of *Jatropha,* that have dried up should be cut and disposed off. Branches that have grown improperly or those leaning down, should also be removed.

Some natural materials can be used to cover the land between the two plants. This can be husk, small branches, stocks of rice and wheat etc. This reduces evaporation of water from the soil.

MAINTANANCE OF PLANTS

The rising top of the tree should be cut once the tree is 1 meter tall. This will lead to branching of the tree. More the branches, more the production of fruits and seeds. Every year branches grow near the base, and these should be removed and replanted elsewhere. It is very important to cut the tree in time and keep it in proper shape. The plant tops should be cut in proper way, so that it will grow like an umbrella. Care should be taken from the beginning.

Normally *Jatropha* can naturally flower only once a year, but with modern techniques it can be forced to flower twice or thrice a year. To do this watering of the plants is stopped for a period. During this period half the leaves are shed by the tree. Water supply is restarted at this point and tree starts flowering again. When watering is started again, the quantity of water is increased slowly day by day and NPK fertilizers are provided. Normally, flowering takes place after 21 days.

FERTILZERS

In case of regular plantation, organic and chemical fertilizers should be provided in proper quantity as per the age of the tree. Lot of nutrients are required in the initial phase of plant. Growth and bearing of good fruits depend on the nutrients and weather. Out of NPK, nitrogen is required in larger quantity. NPK ratio should be 46 : 48 : 24 kgs per hector. As the roots grow longer, fertilizers are applied away from the base of the tree.

WATER MANAGEMENT

Plants get the nutrients from soil as water solution. Hence its successful growth depends on water content of soil, or timely watering of the plants. In the initial stages it is sensitive and hence, water should be provided as per the requirement. Watering for poorer soils is done every 5 to 6 days, medium soils 7 to 10 days, and good soils every 10 to 12 days. In monsoon the trees bloom and flowering and bearing of fruits can be achieved with rain water.

For plantations, it is necessary to erect small boulder check dams, to create small and big water bodies. This water can be used after the monsoon. Drip irrigation can enhance the yield. Through this controlled amount of water and fertilizer can be provided all the time. With drip irrigation, 3 crops can be obtained in a year. Water should wet only the area under the tree and rest should be dry. Hence initial requirement of water is very small. If monsoon rain is at regular interval of few days, rain water is sufficient for it.

PLUCKING OF FRUITS

Fruits should be plucked at appropriate time and in appropriate manner. Plucking time is generally at the end of December or beginning of January. All the fruits on tree are not ready for plucking and only ripe one should be plucked. Latex drops down from the point of plucking of fruit and care should be taken that it does not fall on body.

24

Bio Gas Plant

Disposal of Cake of *Jatropha* Seed is one of the major problems being faced by bio diesel Producers across the World. Seed cake is not a problem but it is a big asset. There are two ways of processing these to produce Organic Fertilizer.

Bio-Gas Plant : In this case the Bio-mass is digested in a simple plant and BioGas produced is stored and used. The area required for plant is very small.

Composting: Here the Bio-mass is digested underground but Bio-Gas produced is wasted. Needs large area of land.

A1 tone per day biodiesel plant, produces 3.5 to 4 tones of seed cake. If we carefully analyze this waste, we will realise that majority of it is biodegradable. Oil seed cake is a by-product obtained from the oil extraction process and can be converted to valuable organic fertilizer. The cake has the following properties and nutrients :

- Moisture: 4.58%
- Nitrogen: 3.2 - 6.0% (N_2)
- Phosphorus: 1.4 - 2.75 (P_2O_5)
- Potassium: 0.94 - 1.68% (K_2O)
- Crude Protein: 58%.

When compared with other organic sources, (manure, seed and oil cakes), oil seed cake from *Jatropha* provides essential nutrients at comparable levels. The seed cake is unusable as feed for livestock due to it's toxicity. This biodegradable waste, if handled properly would maintain the natural balance of essential elements and thereby promote more harvests from nature. Disposal of Seed Cake of *Jatropha,* can be achieved by several other means like incineration, landfills, dumping in the sea or other water bodies etc. These methods have their own hazards. Incineration can lead to respiratory illnesses. Moreover, it may lead to disruption of biogeochemical cycles of several elements and will have long term effects on biosphere. Landfill and dumping can pollute water bodies.

Bio Gas Plant would serve many purposes such as :

- Environment friendly disposal of waste, which is need of hour considering mass pollution everywhere.
- Generation of fairly good amount of fuel gas, which will definitely support the dwindling energy resources.
- Generation of high quality manure, which would be weedless and an excellent soil conditioner. This is very important for replenishing fast decreasing resources of productive soils. It must be noted that need for replenishing the soil with high quality organic manure has been identified in plan documents.
- Bio gas is a colourless, odourless and inflammable gas. The gas generated in this plant can also be used as a source of natural gas.

The composition of biogas is.

- Methane (CH_4): 70-75%
- Carbon Dioxide (CO_2): 10—15%
- Water vapours: 5—10%.

Operation

The material to be processed is brought to the plant site every day. Two workers are needed for the operation of the plant. The important tasks to be done are :

- Transport of waste materials.
- Processing the waste in mixer.
- Routine operations for pre-digester and digester tanks.
- Manure pits.

Infrastructure Required

Infrastructures required to set-up a Bio-gas plant of a capacity of 1 tone/day of Oil Cake :

- Area of Plot: 300 m^2.
- Manpower: Two unskilled persons.
- Power supply: 1 KW.
- Water Supply: 1200 liters.
- Cost: Rupees 500,000.

CONSTRUCTION OF A BIO-GAS PLANT

Criteria for Bio Gas Plant

- Bio Diesel plant-owner who wants to build a bio-gas plant must have oil seed cake to sustain the operation of the plant. The minimal amount of cake should be 3 to 4 tones per day.
- Cake storage enclosure which is not more than 20 meters from the bio gas construction area.
- There must be drainage alley from cake storage area, connected directly to the bio gas plant.
- Access to ground water all year round and the water source should not be farther than 20 meters from the bio gas plant.
- Bio gas usage should not be placed further than 100 meters form the plant.
- The owner must have interests in using gas, fermented manure and want to build a bio gas plant to reduce the pollution in environment.
- Required budget, materials and labour to build bio-gas plant.
- Time and labour in maintenance bio-gas plant.

Design of Bio gas Plant

The fixed dome of bio-gas plant is buried underground. There are 3 main connecting parts :

- ***Mixing Chamber :*** where oil seed cake is mixed with water before it is poured into digester chamber.
- ***Digester chamber :*** Where oil seed cake is fermented. Methane

and other gases will be produced in the chamber and these gases will push manure and slurry at bottom of the floor into expansion chamber.

- ***Expansion Chamber :*** Which collects excess manure and slurry. When gas is being used, manure arid slurry will flow back into digester chamber to push gas up for usage. When the excess manure exceeds the volume of the chamber, the manure will be drained out.

This system is called dynamic system, when gas is produced inside the pit, the gas pressure will push manure and slurry at the bottom of the pit to flow up into expansion chamber. When this gas is used the slurry in the expansion chamber will flow back into the digester chamber to push the gas up for usage. This happens consistently. The plant will be operated efficiently for a long period of time if the gas pit does not get cracked and the system runs regularly. In each case the strength of the plant depends on fine construction, specification of materials, and strict adherence to the maintenance of the bio gas plant.

Location of the Bio Gas Plant

The plant should not be located further than 5 meters from the oil seed cake enclosure. The digester chamber must be in an open area and should not be near any water source or natural water as water coming out from Bio Gas plant may seep into underground water. The plant should also be situated on a slope and not on the low land to avoid the danger of floods. The excess manure from expansion chamber should flow into the open pit or the storage tank and not into natural water bodies such as rivers to avoid the risk of pollution. The bio gas plant must have a concrete slab floor enclosure with a drainage alley with 1 % gradient. If the floor is not on slope, it must be elevated.

Construction of Bio Gas Plant

- Locate the lowest point of drainage alley and mark 30 cm above this point. Mark a peg on the opposite side and balance the level between the peg and the mark over the alley with level adjusting hose. From the mark on the level line, set the center of digester chamber on the ground surface by using plumb. Draw the line to mark the size of digester chamber.
- To locate the storage tank, measure from the center of digester chamber. Find the lowest point to set the outlet point which is 60

cm lower than the level line and at least 15 cm over the ground to prevent the outside water to flow into the chamber. If the lowest point can not be located, check the drainage alley for the possibility of being elevated or excavated. When the outlet point is found, the temporary level line becomes level line. Cross another permanent level line to the first line at the center of the digester chamber to locate the center of digester chamber. The location of expansion chamber should be on the opposite side of the mixing chamber or not over 45°.

- ***Think before excavating :*** Ensure that the diameter of the pit is excavated consistently with diameters begin equal at the top and the base, and at depth below level line. Place excavated soil 50 cm away from the edge of the pit and do not put it on the ground where the expansion chamber, mixing chamber or outlet pipe will be constructed. It is a waste of time to have to remove this pile of soil later. Do not excavate deeper as the base of the chamber may not be strong enough. If there is any seepage, a small trap pit must be dug next to the outer edge of digester chamber base. The floor of the trap pit should be lower than the digester chamber so that ground water can flow into the trap pit. When the required final depth is obtained, set the center at the base of digester chamber by crossing the level line and use a plumb to locate the center of the digester chamber. Excavate soil in the outer circle to a depth of 25 cm deep and draw another circle. Excavate soil in the inner circle to a depth of 5 cm deep.

25

Biodiesel from Algae

INTRODUCTION

Currently most research into efficient algal-oil production is being done in the private sector, but if predictions from small-scale production experiments bear out then using algae to produce biodiesel may be the only viable method by which to produce enough automotive fuel to replace current world gasoline usage. Microalgae have much faster growth-rates than terrestrial crops. The per unit area yield of oil from algae, (estimated to be from between 5,000 to 20,000 gallons per acre, per year), is 7 to 31 times greater than the next best crop, palm oil (635 gal). Algal-oil processes into biodiesel as easily as oil derived from land-based crops Research into algae for the mass-production of oil is mainly focused on micro algae. This preference towards micro algae is due largely to its less complex structure, fast growth rate, and high oil content- (for some species). Some commercial interests into large-scale algal cultivation systems are looking to tie-in to existing infrastructures, such as coal power plants.

CULTIVATION

Like plants, algae require primarily two components to grow: sunlight and carbon-dioxide. Like plants again, they use the sunlight for the process of photosynthesis. Photosynthesis is an important biochemical process in which plants, algae, and some bacteria convert the energy of sunlight to chemical energy. This chemical energy is used to drive chemical reactions such as the formation of sugars or the fixation of nitrogen into amino acids, the building blocks for protein synthesis. Algae can be cultured in raceway-type ponds and lakes.

Raceway pond : A raceway pond is a long, relatively shallow open-pond made up of channels that wind around, sometimes in the pattern of an automotive raceway, though many ponds look like a very simple maze if looked at from above. Raceway ponds use paddle wheels to agitate the water and give it a direction of flow.

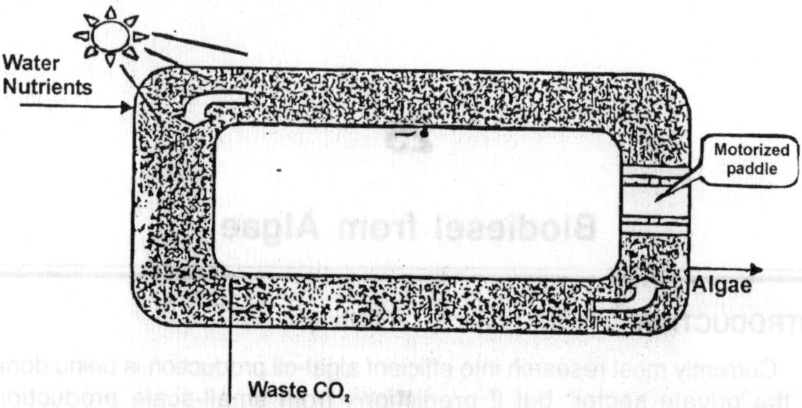

Fig. 25.1 : Raceway Pond.

The Department of Energy's Aquatic Species Programme experimented with raceway ponds for the cultivation of algae. Many commercial producers of Spirulina, (blue-green algae), still use raceway ponds as their prime means of cultivation.

Due to the fact that these systems are "open" to the elements, sometimes called "open-pond" systems, they are much more vulnerable to being invaded by other algal species and bacteria. The number of species that have been successfully cultivated for a given purpose, (i.e. : as a food source, for oil production, or for pigments.), in an outdoor system, are relatively small. In open systems ones does not have control over water temperature and lighting conditions. The growing season is largely dependent on location and, aside from tropical areas, is limited to the warmer months. Some of the benefits of this type of system are that it is one of the cheaper ones to produce - at the most basic one needs only to dig a trench or pond. It also has one of the largest production capacities compared to other systems, depending on how large it's made. A variation on the basic "open-pond" system is to close it off, to cover a pond or pool with a greenhouse. While this usually results in a smaller system, (for economic reasons), it does take care of many of the problems associated with an open system. It allows more species to be grown, it allows the species that are being grown to stay dominant, and it extends the growing season, only slightly if unheated and if heated it can produce year round.

Fig. 25.2 : The large open ponds used for the cultivation at Hutt Lagoon, Western Australia.

Fig. 25.3 : Raceway Ponds used for the cultivation in Calipatria, California.

Algae can be grown in a photobioreactor. A photobioreactor is basically a bioreactor which incorporates some type of light source. While almost anything that it would be possible to grow algae in could technically be called a photobioreactor, the term is more commonly used to define a closed system, as opposed to an open tank, or pond. Because these systems are closed, when used to cultivate algae, everything that the algae need to grow, (carbon dioxide, nutrient-rich water and light), all must be introduced into the system. A pond covered with a greenhouse could be considered a photobioreactor.

In most algal-cultivation systems, light only penetrates the top 3-4 inches of the water. This is because as the algae grow and multiply they become so dense that they block light from reaching deeper into the pond or tank. Algae only need about 1/10 the amount of light they receive from direct sunlight. Direct sunlight is often too strong for algae. In order to have ponds that are deeper than 4 inches algae growers use various methods to agitate the water in their ponds, exposing the algae below to light and keeping algae on the surface from being over-exposed. Paddle wheels can be used to circulate the water in a pond. Compressed air can be introduced into the bottom of a pond or tank, bringing algae from the lower levels up to the top to receive its share of light.

Fig. 25.4 : A greenfuel technologies bioreactor in operation.

Aside from agitation, another means of supplying light to algae is to place the light in the system. Glow plates are sheets of plastic or glass that can be submerged into the water of a tank, providing light directly to the algae at the right concentration.

HARVESTING

Froth Floatation Process

Air is introduced into the bottom of the cylinder through a porous diffuser plate. The rate of aeration is controlled with float type rate meters. The culture to be harvested is introduced into the bottom of the device by gravity flow from an elevated reservoir. Aeration is applied and the froth formed rises up the tube and is delivered through the side arm. Operation may be batch or continuous. In the batch process, the desired amount of culture is introduced into the column, aeration is started and harvesting continues until the froth no longer rises to the elevation of the side arm. The continuous process permits the maintenance of any desired feed concentration in the column. This is achieved by balancing feed against withdrawal to maintain concentration and volume equilibria in the column. This simple apparatus has permitted the investigation of a number of important parameters affecting the quantities and concentrations of algae which may be harvested from suspensions.

Flocculation

Flocculation refers to a process where a solute comes out of solution in the form of floc or "flakes". The term is also used to refer to the process by which fine particulates are caused to clump together into floc. The floc may then float to the top of the liquid, settle to the bottom of the liquid, or can be readily filtered from the liquid. In geology, flocculation is a condition in which clays, polymers or other small charged particles become attached and form a fragile structure, a floc. In dispersed clay slurries, flocculation occurs after mechanical agitation ceases and the dispersed clay platelets spontaneously form flocs because of attractions between negative face charges and positive edge charges

Alum and ferric chloride are chemical flocculants used to harvest algae. Chitosin can be used as a flocculant. The shells of crustaceans are ground into powder and processed to acquire chitin, a polysaccharide found in the shells, from which Chitosin is derived. Chitosin is commonly used for water purification.

The more brackish or saline the water that the algae is being grown in, the more chemical flocculant will be required to induce flocculation. Harvesting by chemical flocculation is a method that is often too expensive for large operations.

Ultrasound Technique:

When algae are exposed to an ultrasonic standing wave (Fig. 25.5a) they experience a force that almost instantaneously drives them into the planes of the pressure nodes (Fig. 25.5). Subsequently, agglomeration of the cells occurs into the knots of the ultrasonic field (fig. Sc). When the field is switched off, the aggregated cells sediment rapidly from the fluid due to gravity forces.

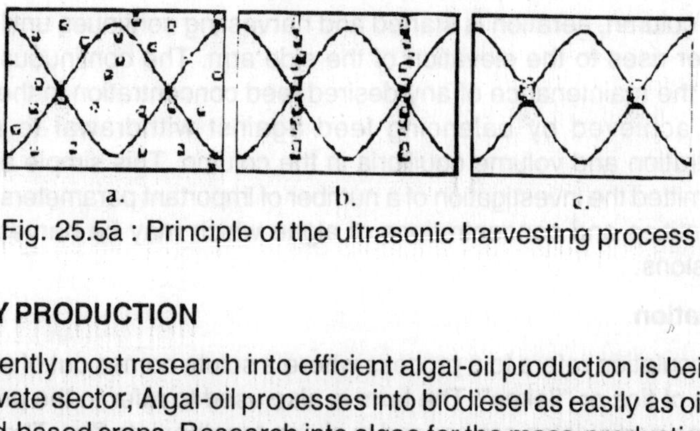

Fig. 25.5a : Principle of the ultrasonic harvesting process

ENERGY PRODUCTION

Currently most research into efficient algal-oil production is being done in the private sector, Algal-oil processes into biodiesel as easily as oil derived from land-based crops. Research into algae for the mass-production of oil is mainly focused on micro–algae, (which is a term generally referred to as organisms capable of photosynthesis that are less than 2 mm in diameter, including the diatoms and cyano–bacteria), as opposed to macro–algae, (i.e. seaweed). This preference towards micro–algae is due largely to its less complex structure, fast growth rate, and high oil content- (for some species).

The major problem associated with the use of oil from algae as fuels for diesel engines is caused by high fuel viscosity in compression ignition. Algal oil is highly viscous, with viscosity ranging 10–20 times those of no. 2 Diesel fuel. Due to their high viscosity and low volatility, they do not burn completely and form deposits in the fuel injector of diesel engines.

Dilution, micro-emulsification, pyrolysis and trans–esterification are the four techniques applied to solve the problems encountered with the high fuel viscosity. Amongst the four techniques, chemical conversion of the oil to its corresponding fatty ester is the most promising solution to the high viscosity problem. This process–chemical conversion of the oil to its corresponding fatty ester, and thus biodiesel is called transesterification.

Trans–esterification of Algal Oil into Biodiesel

Transesterification of algal oil is normally done with ethanol and sodium ethanolate serving as the catalyst. Sodium ethanolate can be produced by reacting ethanol with sodium. Thus, with sodium ethanolate as the catalyst, ethanol is reacted with the algal oil (the triglyceride) to produce bio–diesel and glycerol. The end products of this reaction are hence biodiesel, sodium ethanolate and glycerol. This end-mixture is separated as follows : Ether and salt water are added to the mixture and mixed well. After sometime, the entire mixture would have separated into two layers, with the bottom layer containing a mixture of ether and biodiesel. This layer is separated. Biodiesel is in turn separated from ether by a vapourizer under a high vacuum. As the ether vapourizes first, the biodiesel will remain. The biodiesel from algae is now ready for use.

Why Microalgae Technology?

There are a number of benefits that serve as driving forces for developing and deploying algae technology. Some of these benefits have already been mentioned. Four key areas are :

(a) Energy Security; (b) Climate Change; (c) The Synergy of Coal and Microalgae; (d) Terrestrial versus Aquatic Biomass.

26

Processing Technology for Biodiesel from Jatropha Seeds

INTRODUCfION

Biodiesel is a fatty acid of ethyl or methyl ester made from virgin or used vegetable oils (both edible and non-edible) and animal fats. The main commodity sources for Bio diesel in India can be non-edible oils obtained from plant species such as Jatropha curcas (Ratanjyot), Pongamia pinnata (Karanj), Calophyllum inophyUum (Nagchampa), Hevcca brasiliensis (Rubber) etc. Biodiesel contains no petroleum, but it can be blended at any level with petroleum diesel to create a Biodiesel blend or can be used in its pure form. Just like petroleum diesel, biodiesel operates in compression engine; which essentially require very little or no engine modifications because biodiesel has properties similar to petroleum diesel fuels. It can be stored just like the petroleum diesel fuel and hence does not require separate infrastructure. The use of biodiesel in conventional diesel engines results in substantial reduction of un-brunt hydrocarbons, carbon monoxide and particular matters. Biodiesel is considered clean fuel since it has almost no sulphur, no aromatics and has about 10% built-in oxygen, which helps it to burn fully. Its higher cetane number improves the ignition quality even when blended in the petroleum diesel.

Jatropha curcas is a potential crop for production of biodiesel. The Jatropha seed has oil content of about 30–40%. The oil can be combusted as fuel without being refined or can be trans–esterified for producing the biodiesel.

Fruits are produced in winter or even through out the year if soil moisture is good and temperatures are sufficiently high. Each inflorescence yields a bunch of approximately 10 or more ovoid fruits. A three, bi-valved cocci is formed after the seeds mature and the fleshy exocarp dries. The seeds become mature when the capsule changes from green to yellow, after two to four months of fertilization. Blackish, thin shelled seeds are oblong and resemble to small castor seeds.

JATROPHA PROCESSING

Jatropha oil can be obtained by different processing operation like fruit harvesting, drying, fruit decapsulation, seed dehulling and oil expelling. Other processing operations to produce biodiesel from Jatropha involve trans-esterification, separation of glycerol and biodiesel, washing of biodiesel, drying and storage of biodiesel.

HARVESTING OF JATROPHA FRUIT

Ripe Jatropha fruits are yellow. The fruit dries and the hull becomes hard and black. The dry fruits remain on the branches. The fruits are hand picked or harvested by hitting the fruits by a long stick. At times, the younger trees are harvested by shaking the tree/ branches. The best way of harvesting the Jatropha fruits is to use some sort of a modified fruit picker, i.e. a long wooden stick with a circular comb and a cotton bag at one end. With this harvesting tool, the dry fruits can be picked from the trees, the fruits fall into the bag and do not have to be found in the grass.

DRYING OF JATROPHA FRUIT

Before dehulling, the seeds have to be dried. The fruits are just heaped outside the house or in the field for 7–10 days for drying. It is seldom spread on a threshing floor for drying. The best method is to spread a thin layer of fruits on a plastic sheet or on a surface of concrete for sun drying. If the seeds are to be planted they should not be dried in full sunshine, because the heat can reduce the germination capacity. If the seeds are going to be used for oil extraction, they may be dried to lower moisture content. It is important to keep the seeds free of sand or small stones, as it may damage the processing or oil extracting machines and also results in poor quality oil and cake.

DECAPSULATION OF JATROPHA FRUIT

Decortication of Jatropha fruits is in general done by beating the dried fruits with sticks on threshing yard. Decapsulation by hand is a time consuming process. A small tool makes this task much easier. The dried fruits are placed in a thin layer on a hard surface, i.e. on a table or on a concrete floor. If a small wooden board is moved over them while pressing it down, the fruit husk split and the seeds come out. The husk and seeds can be separated by winnowing and sieving.

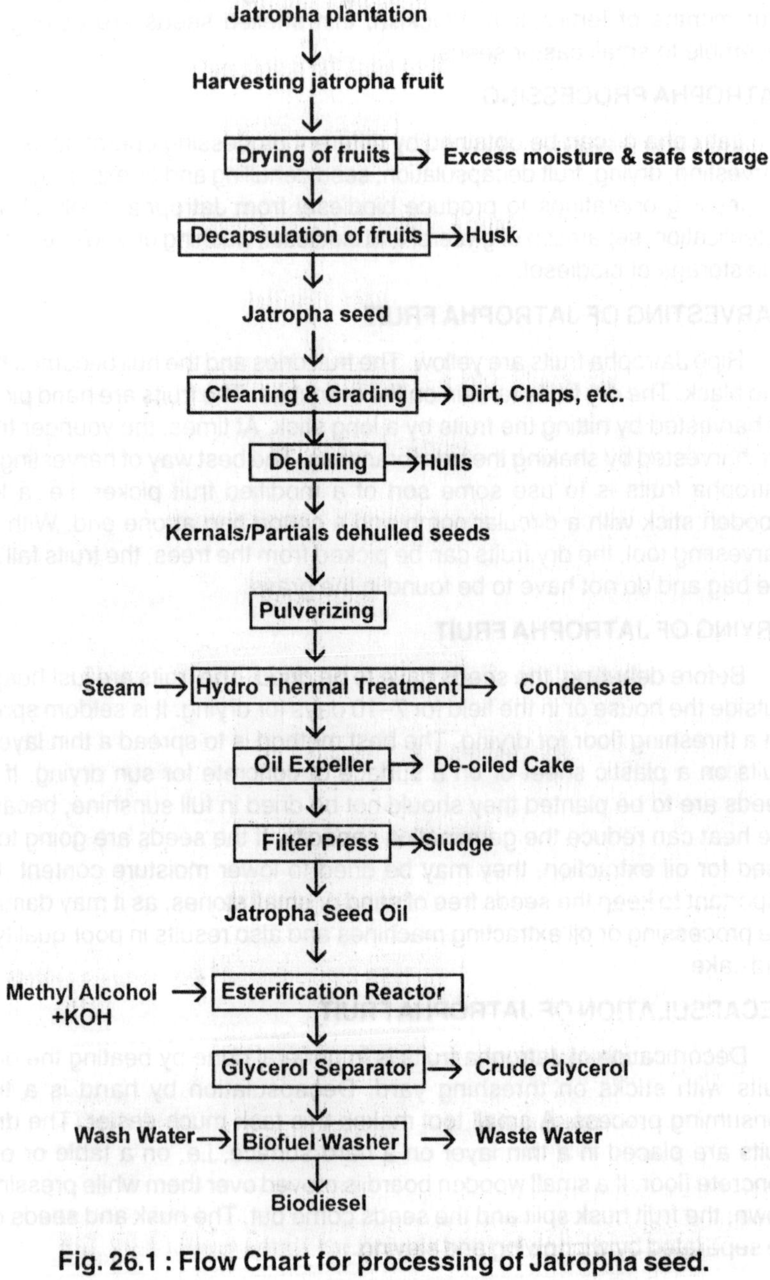

Fig. 26.1 : Flow Chart for processing of Jatropha seed.

STORAGE AND VIBILITY OF SEED

The seeds should be dried to low moisture content (5–7%) and stored in air-tight containers. At room temperature, the seeds can retain high viability for about one year. However, because of the high oil content the seeds cannot be expected to be stored for long as most of the other orthodox species.

DEHULLING OF JATROPHA SEED

Jatropha seed contains about 38 % hull/shell. The hull doesn't contain oil and rather obstructs the oil extraction/expression from the kernel inside. So it is necessary to dehull the Jatropha seeds before the oil extraction. At present, no machine or technology is available for dehulling the Jatropha seeds, on large scale.

Dehulling is the process of removing the hull from a grain or seed. Whenever a force applied on a seed exceeds the sum of the forces, which tend to retain the hull with kernel, dehulling occurs. Breakage-free kernel would result if the force is selective and is applied only to the hull. Three general categories of methods for obtaining the dehulling force are as follows: (a) mechanical methods such as abrasion or attrition, (b) impact or impulsive acceleration methods, and (c) shearing or non-impulsive acceleration methods. Usually, dehulling is accomplished in conventional dehulling mechanisms by the use of more than one type of force with such machines as hullers, stone mills, under runner disc hullers, roll dehuller and centrifugal dehuller. These machines have wide variations in the qualitative and quantitative output, cost and suitability to different grains.

The Jatropha seed is oblong in shape and has fragile cotyledons enclosed in a thick-walled tough hull with a relatively thicker ring around the edges. Because of this it is very difficult to mechanically dehull the seed without causing a high proportions of brokens. Thus its peculiar non-spherical shape, fragile cotyledons and a tough covering structure would seem to lend itself to manipulation for dehulling only by combined mechanisms capable of exerting compression or impact associated with shearing action, either separately or jointly.

OIL EXTRACTION/EXPRESSION FROM JATROPHA SEED

The ghanies or screw presses are used for expression of oil from Jatropha seed. There is no standard method for extraction/expression of Jatropha oil from its kernel and hence the recovery of oil is very poor. The technology

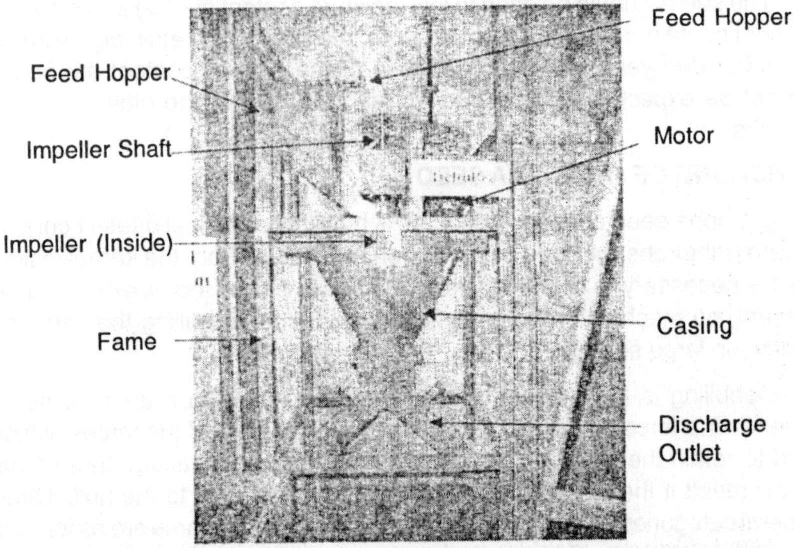

Fig. 26.2 : Oil expeller for expelling oil from Jatropha Seed.

Fig. 26.3 : Experimental plant for biodiesel production from Jatropha seed.

has been standardized after extensive experimental investigations and large scale trials in the experimental plant. The pretreatments including dehulling, size reduction and steaming are necessary for efficient extraction of oil from Jatropha seed.

TRANS–ESTERIFICATION OF JATROPHA OIL

The trans–esterification process involves mixing at room temperature methanol (50% excess) with NaOH (100% excess), then mixing vigorously with vegetable oil and allowing the glycerol to settle (about 15% of the biodiesel mix). The supernatant is biodiesel and contains a mixture of methylated fatty acids and methanol, the catalyst remaining dissolved in the glycerol fraction. Industrially, the esters are sent to the dean-up or purification process which consists of water washing, vacuum drying, and filtration.

27

Tapioca–Renewable Energy Source of Bio-Fuel for India

BIOMASS–TAPIOCA

Climate

Cassava grows best in areas with a mean temperature of 25–29°C, and a soil temperature of about 30°C; below 10°C the plant stops growing. While the crop grows best in areas with an annual well-distributed rainfall of 1000-1500 mm, it can tolerate semi-arid conditions with rainfall as low as 500 mm, and may have a competitive advantage over other crops under those conditions. Cassava can grow on a wide range of soils, but is best adapted to well-drained, light-textured, deep soils of intermediate fertility. Under high fertility conditions top growth may be stimulated at the expense of root growth. Optimum soil pH is between 4.5 and 6.5. The crop does not grow well in poorly drained soils, gravelly or saline soils, or in soils with a hardpan. These conditions are available in the southern region of India, throughout the year, hence the yield is high.

The average crop yield of roots and tubers for world is about 12,958 kg per ha whereas it is relatively high for India i.e. about 16,906 kg/ha. Therefore the present investigation proposes in developing an alternate eco-friendly source for alcohol from starch.

Tapioca starch is selected as the fermentation substrate. Because compared with the other starches, it has very less protein, hence eliminating de-proteination step in the fermentation. Absence of proteins makes cassava an interesting candidate as a substrate for a number of fermentation processes, especially when the world price for cassava starch is currently half of maize starch. Tapioca also has higher starch content compared with other tubers.

Modification of cassava starch to improve the functional properties such as viscosity, gelatinisation temperature, solubility and digestibility has been well established. However, the present chemical modification methods produce unwanted by-products and above all, the chemicals can have harmful effects. Bio–technological techniques can be useful in overcoming these problems. Typical example is esterification of starch or lowering the level of saccharides by treatment with lipids in the presence of lipases and esterases. These enzymes, being specific in their action, can bring about substitution at particular carbon atom thus providing products with special characteristics.

Starch and sago is used as the major food for people in considerable part of India. But the present methodology of tapioca conversion poses many problems in process as well as in effluent treatment. This requires an efficient and environmental friendly process for such conversions.

Yield

Cassava is not usually grown on soils where it would be most productive–that is, the light sandy loams, fertile and deep, which are reserved for other crops less tolerant of poor soils. When cassava is grown by traditional tropical methods, yields lie between 5 and 20 tones per hectare, varying with the region, the variety, the soil and other factors. However, when the crop is given more attention, yields of 30–40 tons per hectare are obtained. It has been reported that it is normal for some varieties, under appropriate cultivation methods, to yield over 60 tones per hectare.

The high yields frequently achieved at agricultural experiment stations and occasionally by some active farmers show what might be accomplished with improved varieties and better cultural practices.

Nevertheless, cassava yields in total calories per hectare compare very favourably with those of other starchy staples, as shown in Table 27.1.

TABLE 27.1
Average yields of tropical starchy staples, 1948-1952
Millions of calories per hectare

	Brazil	Java	India	China (province of Taiwan)
Maize	4.4	2.4	2.3	5.0
Rice	3.9	3.9	2.8	5.5
Yams and sweet potato	7.5	5.4	5.6	8.6
Cassava	14.2	7.1	5.8	11.6

Biochemical constituents of cassava (%)

For industrial development, many efforts are being made to organize research and experiments in various geographical regions for the selection of new varieties with high yields of roots and higher starch content.

TABLE 27.2

Average composition of the cassava root (common varieties at harvest time)

Composition	Percentage
Moisture	70.25
Starch	21.45*
Sugars	5.13
Protein	1.12
Fats	0.41
Ash	0.54

*Bitter varieties usually average about 30 percent starch content.

Importance of Tapioca in the context of current status

The production of starch from tropical root and tuber crops could be a way to get higher economic gains in developing countries. The present method produces starch, which includes tuber crushing, sieving, sedimentation and drying. This leads to starch loses up to 20% and also involves high-energy inputs, the use of much water, and expensive machinery. Hence this introduces the following problems in tapioca starch and sago industries,

- High energy consumption.
- Effluent problem.
- High water consumption.

In the current status, nowhere bio–process is applied for conversion of tapioca to starch (or) tapioca to higher alcohols in India. Hence finding out the feasibility of starch processes will definitely improve the utilization of biomass overcoming the environmental problems.

The energy required for operating the plant would be met substantially from biogas generated from biomass formed after extraction of alcohols. Further the bio-methanated biomass could be recycled to the field as manure. Thus the entire process becomes eco-friendly without producing any new CO_2 and is sustainable.

TABLE 27.3

Tapioca potential in Tamil Nadu

	District	Tapioca (in Tonnes)
1.	Chennai	0
2.	Kancheepura	211
3.	Thiruvallur	3346
4.	Cuddalore	171925
5.	Villupuram	244582
6.	Vellore	3475
7.	Thiruvannamalai	20093
8.	Salem	841484
9.	Namakkal	880110
10.	Dharmapuri	395229
11.	Krishnagiri	
12.	Coimbatore	39921
13.	Erode	176187
14.	Tiruchirapalli	251997
15.	Karur	23736
16.	Perambalur	104769
17.	Pudukottai	601
18.	Thanjavur	3042
19.	Thiruvarur	3042
20.	Nagapattinam	6355
21.	Madurai	4154
22.	Theni	2296
23.	Dindigul	13748
24.	Ramanathapuram	0
25.	Virudhunagar	820
26.	Sivagangai	180
27.	Tirunelveli	6901
28.	Thoothukudi	452
29.	The Nilgiris	3271
30.	Kanyakumari	209663
	State	**3410820 tones**

UTILITY OF THE PROJECT

Product-Alcohols

Available Agricultural crop land (ha)	= 169,700
Average crop yield (kg per ha) [9]	= 16,906
Cultivatable land for tapioca is around 50%	
Yield of Starch per tone of tapioca	= 240 kg
Therefore total yield of Tapioca (tons/year)	= 1.43×10^6
Considering fermentation and distillation efficiency starch converted to alcohol per tone of tapioca	= 154 kg
Expected yield of alcohol per kg of starch used as a feedstock	= 1.7 6litre
1 tone of tapioca gives	= 271.04 litre of alcohol
Hence, maximum alcohol that could be produced per year	= 462.6×10^6 litres
42 gallons of crude oil	= 44 gallons of pertoleum product
4.62.6 x 106 litres alcohol	= 4.37.8 x 106 litres of crude oil

- **437.8 x 106 litres of crude need not to be imported.**

Reduction in CO_2 Emission

1.16 kl	= 1 tone of crude oil
4.378.8 x 10^6 litres	= 3.77×10^5 ones of crude oil
Energy content of crude oii	= 41.87 GJ/tone
CO_2 emmission for crude oil	= 73.3 Kg/GJ
• **CO_2 prevented/annum**	**= 1.16×16^6 tones**

Bioproducts

1. Biogas

Starch carried out with effluent per tone of stapioca processed	= 96 kg
Yield of starch for 1.43 x 106 tone/year of tapioca processed	= 137.28×10^6 kg
1 kg of starch	= 0.8 m^2
Calorific value of Biogas	= 20 MJ/m^3
Biogas to be produced	= 109.8×10^6 m^3

If biogas is used for power production of

30% efficiency = 21 MW

The exhaust heat from the power plant is used for distillation.

2. Manure

Biosludge produced in the process of biogas production will be utilized as manure.

Manure to be produced = 34.32 x 106 tones

3. CO_2 credit

Every ton of CO_2 reduction reduces the cost of process by an average value of 5 Dollars.

Hence total cost gain in terms of CO_2 reduction is 4.9×10^6 dollars.

- Economical calculations made shows that a minimum of Rs. 15000/ tone of tapioca will be the gain profit for the project, besides the carbon credit.

Outcome of the project basis : 1 Year

	Units	Value
Tapioca production	Tones	$1.4^3 \times 10^6$
Alcohols production	Litres	462.6×10^6
Biogas	m^3	109.8×10^6
Manure	Tones	34.32×10^6
Power generation	MW	21
CO^2 prevented	Tones	1.16×10^6
CO^2 Credit	Dollars	4.9×10^6
Crude saved	Litres	437.8×10^6

28

Preparation of Biodiesel from *Jatropha circus*

INTRODUCTION

The trend towards dieselization of motorcar has grown rapidly over the last few years. The sole factor responsible for this is the low'running cost. Our country uses billions of gallons of diesel every yoear. As a result of combustion of this fuel tones of pollutant are dispersed into the air annually.

For supply the energy need of future, biodiesel shows much promise and its demand is growing with increasing use of the technology. "Producing biodiesel from Jatorpha could provide more environment friendly alternative by reducing the pollutants, low cost and renewable resources that reduce dependence on imported oil.

Jatropha Curcus

Jatropha curcus is a native of Mexico and tropical South America but naturalized now through out tropical to sub tropical Asia and Africa. It is commonly known as physics nut, Rat jot, Jamalghota, Jangaliaarandi or kala-aranda and is a multi–purpose, deciduous large 3-4 feet high shrub. It is reported to be cultivated in central and western regions 2.5 cm long, ovoid black and 2-3 halved .The 100 seed weight of is 63.01gm. It flowers in hot and rain season and set fruits in winter when it is leafless. Fruits mature by September- October The seed resemble castor oil in shape but smaller in size. The dry fruits are plucked by farmers or tribal people and sold in nearby market. It was nearly 422 fruit /kg and 1587 seed/kg Jatropha is a tropical plant. It can be very well grown in a wide range of agroclimatic conditions including moderate to high temperature areas. It can be planted in any kind of soil. It grows almost anywhere, in sandy and saline soils. Its water requirement is extremely low and it can withstand long period of drought by shedding most of its leaves to reduce transpiration loss.

PREPARATION OF BIODIESEL BY TRANSESTERIFICATION OF *JATROPHA CURCUS*

Trans–esterification is the process of converting the tri glycerides of the oils into methyl ester. Biodiesel is a methyl ester. Formed by of the oil with methanol in the presence of a catalyst to yield methyl ester and glycerol, Sodium hydroxide (NaOH) is most commonly used catalyst, though potassium hydroxides (KOH) can also be used.The methanol and NaOH are premixed with oil. Mixed for few hours and left to gravity settle for about eight hrs. The biodiesel comes to top leaving glycerin to settle in the bottom.

$$100 \text{ Kg oil} + 24 \text{ Kg Methanol} + 2.5 \text{ kg NaOH} \rightarrow 100 \text{ kg biodiesel} + 2.5 \text{ kg glycerin}$$

The overall potential of biodiesel is 50%less than the diesel fuel. Methanol used is a very active chemical against which the human body has no means of defense. It is absorbed easily through the skin and there is no means of elimination from the body. So levels of methanol dissolved in the blood accumulate. But the fact is 30 lit of fruit juices will probably contain up to 20 gram of methanol, near the official minimum lethal dose. Methanol is in the food we eat in fresh fruit and vegetables, beer and wine, diet drink.

Hydrogen as a fuel has received widespread attention in the media of late, particularly ever since the Bush administration proclaimed that developing a hydrogen economy would clean our air, and free us of oil dependence. There are many problems with using hydrogen as a fuel. The first, and most obvious, is that hydrogen gas is extremely explosive. To store hydrogen at high pressures for as a transportation fuel, it is essential to have tanks that are constructed of rustproof materials, so that as they age they won't rust and spring leaks. Hydrogen has to be stored at very high pressures to try to make up for its low energy density. Diesel fuel has an energy density of 1,058 kBtu/cu.ft. Biodiesel has an energy density of 950 kBtu/cu.ft, and hydrogen stored at 3,626 psi (250 times atmospheric pressure) only has an energy density of 68 kBtu/cu.ft.1 So, highly pressurized to 250 atmospheres, hydrogen's volumetric energy density is only 7.2% of that of biodiesel. The result being that with similar efficiencies of converting that stored chemical energy into motion (as diesel engines and fuel cells have), a hydrogen vehicle would need a fuel tank roughly 14 times as large to yield the same driving range as a biodiesel powered vehicle. To get a 1,000-mile range, a tractor-trailer running on diesel needs to store 168 gallons of diesel fuel.

When biodiesel's slightly lower energy density and the greater efficiency of the engine running on biodiesel are taken into account, it would need roughly 175 gallons of biodiesel for the same range. But, to run on hydrogen stored at 250 atmospheres, to get the same range would require 2,360 gallons of hydrogen. Biodiesel of vegetable oil was evaluated as a fuel in CIE by researchers. They concluded that the performance of ester of vegetable oil did not differ greatly from that of diesel fuel. The brake power was nearly same as with diesel fuel, while the specific fuel consumption was higher than that of diesel fuel. Most vegetable oil esters are suitable as diesel substitutes but studies are necessary for commercial utilization, based on crankcase oil analysis, engine wear rates were low but some oil dilution did occur. Carbon deposits inside the engine were normal, with the exception of intake value deposits. Biodiesel has become more attractive recently of its environmentally benefits.

The cost of biodiesel is however the main obstacle to commercialization of products. With cooking oil used as raw material, the viability of a continuous trans–esterification process and recovery of high quality glycerol as a biodiesel by-product are primary options to be considered to lower the cost of biodiesel. Most of the biodiesel that is currently made uses soybean oil, methanol and an alkaline catalyst. The high value of soybean oil as a food product makes production of a cost effective fuel very challenging. Accepted molar ratios of alcohols to glycerides are 6 :1–30 :1. Pyrolysis produces more biogasoline than biodiesel fuel. Soap pyrolysis products of vegetable oils can be used as alternative diesel engine fuel. Specific weight is higher for biodiesel heat of combustion is lower and viscosities are 1.3-2.1 times that of D2 fuel.Pour point for biodiesel vary from 274-298K higher for biodiesel fuels depending on the feedstock. SC for biodiesel fuel is 20–50% that of D2 fuel. The ester has higher levels of injector coking than D2 fuels.

One of the biggest advantages of biodiesel compared to many other alternative transportation fuels is that it can be used in existing diesel engines with some. Modification, and can be blended in at any ratio with diesel. This completely eliminates the "chicken-and egg" dilemma that other alternatives have, such as hydrogen powered fuel cells. With biodiesel, since the same engines with some modification can run on conventional diesel, manufacturers can comfortably produce diesel vehicles before biodiesel is available on a wide scale same can be said for flex-fuel vehicles capable of running on ethanol, gasoline, or any blend of the two. As biodiesel production continues to ramp up, it can go into the same fuel distribution infrastructure, just replacing petroleum diesel either wholly (as B100, or 100% biodiesel), or blended in with diesel. Not only does this eliminates the chicken-and-egg problem, making biodiesel a much more feasible alternative than hydrogen, but also eliminates the huge cost of revamping the nationwide fuel distribution infrastructure.

NEERI's research showed that one quad (7.5 billion gallons) of biodiesel could be produced from 200,000 hectares of desert land (200,000 hectares is equivalent to 780 square miles, roughly 500,000 acres), if the remaining challenges are solved (as they will be, with several research groups and companies working towards it, including ours at UNH). The country witnessed the launch of the first commercial production of biodiesel from karanja pongania seed by the Maharashtra Energy Eevelopment Agency [MEDA] in Pune. Produced and marketed by city based mint Biofuel, the company plans to set up a 30 crore plant at chiplyn, which will have a capacity of producing 5000 tones of fuel per day. Plans are on to increase the capacity of the plant to one-lakh tones within four year.

In order to provide the necessary impetus for the growth of biodiesel in the state of Maharashtra, MEDA is also planning to set up a biodiesel park at Tatawade Dairy near Pune, The park estimated to cost Rs 5 crore, will comprise a research laboratory as well as plantation area for different species of oil producing plants like Jathorpha, Karanja and castor. Besides research, the parked for publicity and for training of farmers on biodiesel.

Besides pongania seed, the country has substantial reserves of other non-traditional oil seeds and oil-bearing material. One of this is rice bran. The Chennai based Central Leather Research Institute (CLRI) recently obtained global patent for developing bodies from rice bran. CLRI initiated a pilot project with a daily production capacity of 150 liters and the biodiesel produced was certified by the Indian Institute of Petroleum, Dehradun, The biodiesel from the pilot plant was successfully used to Metropolitan Transport Corporation Buses in Chennai The performance of the engine was found to be on par with that of the normal petroleum diesel engine. The success of the pilot project has resulted in the technology being transfer diesel to Vel Biodiesel Energy Pvt .Ltd, which is setting up a 60,000 liter capacity plant in Pudukkottia district of Tamil Nadu at a cost of Rs. 8 crore.

India's biodiesel programmed is also receiving government support as is evident from the new purchase policy announced by the ministry of petroleum. It states that Public Sector Oil Marketing Companies (OMCS) will have to purchase biodiesel extracted from plants such as jathorpha and pongania for mixed with conventional diesel from January 2006, at the rate of Rs. 25 per liter. According to the policy, OMCS such as Indian Oil Corporation and Bharat Petroleum Corporation would buy product at a uniform price decided by them depending by on market condition. The price would be inclusive of any taxes and duties and transportation cost for delivery of biodiesel at the purchase centers. Initially 5 per cent of the biodiesel BO5 that should meet the fuel quality standard prescribed by the Bureau of Indian standard by the (BIS) would be mixed with diesel during trial runs and the percentage would be increased to 20% in phases.

The American State of Indiana will soon have the world's largest plant capable of producing up to 2,30,000 gallons of biodiesel/day is more than 80million gallons of biodiesel per year to be located. The ninth plant to be developed in the state will use soybeans as raw material. Indiana is the nation's fourth producer of corn.

The plant will be built in two phases 1st a 50 million bushel/day soybeans processing facility will be set up followed by a biodiesel production plant. About 260000 metric tones of soybeans oil from the plant will be used each year for biodiesel production. In addition, 1 million tones of Protein rich soybean meal produced each year will be used by the livestock and poultry industry.

The Claypool plant, which would be completed in 18 months, is expected to create around 85 additional jobs. With the facilities under contraction, the state will produce an additional 95 million gallons of biodiesel and 400 million gallons of ethanol annually, Indian's goal to produce a combine 1 billion gallons of ethanol and biodiesel annually.

Test run drive

1. Field trial (3, round trips) done on Luknow Allahabad Jan Shatabadi by using B10 (10% biodiesel) run was successful in term of haulage and other performance characteristics.
2. Shatabadi train was run from Delhi to Amritsar using B5 (5% biodiesel) blends. No loss of hp. Acceleration or any other problem was observed during the run.

3. Mercedes Benz c 220 cedi vehicle was run in various states of the country (> 10,000km) without any engine modification using 100% biodiesel by CSMERI, Bhawnagar. No problem was encountered in the trip and average mileage of 13.5 km per liter was achieved which is comparable with fossil fuel.

29

Biodiesel Production from *Jatropha Circus (SVO) Oil*

INTRODUCTION

Vegetable oils are transferred to methyl esters to improve the viscosity and volatility, and are applied to diesel engines. Also, in order to reduce NOx and smoke emissions from diesel engines, emulsified fuels with water are proposed as diesel fuel. Emulsified rapeseed oil with 20 % water, made by one of authors, shows the reductions of NOx and smoke emissions from diesel engines.

Water-diesel fuel emulsions have the potential to break the NOx-PM trade-off. Experiments have shown that if the injection pressure is kept constant as with diesel fuel, water-diesel fuel emulsions lower both NOx and PM emissions (10% water in the emulsion fuel corresponds to ca. 10% NOx reduction). On the other hand, if water-diesel fuel emulsions are used maintaining equal fuel energy flow rate as with diesel fuel, the NOx emissions are constant and do not depend on the water content in the fuel. This applies for any initial setting of injection pressure and start of injection at low and medium engine loads.

Water-diesel fuel emulsions lower the peak flame temperatures and enhance the fuel/air mixing during the diffusion combustion phase. The use of water-diesel fuel emulsions permits to operate the combustion at much lower global air/fuel ratios while maintaining PM constant (in combination with EGR this means higher EGR rates, lower NOx at constant PM and BSFC.

In this work, a novel technique of water fumigation along with the suction air to the engine is implemented to study the engine performance, emissions and vibrations.

The following investigations are carried out with diesel fuel, JME, and JME with water fumigation ranging from 0.25 kg/hr – 0.75kg/hr at no load and three fourth full loads.

- Engine Performance,
- Combustion Pressures,
- Heat Release Rates,
- Exhaust Emissions,
- Engine Cylinder Vibrations.

CHARACTERIZATION OF THE JATROPHA METHYL ESTER

Mike Pelley's recipe is used in the biodiesel preparation from the raw Jatropha oil. It comprises first methanol treatment with acid catalyst to remove free fatty acids and then base treatment using sodium hydroxide and methanol followed by water washing.

The properties are enlisted in the Table below :

TABLE 29.1

Fuel oil	Density in kg/cubic. Meter	Viscosity in cst	Cetane Number	Calorific Value, MJ/kg	Flash Point in °C
Diesel	0.83	2.75	45	43,000	50
JME	0.88	4.38	50	38,800	170

EXPERIMENTAL TEST RIG AND INSTRUMENTATION

The experiment is conducted on a vertical single cylinder four stroke, water cooled, direct injection diesel engine. The engine specifications are: hp. 5, rpm 1500, bore; 80 mm, stroke :110 mm, Kirloskar make with eddy current dynamometer (SAJ Froude make). Delta 1600-L exhaust gas analyzer made in Germany is used to monitor the exhaust emissions. DIESELTUNE 114 smoke density tester is used to measure the exhaust soot. Water fumigator with automatic temperature control and water metering designed by Legion Brothers, Bangalore is used. Vibration spectra and time wave forms are measured using DC-11 vibration analyzer made in Canada. On-Time and Vast-an vibration software developed by Epredict Corp., Argentina and Russia respectively is used to analyze the engine cylinder vibration. Apex, Engine Recorder, Pune with C7112 software is used to monitor and record the pressure signatures on line.

RESULTS AND DISCUSSION

- The pressure crank angle diagram at 3/4 load indicates higher peak pressures (with a difference of 5.3 bar) for JME with water fumigation and almost same Indicated horse power generated. The water vapour induction rate is 0.75 kg/hr. [Fig. 29.1]. This is due to the higher cetane value of JME.

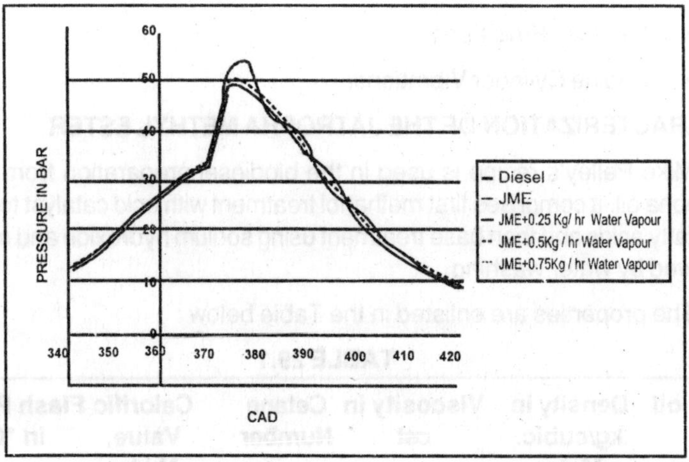

Fig. 29.1 : Comparison of Combustion Pressures.

- Marginal increase in SFC is observed with the increase in the flow rate of water vapour with JME. [an increase of 23% is recorded] [Fig. 29.2]. This is because of the lower calorific value of JME.
- Decrease in the brake thermal efficiency is observed because of water fumigation. [Fig. 29.3.]
- Much variation of the net heat release rate with respect to the crank angle in the diffused combustion zone is observed in the case of JME +0.75 kgjhr water. These quantum releases can be attributed to the presence of water vapour. [Fig. 29.4]
- There is significant decrease in the NO emissions with water fumigation. There is also significant decrease in HC and CO_2 emissions. It is observed marginal increase in the emission of CO because of the presence of water. The NO emissions for diesel at 3/4 full load is measured as 171 ppm and 59 ppm for JME +0.75 kg/ hr water. Hence a significant reduction of 65% lower NO emissions

is recorded [Fig. 29.5]. The reduction in HC and CO_2 emissions are 74.1 % and 40.7% respectively [Fig. 29.6 and 29.7]. The smoke value has increased from 57 HSU to 70 HSU for the diesel and JME +0.75 kg/hr water [Fig. 29.8).The smoke level incidentally has decreased at water fumigation of 0.25 kg/hr with JME by a margin of 1.5%.

- The Time wave forms (TW) and *FFT* [Fig.29.9 to 29.14] indicate that there is no abnormal combustion with the addition of water vapour at the suction and with JME fuel oil. Any sign of engine knock or detonation appears in the form of rise in the amplitude levels in

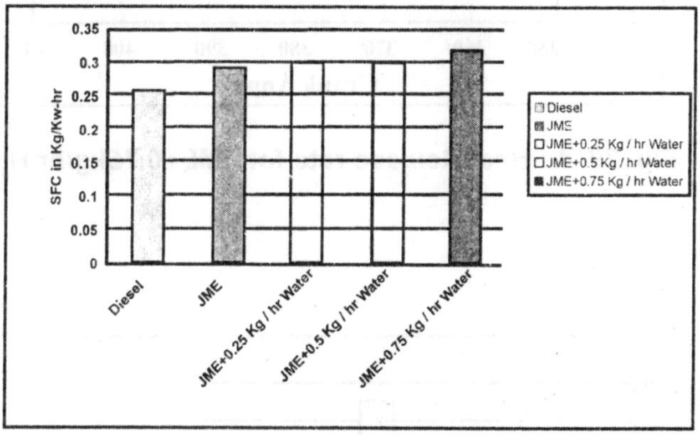

Fig.29.2 : Comparison of SFC at 3/4 Load with water fumigation.

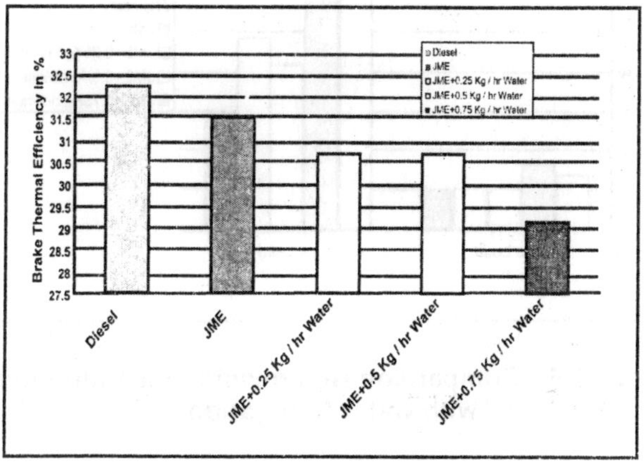

Fig. 29.3 : Comparison of brake thermel efficiency.

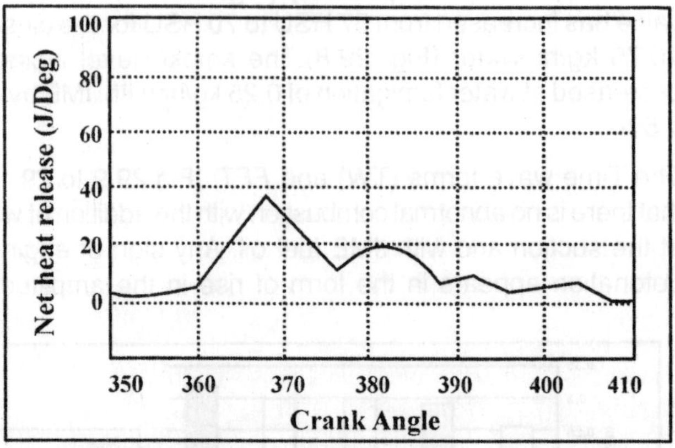

Fig. 29. 4 : Heat Release rate for JME+0.75kg/hr H_2O.

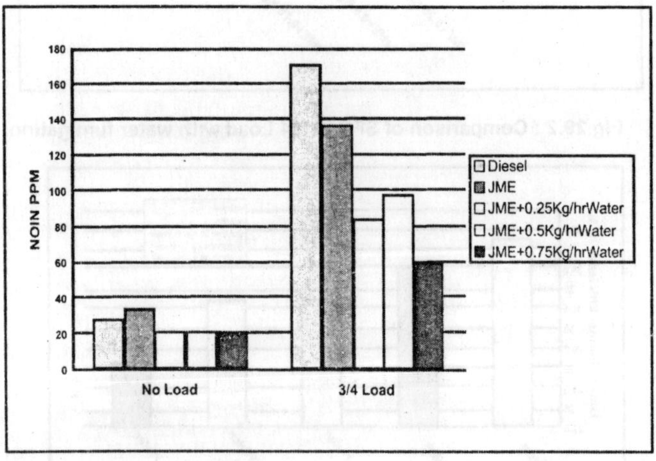

Fig. 29.5 5 : Comparison No emission measurements with water fumigation.

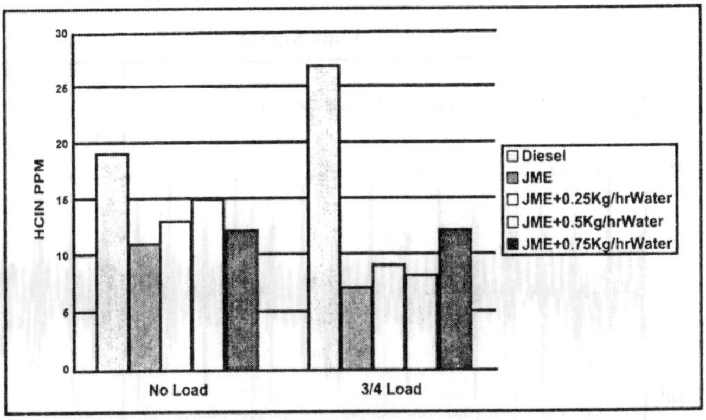

Fig. 29.6 : Comparison 'HC' measurements with water fumigation.

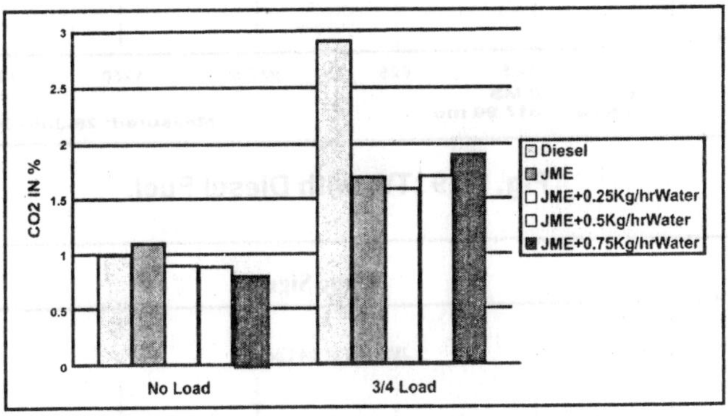

Fig. 29.7 : Comparison 'CO2' emission measurements with water fumigation.

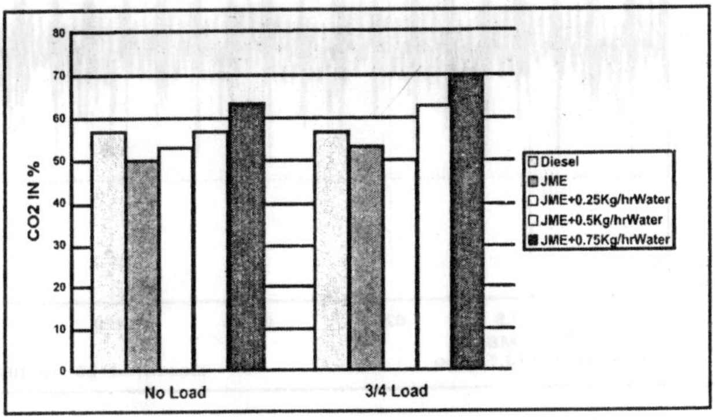

Fig. 29.8 : Exhaust smoke measurements with water fumigation.

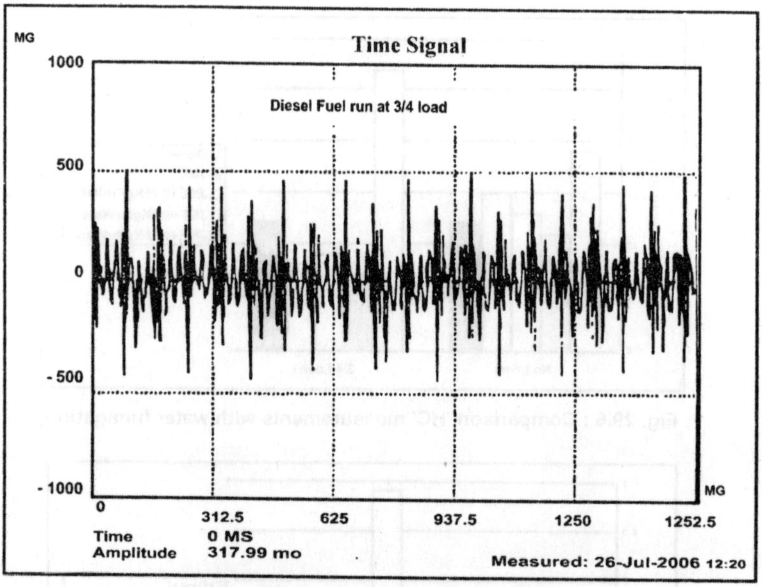

Fig. 29.9 :TW with Diesel Fuel.

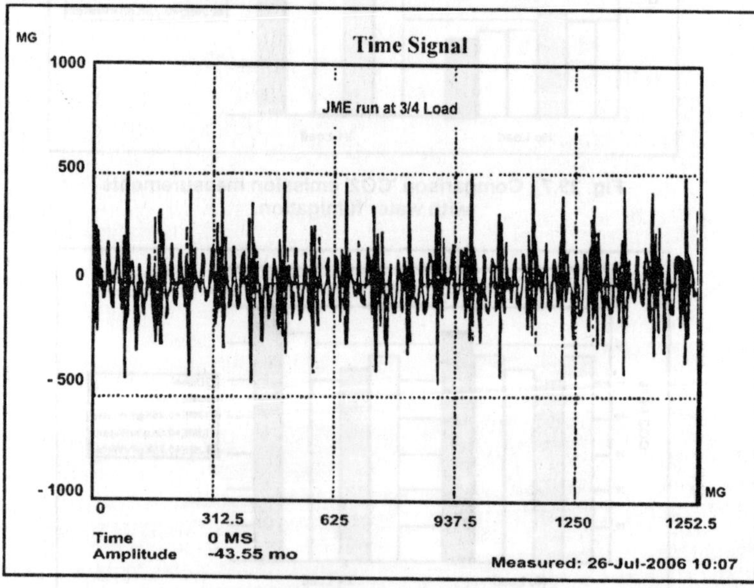

Fig. 29.10 :TW with JME.

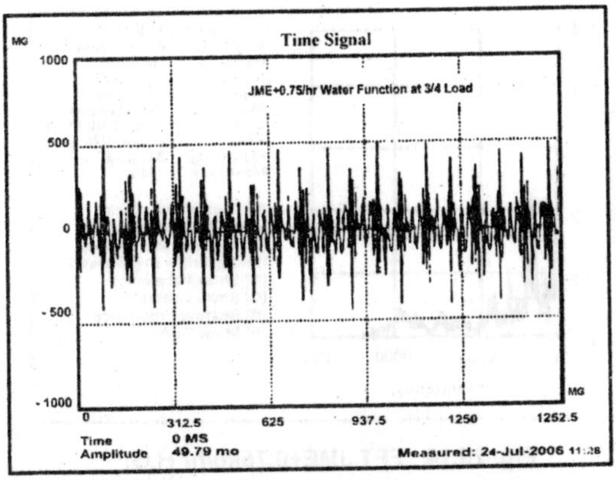

Fig. 29.11 : TW with JME+0.75kg/hr H_2O.

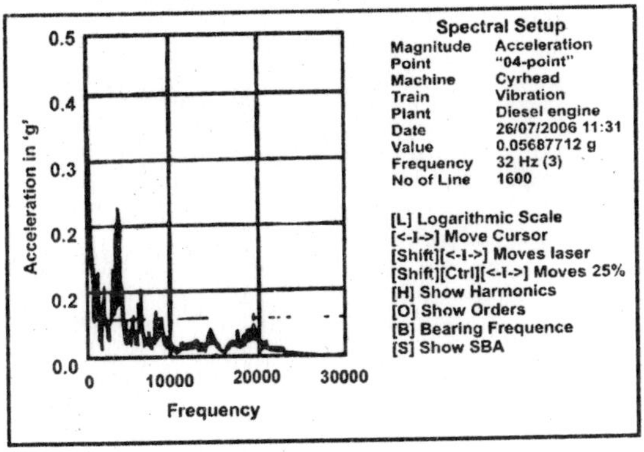

Fig. 29.12 : FFT with Diesel.

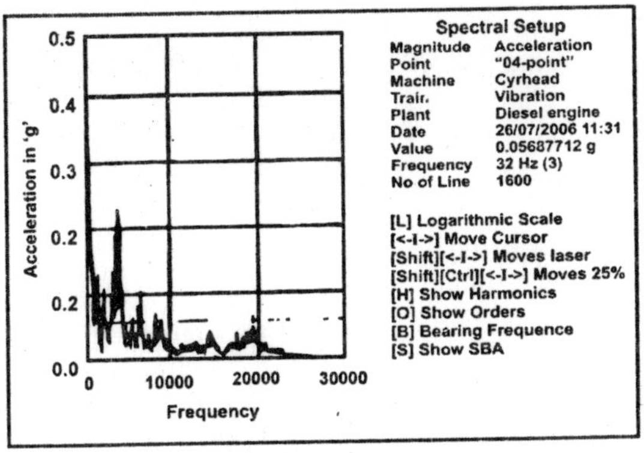

Fig. 29.13 : FFT with JME.

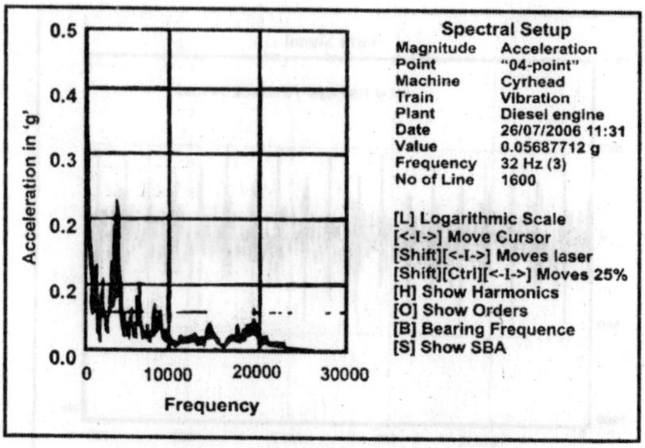

Fig. 29.14 : FFT JME+0.75kg/hr H_2O.

30

Gasification of Biomass and Waste

INTRODUCTION

With respect to global issues of sustainable energy and reduction in greenhouse gases, biomass is getting increased attention as a potential source of renewable energy. According to the World Energy Assessment report, 80% of the world's primary energy consumption is contributed by fossil fuel, 14% by renewable (out of which biomass contributes 9.5%) and 6% by nuclear energy sources. A sustainable energy future requires combination of factors such as renewable resources and advanced energy technology. Biomass is being traditionally used as energy source especially for cooking and heating particularly in the developing countries.

The advantages of "High Temperature Gasification of biomass and waste" over other existing technologies are as follows:

Biomass and wastes makes possible of high calorific gas (syngas-synthetic gas) production, which in traditional methods is obtained only by use of pure oxygen, utilization of oxidizer (air or air and steam mixture) with temperature above 1000°C causes decreasing dimensions of devices to energy conversion and flue gas cleaning systems, amount of syngas production and increasing of its calorific value.

- In energy conversion system, as fuel, biomass and different kind of municipal wastes or poor quality solid fuels are used.
- Mineral matters are solidified (temperature level, at which process goes is higher than melting temperature of mineral matter), most of organic compounds in liquid slag form are harmless for environment and are used in building industry.

- There is expectation of low emission of dioxins and heavy metals and increased calorific value of syngas in relation to gas obtained by classic methods.

DESCRIPTION OF THE PROCESS

Direct combustion of biomass and waste (for example on the grate) is not acceptable due to different pyrolysis and oxidative pyrolysis times for the various materials present in the stream of waste. In essence it is difficult to design a gasifier without any knowledge on the type of fuel that will be used. Application of this technology results in very expensive flue gas and ash treatment installations to comply with obligatory legislation. Latest research on High Temperature Air Combustion (HTAC) of gas and liquid fuels was followed by development of a new solid fuel gasification technology. Particular progress has been made in the area of High Temperature Air Combustion and in designing of highly efficient regenerative air and steam ceramic preheaters, which made this development faster. Such progress has created the possibility to begin a systematic research on gasification processes with high temperature air and steam called High Temperature Air/Steam Gasification (HTA/SG). Gasification involves partial oxidation of the feedstock to obtain a mixture of hydrogen, carbon oxides, water, nitrogen if air is used and small amounts of methane and higher hydrocarbons. The product gas also contains variable amounts of ash particles, volatile alkali metals and tar, which is a complex mixture of aromatics that includes a significant fraction of polycyclic aromatic hydrocarbons. Temperature is an important variable with regard to the final composition of the gases. It has recently been found that addition of steam is effective in increasing cracking rates in the temperature range of 950–1250°C. Oxygen at 600–700°C accelerates the destruction of primary products, and inhibits the formation of aromatics; however, once benzene, the primary component of aromatic compounds in tar, is formed it cannot be destroyed by oxygen. Moreover, steam biomass reaction rates may be enhanced relative to the completing reactions by increasing the gasifier steam concentration. Higher temperature will also result in higher rates of reaction and reduce required residence times.

In Fig. 30.1 the general process for high temperature air/steam gasification of biomass to hydrogen rich gas production is presented. Fig. 30.1. The scheme of the high temperature air/steam gasification of biomass process. During the gasification process the following three phases could take place. Energy release for this process is described by simplified

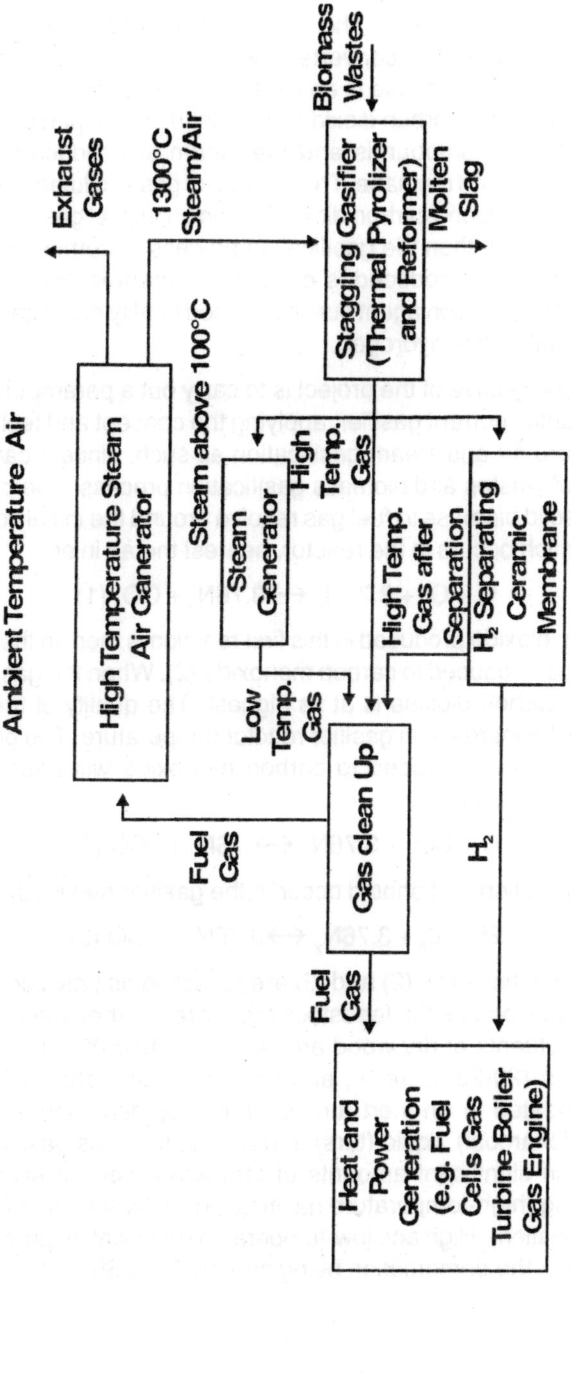

Fig. 30.1 : The Scheme of the high temperature air/steam gasification of biomass process.

combustion mechanism below. The first phase is a process of pyrolysis, during which the biomass is converted by heat into charcoal and volatile compounds. The second phase is an exothermic reaction, in which part of the carbon is oxidized to carbon dioxide. In the third phase, part of the carbon dioxide, the volatile compounds and the steam are reduced to carbon monoxide, hydrogen and methane. This mixture of gases diluted with nitrogen from the air and unreduced carbon dioxide is known as fuel gas. If the original feedstock is charcoal, then the gasification process becomes two phased, and the amount of tar produced is cut down. Steam is one of the most commonly used gasification agent due to the good quality of the gas obtained, with a high percentage of hydrogen.

The overall objective of the project is to carry out a parametric study on a fixed bed counter-current gasifier, applying the concept and technology of high temperature air and steam gasification as such, since it can improve the efficiency of wastes and biomass gasification process. The conversion process from solid biomass to fuel gas resolve around the initial combustion reaction (1), which occurs in the reactor, nearest the air inlet.

$$C + O_2 + 3.76N_2 \leftrightarrow 3.76N_2 + CO_2 \ (1)$$

The carbon dioxide produced in this first reaction is then, in the presence of glowing carbon, reduced to carbon monoxide (2). When the gasifier is first lit, the level of carbon dioxide is at its highest. The quality of the fuel gas increases with the increase in gasifier reactor temperature. The percentage of the carbon dioxide reduced to carbon monoxide will depend on the temperature in the .gasifier.

$$C + CO_2 + 3.76N_2 \leftrightarrow .76N_2 + 2CO \ (2)$$

The ideal reaction that should occur in the gasifier bed is (3);

$$2C + 0_2 + 3.76N_2 \leftrightarrow 3.76N_2 + 2CO \ (3)$$

Chemical reactions (1), (2) and (3) are regarded as only occurring with carbon, and with wood as the feedstock there are other elements involved. The main constituents of dry wood are cellulose (40–50%), hemicellulose (20–30%), lignin (20-25%), resin, and trace mineral matter. When these residues are heated in an inert atmosphere they decompose into three phases: solid (charcoal), liquid (tars) and gas. In biomass gasification, the gas can contain significant amounts of tars which can be eliminated by thermal cracking (high-temperature gasification) or by the use of a catalyst (catalytic gasification). High and low-temperature gasification processes can be distinguished, the demarcation being around 700-750°C. An increase in the gasification temperature causes an increase in the gaseous product yield and a decrease in the tar yield. Despite this lower tar content, the remaining tars must be eliminated in order to be able to use the gas obtained. These tars are mainly polyaromatic hydrocarbons (PAH), which are difficult to convert, and the relative proportion of PAH increases with the gasification temperature.

The main secondary reactions involved are :

$C + H_2O \leftrightarrow H_2 + CO$ (4)

$CO + H_2O \leftrightarrow H_2 + CO_2$ (5)

$C + CO_2 \leftrightarrow 2CO$ (6)

$CO + 3H_2 \leftrightarrow CH_4 + H_2O$ (7)

$C + 2H_2 \leftrightarrow CH_4$ (8)

$Tar + H_2O \leftrightarrow H_2 + CO$ (9)

Tar + H2 $\leftrightarrow$ light hydrocarbons + gases (10)

Equations (4) and (6) represent the gasification reactions of carbon deposits with H_2O and CO_2. These reactions become significant at 700°C. In addition to being endothermic, reaction (4) is relatively slow compared to carbon-oxygen or carbon-carbon dioxide (Boudouard-reaction 6). Steam-biomass reaction rates may be enhanced relative to the competing reactions by increasing the reactor steam concentration. Higher temperatures will also result in higher rates of reaction and reduce required residence times.

EXPERIMENTAL PROCEDURE

Start-up of the gasifier includes all operations required until a steady state, whereby the pre-set feed gas temperature is stable. Pre-weighed batches of feedstock are loaded on top on the ceramic beads from the top side of the gasifier. Initial height of the bed was equal to about 0.35 m and diameter was equal to 0.4 m. Fuel is ignited immediately after closing the conversion system. The common feature of the experiments is that ignition occurs on the bottom of the fuel bed. Shut down procedure includes all the actions to safely seal the gasifier. Computer, steam boiler, heat up process of the feed gas preheater are shut down in an orderly sequence with the 150 kW safety burner on the afterburner remaining on using a propane gas until no combustible gas is produced. Shut down of all fans is the last procedure following cooling of feed gas pre heater and of the gasifier. After the reactor cooled down, the top section of the gasifier was opened so that all ash any or slag were carefully removed and monitored.

The following parameters are measured:

- Temperature of preheated feed gas, reacting fixed bed (Tb1, Tb2), and of the fuel gas (Tog 1), by means of type N thermocouple, and temperature of flue gas by means of type B thermocouple.
- Fuel gas composition with help of micro Gas Chromatograph (GC) connected to the gas sampling probe.
- Pressure along the air lines.

The following gas components of the fuel gas are measured: hydrogen (H_2), carbon monoxide (CO), carbon dioxide (CO_2), nitrogen (N_2), oxygen (O_2), methane (CH_4) and higher hydrocarbons (CxHy). The composition of fuel gas was determined from gas samples taken at the gasifier outlet. All measurements were performed using a sampling frequency of one sample per 115 seconds. The run time of 115 seconds is built up in a sampling time of 15 seconds and an analysis time of 100 seconds. In this work, influence of the air to steam ratio in the feed gas was investigated during gasification of wood pellets and charcoal, while the influence of other main parameters, such as feed gas temperature and flow rate of feed gas on the phases of gasification process of wood pellets were investigated and reported else where. Experimental conditions for the biomass fuels gasification carried out in a fixed bed gasifier whose results are object of study in this paper are presented in Table 30.1 gives the operation

TABLE 30.1 Operation conditions on the fixed bed gasification of charcoal and wood pellets 12 mm.

Case number	Fuel type	Temperature of the feed gas	Total flow of feed gas	Molar fraction of steam in the feed gas	Mass of fuel
[-I	[-]	[oC]	[Nm_3/h1	[%1]	[kg]
Ch-1	Charcoal	360	50	0%	6.11
Ch-2	Charcoal	360	50	10%	6.11
Ch-3	Charcoal	360	50	20%	6.11
Ch-4	Charcoal	360	50	25%	6.10
WP-1	Wood pellets	830	50	0%	20
WP-2	Wood pellets	920	55	25%	20
WP-3	Wood pellets	900	53	52%	20
WP-4	Woad pellets	900	56	83%	20

conditions for the case of gasification of charcoal in the experiments with air and mixture of air and steam used as feed gas. Mass of charge was kept constant and equal to 6.11 kg. For the same volume flow rate of the feed (50 Nm^3/h) and same temperature (360°C), the molar fraction of steam was varied from 0 up to 25%.

Table 30.1 also shows operation conditions of 4 selected gasification runs of wood pellets (sized 12 mm in diameter). The mass of charge was constant and equal to 20 kg. Temperature of the feed gas was slightly varied from 830 up to 930°C whereas its flow rate was slightly varied from 50 to 56 Nm^3/h. Molar fraction of the steam in the feed gas was varied from 0 up to 83%. The type of biomass largely determines the nature of the tar produced, which is also influenced by the gasification process and the operating conditions. Air gasification produces a low viscosity/low reactivity tar, while steam gasification produces a liquid tar with a low molecular weight. High temperature gasification gives a tar with low oxygen content, consisting mostly of hydrocarbons ..

PROCESS TEMPERATURE

For the sake of simplification, gasifier temperature (or reaction temperature) and temperature of the fuel gas exiting the gasifier are called process temperature in this study. The importance of both temperatures and the corresponding profiles as a result of variation of molar fraction of steam in the feed gas are discussed in this section.

Figure 30.2 and Figure 30.3 show the impact of the preheated feed gas on the reaction temperature referred as temperature of the fuel bed. The sensible heat of the preheated air brought to the reactants induces an increase in the temperature of the fuel bed. During gasification of wood pellets (Fig. 30.3), it goes up to about 1350°C when temperature of the feed gas (only air) is kept constant at 900°C. However, this temperature does reduce to about 830°C and 780°C when molar fraction of steam is increased up to 52% and 83%, respectively. As shown in (Figure 30.22), temperature of the gasifier bed as higher as 1450°C is seen during gasification of charcoal when the feed gas enters the gasifier with temperature of 360°C. Figure 30.2 shows that the use of 10% and 25% of molar fraction of steam in the feed gas does significantly decrease the temperature of the fuel bed down to about 1200°C and 1000°C, respectively.

High gasifier bed temperature shown in Figures 30.2 and 30.3 favours the endothermic Boudouard reaction ($C + CO_2$ B $\leftrightarrow$ 2CO). This reaction requires high temperatures and produces only CO above 1000°C, which is

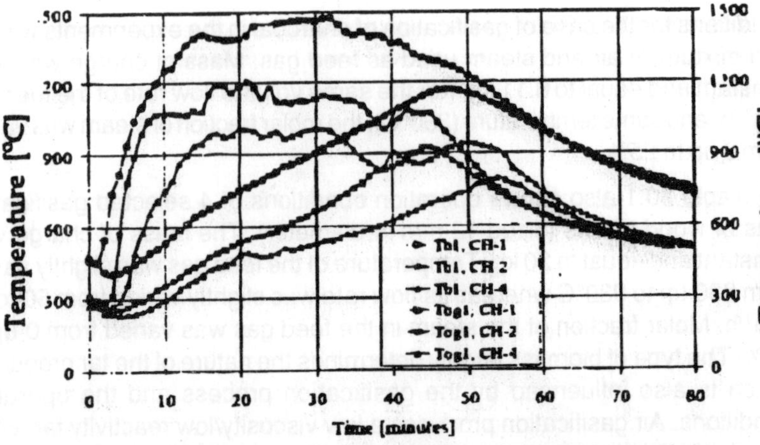

Fig. 30.2 : Influence of steam on the temperature of the fuel and (Tb1) and fuel gas at the exit point of gasifier (Tgo1) during gasification of charcoal (refer to Table 30.2).

the reason of high molar fraction of CO using only air and low molar fraction of CO and high molar fraction of CO_2 when mixture of air and steam is used as feed gas.

In some gasifiers, the injection of water in the bed allows to control temperature of the gasifier bed (temperature of reaction) and favours the formation of CO and H_2 according to the following reaction: $C + H_2O \leftrightarrow CO + H_2$. As discussed above, the increase of the amount of water in the

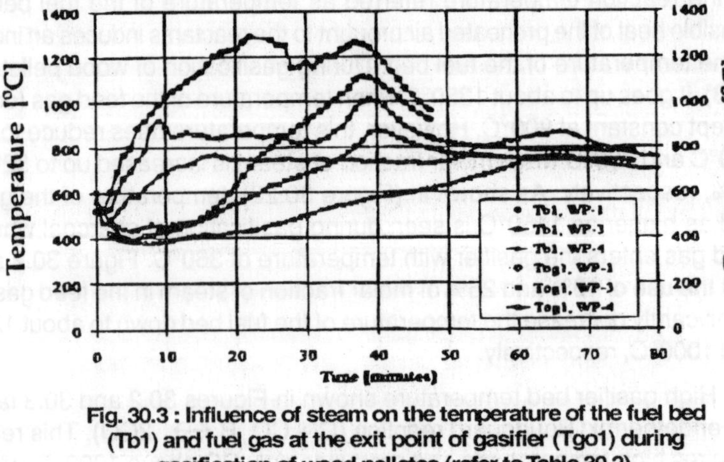

Fig. 30.3 : Influence of steam on the temperature of the fuel bed (Tb1) and fuel gas at the exit point of gasifier (Tgo1) during gasification of wood pelletes (refer to Table 30.2).

gasifier bed leads to more production of H_2 and CO_z in expenses of the generation of CO by the following water gas shift reaction, $CO + H_2O \leftrightarrow CO_2 + H_2$. This is caused by the participation of the steam in gas phase reactions and in the char reactions.

The results obtained in this study correspond to two levels of temperature of the feed gas. 360°C for charcoal and around 900°C for wood pellets. As for tar removal, it has been stated that a uniform and high gasifier temperature has been found to be the ideal combination to achieve the total cracking of tar . In the previous works [3, 4], high temperatures of pre heated feed gas increases the temperature of the gasifier bed. It was noticed that little or no tar is produced from this thermal gasification process. From the mass balance performed, the higher temperature also gave a significant reduction in the yield of carbon into soot, tars and an equally significant reduction in CO_2 production with a corresponding increase in CO yield.

Concerning effect of steam in the gasifier temperature, in both cases (wood pellets and charcoal), the increase of the H_2 content with decrease of Tbl is observed because endothermic reaction takes place. The importance of the temperature of the gasifier bed is justified in the study of Cummer who stated that addition of steam and/or oxygen is effective in increasing cracking rates in the temperature range of 950–1250°C.

31

Biodiesel from Used Soya Oil

INTRODUCTION

The search for an alternative fuel, which promises a harmonious correlation with sustainable development, energy conservation, management, efficiency and environmental preservation, has become highly pronounced in the present context. For the developing countries of the world, fuels of bio-origin can provide a feasible solution to the crises. The fuels of bio-origin may be alcohol, vegetable oils, biomass, and biogas. Some of these fuels can be used directly while others need to be formulated to bring the relevant properties close to conventional fuels. The power used in the agricultural and transportation sector is essentially based on diesel fuels and it is, therefore, essential that alternatives to diesel fuels be developed. Given the recent widespread use of diesel fuel in various sectors, this study concentrates on assessing the viability of using vegetable oils in the existing diesel engines. Vegetable oils have comparable energy density, cetane number, heat of vaporization, and stoichiometric air/fuel ratio with mineral diesel fuel. The large molecular sizes of the component triglycerides result in the oils having higher viscosity compared with that of mineral diesel fuel. The viscosity of liquid fuels affects the flow properties of the fuel, such as spray atomization, consequent vaporization, and air/fuel mixing. The problem of viscosity has an adverse effect on the combustion of vegetable oils in the existing diesel engines. Besides some problems crop up in the associated fuel pump and injector system. An acceptable alternative fuel for engines has to fulfill the environmental and energy security needs without sacrificing operating performance.

BIODIESEL DEVELOPMENT AND CHARACfERIZATION FOR USE AS A FUEL IN COMPRESSION IGNITION ENGINES

Neat vegetable oils pose some problems when subjected to prolonged usage in CI engine. These problems are attributed to high viscosity, low volatility and polyunsaturated character of the neat vegetable oils. These problems are reduced to minimum by subjecting the vegetable oils to the process of trans–esterification. Various properties of the biodiesel thus developed are evaluated and compared in ·relation to that of conventional diesel oil. These tests for biodiesel and diesel oil include density, viscosity, flash point, aniline point/cetane number, calorific value, etc. The prepared biodiesel was then subjected to performance and emission tests in order to evaluate its actual performance, when used as a diesel engine fuel.

Methanol and ethanol are two abundantly available alternative fuels, which possess the potential to be produced from biomass sources. These fuels can be successfully used as diesel engine fuels by preparing biodiesel. Trans–esterification process utilizes methanol or ethanol and vegetable oils as the process inputs. This indirect route of utilizing alcohol as a diesel engine fuel is definitely a superior route as the toxic emissions containing aldehydes are drastically reduced. The problem of corrosion of various engine parts utilizing alcohol as fuel is also solved by way of trans–esterification.

The present work is carried out using used soya oil by formulating its properties closer to the conventional diesel oil. System design approach has taken care to see that these modified fuels can be utilized in the existing diesel engine without any substantial hardware modifications. The Indian Scenario is different from Europe and USA where refined vegetable oils, waste frying oils and tallow are used to produce biodiesel. In India, non-edible oils are likely the preferred feed stock. India is producing around 6.7 x 10^6 tones of non-edible oils such as linseed, castor, karanji (Pongamia glabra), neem (Azadirachta indica), palash (Butea monosperma), and kusum (Schlelchera trijuga). Some of these oils produced even now are not being properly utilized, and it has been estimated that some other plant-based forest derived oils have a much higher production potential. But it is just a fraction of diesel required.

BIODIESEL BY TRANS–ESTERIFICATION

Biodiesel fuel can be made from new or used vegetable oils and animal fats, which are non-toxic, biodegradable, renewable resources. Fats and oils are chemically reacted with an alcohol (methanol is the usual choice) to produce chemical compounds known as fatty acid methyl esters. Biodiesel is the name given to these esters when they're intended for use as fuel. Glycerol (used in pharmaceuticals and cosmetics, among other markets) is produced as a co-product.

Biodiesel can be produced by a variety of esterification technologies. The oil and fats are filtered and pre–processed to remove water and contaminants. If free fatty acids are present, they can be removed or transformed into biodiesel using special pre–treatment technologies. The pre–treated oils and fats are then mixed with an alcohol (usually methanol) and a catalyst (usually sodium or potassium hydroxide). The oil molecules (triglycerides) are broken apart and reformed into esters and glycerol, which are then separated from each other and purified. Approximately 55% of the biodiesel industry in USA can use any fat or oil feedstock, including recycled cooking grease. The other half of the industry is limited to vegetable oils, the least expensive of which is soy oil. The soy industry has been the driving force behind biodiesel commercialization because of excess production capacity, product surpluses, and declining prices. Similar issues apply to the recycled grease and animal fats industry, even though these feed stocks are less expensive compared to soy oils.

EXPERIMENTAL SETUP

Reaction or trans–esterifaction was carried out in a system, as shown in Figure 31.1. Reactor consisted of spherical flask, which was put inside the heat jacket. Oil was used as medium of heat transfer from heat jacket to the reactor. Thermostat was a part of heat jacket, which maintain the temperature of oil and in turn the temperature of the reactants at a desired value. The reaction was carried at around 65–70°C. Spherical flask consisted of four openings. The center one was used for putting stirrer in the reactor. The motor propelled the stirrer. Thermometer was put inside the second opening to continuously monitor the temperature of the reaction. Alcohol was vapourized during the reaction so the condenser was put in the third opening to reflux the vapours back to the reactor to prevent any reactant loss. Fourth opening was used for filling reactants to the reactor.

Biodiesel's Physical Characteristics:

Specific gravity	0.87 to 0.89
Kinematic viscosity @ 40°C	3.7 to 5.8
Cetane number	46 to 70
Higher heating value (btu/lb)	16,928 to 17,996

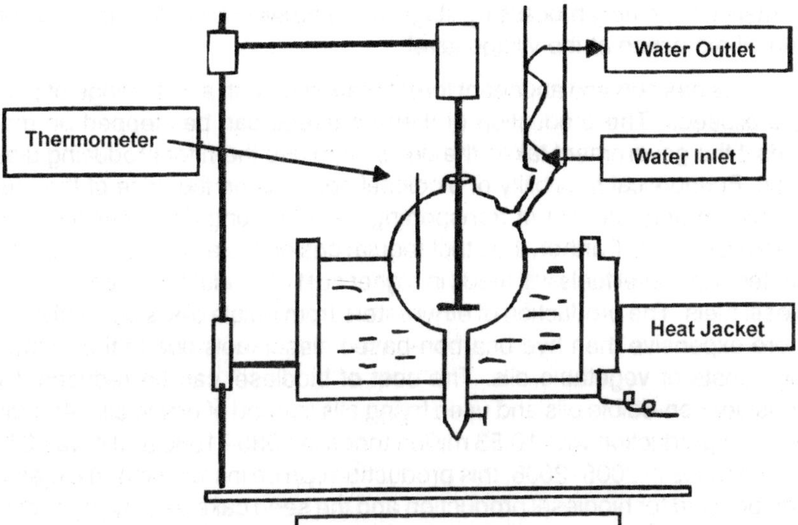

Experimental Setup

Fig. 31.1.

Sulphur, wt%p	0.0 to .0024
Cloud point °C	-11 to 16
Pour point °C	-15 to 13
Iodine number	60 to 135
Lower heating value (btu/lb)	15,700 to 16,735

FEASIBILITY FOR PRODUCTION OF BIODIESEL FROM USED OIL

According to an economic survey conducted by Government of India the cultivation land area of about 175 million hacter has been classified as waste or degraded land which is suitable for cultivation of edible and non–edible oil seeds. Even if 100 million hacter of such land is brought under cultivation, 150 metric tones of seed can be produced which yield upto 37.5 metric tones of oil which is almost 90 % of amount of the diesel being consumed in the country. The by–product such as seed cake which is used as cattle feed, glycerin is used in pharmaceutical industry and soap residue. Part of unemployment problem can also be solved during production. of biodiesel. The center project will be community and farmer driven from plantation to primary processing stage involving seed collection, procurement and oil extraction at the village level.

India has rich and abundant forest resources with a wide range of plants and oilseeds. The production of these oilseeds can be stepped up many folds if the government takes the decision to use them for producing diesel fuels. Economical feasibility of biodiesel depends on the price of the crude petroleum and the cost of transporting diesel to long distances to remote markets in India. Further, the strict regulations on the aromatics and sulphur contents in diesel fuels will result in higher cost of production of conventional diesel fuels. The production of ethyl esters from edible oils is currently much more expensive than hydrocarbon-based diesel fuels due to the relatively high costs of vegetable oils. The cost of biodiesel can be reduced if we consider non-edible oils and used frying oils instead of edible oils. An edible oil seed production was 10.83 million tones in 1985– 1986 and it was 27.28 million tones in 2005–2006, this production can be increased and excess oil can be used for biodiesel production and the seed cake as a by product can used as a cattle feed which is also the problem in many states in India. The soy industry has been the driving force behind biodiesel commercialization because of excess production capacity, product surpluses, and declining prices. Soya seed farming required less water and its cost makes soya the good option for biodiesel production.

With the mushrooming of fast food centers and restaurants in India, it is expected that considerable amounts of used-frying oils will be discarded into the drains. These can be used for making biodiesel, thus helping to reduce the cost of water treatment in the sewerage system and assisting in the recycling of resources.

Acid oil, which is cheaper than both raw and refined oils, is a major by-product of the alkali refining industries and is a potential raw material for making biodiesel.

DRIVING TOWARDS THE CLEANER WORLD

The car industry has taken a good step toward in the development of alternative fuel drive system. Most modern engine is quite capable of running with 5 to 10% ethanol additive to petrol and 5 to 20% biodiesel to diesel. This will not save our currency required for importing the fuel but also reduce pollution.

Biodiesel is a domestically produced, renewable fuel that can be manufactured from vegetable oils or recycled restaurant greases. Biodiesel is safe, biodegradable, and reduces serious air pollutants such as particulates, carbon monoxide, hydrocarbons, and air toxies. Blends of 20% biodiesel with 80% petroleum diesel (B20) can be used in unmodified diesel engines, or biodiesel can be used in its pure form (B100), but may require certain engine modifications to avoid maintenance and performance problems.

The use of biodiesel decreases the solid carbon fraction of particulate matter (since the oxygen in biodiesel enables more complete combustion to CO_2) and reduces the sulfate fraction (biodiesel contains less than 24 ppm sulfur), while the soluble, or hydrocarbon, fraction stays the same or increases. Therefore, biodiesel works well with new technologies such as catalysts (which reduce the soluble fraction of diesel particulate but not the solid carbon fraction), particulate traps, and exhaust gas recirculation. Emissions of nitrogen oxides increase with the concentration of biodiesel in the fuel. Some biodiesel produces more nitrogen oxides than others, and some additives have shown promise in modifying the increases. More R & D is needed to resolve this issue. Biodiesel has physical properties very similar to conventional diesel. Emission properties, however, are better for biodiesel than for conventional diesel.

The flash point of a fuel is defined as the temperature to which the fuel must be heated to produce a mixture that will ignite when exposed to a spark or flame. If the flash point of a fuel is too low, the fuel is considered a fire hazard, which is prone to flashing, possible ignition, and even explosion. The flash point of biodiesel has been tested and reported by various sources. The flash point of biodiesel blends increases as the percentage of biodiesel increases. Therefore pure biodiesel or blends of biodiesel with petroleum diesel is safer to store, handle, and use than conventional diesel fuel. In addition, pure biodiesel is essentially sulfur free and results in a total reduction of SO_2 emissions as well sulfate aerosols in particulate matter. These reductions should assist in increasing both vehicle and catalyst life over time.

32

Characterization of Vegetable Oils for Biodiesel Production

INTRODUCTION

The use of vegetable oils in place of diesel in conventional engines has led to problems such as carbon deposits, oil ring sticking and gelling of lubricating oils. This has necessitated the transformation of vegetable oils into biodiesel prior to their introduction into diesel engines. There are several proven ways of converting vegetable oils into fuel grade products. Physical techniques include dilution and micro-emulsification, whereas catalytic cracking, pyrolysis and trans–esterification are prominent among the chemical methods, of these methods, trans–esterification has found widespread application owing to its relative simplicity and cost advantage. Methyl and Ethyl Esters of different vegetable oils have been found to possess similar fuel properties to those of petro–diesel but with significantly reduced pollutant emissions levels. However, the high cost of production of biodiesel has hampered its widespread application.

Apart from high cost of production arising from high prices of vegetable oil raw materials, another major factor militating against the desired diffusion of biodiesel production and marketing in Nigeria is the availability at relatively low prices of fossil diesel in the country. However, with the country's proven petroleum reserves stabilizing at around 4,635 MMTOE (equivalent to 45 years supply at current rate of exploitation)as new finds appear scarcer, it becomes clear that alternative energy sources, especially biofuels will play an increasing role in the transport sector energy mix. Indeed, fossil diesel prices have been increasing steadily in the country for the past few years to its current value of 65 Naira/litre (about $0.50 per litre). This becomes more imperative when considered along with the country's desire to comply with recommendations of the Kyoto Protocol in future. Previous research work carried out to assess the potentials of palm oil and palm kernel oil as feedstocks for biodiesel production as reported by Anyanwu et al. (2005) has shown good results but the major setback to the idea is the fact that these oils are important edible and industrial oils. This has necessitated the characterization of other vegetable oils such as which are also grown in Nigeria in appreciable quantities.

The present work is, therefore, focused on the study of the aforementioned oils with a view to assessing their potentials as feedstocks for biodiesel production. The inclusion of soybean oil, which is a well established biodiesel raw material particularly in the United States of America was aimed at revalidating its characteristics in comparison with available literature data, which are considered as benchmark figures.

MATERIALS AND METHODS

Although the present work envisages the determination of physical, chemical and fuel properties of both vegetable oils and their corresponding methyl esters, only the physical and chemical properties of the oils were

TABLE 32.1

ASTM D 6751-02 Requirements.

S/No.	Property	Method	Limits	Units
1.	Flash point, closed cup	ASTM D 93	130 min	°C
2.	Water and sediment	D 2709	0.050 max	% volume
3.	Kinematic viscosity, 40°C	D 445	1.9–6.0	mm^2/s
4.	Sulphated ash	D 874	0.020 max	wt. %
5.	Total Sulphur	D 5453	0.05 max	wt. %
6.	Copper strip corrosion	D 130	No.3 max	
7.	Cetane number	D 613	47 min	
8.	Cloud point	D 2500		°C
9.	Carbon residue	D 4530	0.050 max	wt. %
10.	Acid number	D 664	0.80 max	mg KOH/g
11.	Free glycerol	D 6584	0.020	wt. %
12.	Total glycerol	D 6584	0.240	wt. %

assessed at this stage. These are presented in the current communication. Some literature data obtained through recommended standard experimental procedures were also included in the present work. The standard test methods, limits of each parameter determined as well as their units are shown in Table 32.1.

Brief Outline of the Standard Methods

Acid Number

This is essentially the amount of Potassium Hydroxide (KOH) required to neutralize the free fatty acids present in 1 g of the oil sample. The standard test recommended for its determination is ASTM D664, which covers various procedures for the determination of acid constituents of petroleum products and lubricants. The method involves dissolving the sample in a mixture of toluene and iso-propanol that contains a small amount of water. The metre readings are then plotted against the respective volumes of titrating solution and the end points are taken at well defined inflection in the resulting curve (i.e. where it is nearly vertical).

Then, the acid number is given by the expression

$$\text{Acid Number} = 56.1M\,(A\text{-}B)/W \quad \dots (1)$$

Where,

M = Molar concentration of KOH,

A = Volume of KOH needed to reach end-point, corresponding to blank buffer (ml)

B = Volume corresponding to A for blank titration (ml)

W = Mass of sample (g).

Viscosity

Kinematic viscosity, which is essentially a measure of the resistive flow of a fluid under gravity was determined using Cannon-Fenske Routine Viscometer corresponding to ASTM D446 standard method.

Dynamic viscosity data were obtained from the measured Kinematic viscosity figures using the relationship between the two parameters :

$$\eta = \rho \upsilon \quad \dots (2)$$

Where,

= Dynamic viscosity (cP),

= Kinematic viscosity (cSt),

= Density (g/cm^3) at the same temperature.

Elemental Composition

Characterization of elemental composition was also carried out according to standard methods using Perkin-Elmer Series II CHNS/, model TSD 2400 analyser.

Heating Value

Heating value for the vegetable oils were determined using Ika Bomb Calorimeter C 1000 at adiabatic conditions.

Density (Specific Gravity)

Density measurement was carried out using DMA 48 Density meter.

Sulphated Ash

This is a measure of the residue left after the sample has been carbonized at 775 ±25 °C and subsequent residue treated with sulphuric acid. Determination of sulphated ash is done according to ASTM D874 specifications.

Iodine Value

The test measures the degree of unsaturation of a given oil sample and is defined as the number of milligrams of iodine absorbed per gram of oil sample. Thus the greater the total unsaturation, the higher is the iodine number.

Table 32.2

Determined physical and chemical properties of oils.

S. No	Vegetable Oil	Kinematic Viscosity	Heating Value	Specific Gravity	Elemental Composition %			
		mm^2/s	MJ/Kg		C	H	N	O*
1.	Melon Seed Oil	32.5	38.9030	0.9036	68.73	10.60	0.31	20.36
2.	Soybean Oil	36.0	38.0038	0.9072	77.53	12.19	0.36	9.92
3.	Castor Oil	80.2	35.0867	0.9314	69.80	11.81	0.34	18.05
4.	Palm Oil	48.2	38.1999	0.8963	80.18	7.60	0.13	12.09
5.	Palm kernel Oil	29.7	36.2528	0.9043	72.13	7.77	0.14	19.96

• Oxygen content was obtained by difference, i.e. (100-C-H-N).

RESULTS AND DISCUSSION

Results obtained for each of the tested parameters are shown in Table 32.2, whereas fatty acids composition as well as other properties of the vegetable oils obtained for some Nigerian oils are presented in Tables 32.3 and 32.4, respectively.

It can be observed from Table 32.2 that Melon Seed oil possesses the highest heating value among the oils studied. In addition, it has one of the lowest viscosities, which distinguishes it as the most suitable feedstock for fuel production. Its saturated fatty acid composition is also very favourable for biodiesel production via trans–esterification. On the other hand, Castor Oil has the highest viscosity and the lowest heating value, which implies that it is not a suitable raw material for biodiesel production, even though it has a favourable balance of unsaturated fatty acid composition.

TABLE 32.3

Fatty Acid Composition (%) of Various Vegetable Oils

Fatty acid	Red Palm	Palm Kernel	Melon Seed Oil	Soybean	Castor Oil
Capronic 6 : 0	-	0.2	-	-	-
Caprylic 8 : 0	-	3.3	-	-	-
Capric 10 : 0	-	3.5	-	-	-
Lauric 12 : 0	0.2	47.8	-	-	-
Myristic J4 ; 0	1.1	16.3	-	0.1	0.1
Palmitic 16 ; 0	44.0	8.5	12.0	11.0	11.6
Stearic 18 : 0	4.5	2.4	17.0	4.0	3.1
Oleic 18 ; 1	39.2	15.4	17.5	23.4	48.5
Linoleic 18 : 2	10.1	2.4	53.5	53.2	31.4
Linolenic 18 ; 3	0.4	-	-	7.8	-
Arachidic 20 ; 0	0.1	0.1	-	-	1.5
Saturates	49.9	82.1	29.0	15.1	16.3
Mono–unsaturates	39.2	15.4	17.5	23.4	48.5
Polyunsaturates	10.5	2.4	53.5	61.0	31.4

TABLE 32.4

Characteristics of Some Vegetable Oils

Vegetale Oil	Seed Oil	Melting	Refractive	Iodine	Acid
Melon Seed Oil	35–45	-6 to 15	NA	115.6	200
Soybean Oil	11–25	-8 to -18	1.4765 @15°C	120–141	198
Castor Oil	35–55	13	1.4800	81–91	192
Palm Oil	30–70	27 to 54	1.4556	44–58	204-207
Palm kernel Oil	40-50	24 to 31	1.4505	14–22	258-264

Further, the potential for expansion of the quantities of the respective oils produced annually appears to favour melon seed oil, which grows almost all over the country and is not among the major edible oils consumed in Nigeria. Melon seed oil is therefore a potential feedstock for biodiesel production in Nigeria.

33

Process of Biodiesel Production

As per an estimate, India consumed about 40.34 million tones of diesel in 2000-2001, which was 43.2% of the total consumption of petroleum products, and two-thirds of the demand was met by import costing about Rs. 200 billion. With an expected growth rate of diesel consumption of more than 14% per annum, shrinking crude oil reserves and limited refining capacity, India will have to depend heavily on imports of crude. From the point of view of protecting the global environment and the concern for long term supplies of conventional diesel fuels, it becomes necessary to develop alternative fuels comparable with conventional fuels. Diesel fuel is largely utilized in the transport, agriculture, commercial, domestic, and industrial sectors for the generation of power/mechanical energy, and the substitution of even a small fraction of total consumption by alternative fuels will have a significant impact on the economy and the environment. Of the alternative fuels, biodiesel obtained from vegetable oils holds good promises as an eco-friendly alternative to diesel fuel.

Literature shows that a number of studies of acid and base catalyzed trans–esterification have been carried out. Freedman and Pryde and Kusy achieved more than 95% fatty ester yield in 1 h using alkaline catalyst. Freedman et al. found that for maximum ester yield, the requisites are acid value less than 1 mg KOH/g, oil with moisture free alcohol and vegetable oil. Nye and Southwell have studied the effect of catalyst on methyl and ethyl esters of rapeseed oil at room temperature. Boocock et al. developed a new method, which produced methyl ester much faster. Schwab et al. and Liu compared acid and base catalysts. Nye et al. compared base and acid catalysts to produce methyl esters from used frying oil, Kusdiana and Saka have studied the kinetics of trans–esterification of rapeseed oil to biodiesel fuel using super–critical methanol. The present paper is an attempt to review the possibilities of using neat vegetable oils and biodiesel, the processes available, fuel characteristics, performance analysis and economic analysis of biodiesel production,

ALTERNATIVE DIESEL FUELS

Alternative fuels should be easily available, environment friendly and techno–economically competitive. One of such fuels is triglycerides (vegetable oils/animal fats) and their derivatives. Vegetable oils, being renewable, are widely available from a variety of sources and have low sulphur contents close to zero, and hence cause less environmental damage (lower greenhouse effect) than diesel. Besides, vegetable oils and their derivatives are produced widely in the country for food and other purposes.

Table 33.1
Production of Oilseeds in 2002-2003 in India

Oilseed	Production (million tones) World	Production (million tones) India	Total Oil availability (million tone)	% Recovery	Oil Cost (Rs. per tone)
Soyabean	123.2	4.30	0.63	17	4300
Cottonseed	34.3	4.60	0.39	11	3200
Groundnut	19.3	4.60	0.73	40	6200
Sunflower	25.2	1.32	0.46	35	5360
Rapeseed	34.7	4.30	1.37	33	5137
Sesame	2.5	0.62	-	-	6800
Palm Kernels	4.8	-	-	-	-
Copra	4.9	0.65	0.42	65	3035
Linseed	2.6	0.20	0.09	43	-
Castor	1.3	0.51	0.21	42	-
Niger	0.8	0.08	0.02	30	-
Rice Bran	-	-	0.60	15	2000
Total	**253.6**	**21.18**	**1.92**		

Triglyceride as Diesel Fuels

The use of vegetable oils, such as palm, soyabean, sunflower, peanut, and olive oil, as alternative fuels for diesel engines dates back almost nine decades, but due to the rapid decline in crude oil reserves, it is again being promoted in many countries. Depending upon the climate and soil conditions, different countries are looking for different types of vegetable oils as substitutes for diesel fuels. For example, soyabean oil in the US, rapeseed and sunflower oils in Europe, palm oil in South-East Asia (mainly Malaysia and Indonesia) and coconut oil in the Philippines are being considered. The production of oil seeds, percentage oil recovery and their respective cost are given in Table 33.1 , which indicates that the use of vegetable oils as sources of diesel would require more efforts to increase the production of oil seeds and to develop new and more productive plant species with high yield of oil.

Besides, some species of plants yielding non-edible oils, e.g. jatropha, karanji and pongamia may play a significant role in providing resources. Both these plants may be grown on a massive scale on agricultural/degraded/ waste lands, so that the chief resource may be available to produce biodiesel on 'farm scale'.

Chemical Compositions

Vegetable oils, also known as triglycerides, have the chemical structure given in Fig. 33.1 comprise of 98% triglycerides and small amounts of mono- and diglycerides.

Triglycerides are esters of three molecules of fatty acids and one of glycerol and contain substantial amounts of oxygen in their structure. The fatty acids vary in their carbon chain length and in the number of double bonds.

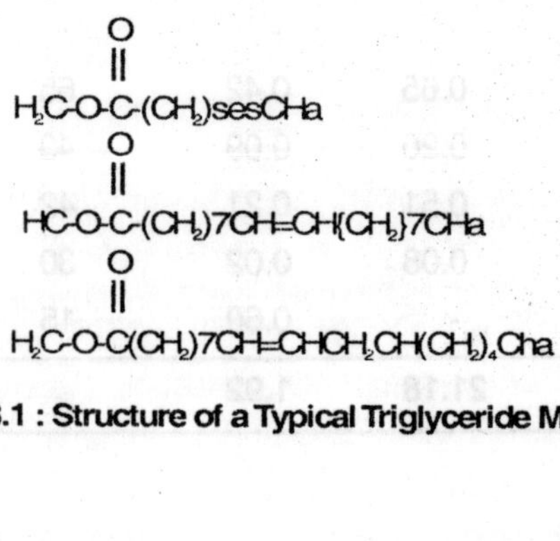

Fig. 33.1 : Structure of a Typical Triglyceride Molecule.

TABLE 33.2
Chemical Structure of Common Fatty Acids

Name of fatty/ acid	Chemical name of fatty acids	structure (xx : y)	Formula
Lauric	Dodecanoic	12 ; 0	$C_{12}H_{24}O_2$
Myristic	Tetradecanoic	14 : 0	$C_{14}H_{28}O_2$
Palmitic	Hexadecanoic	16 : 0	$C_{16}H_{32}O_2$
Stearic	Octadecanoic	18 : 0	$C_{18}H_{36}O_2$
Arachidic	Eicosanoic	20 ; 0	$C_{20}H_{40}O_2$
Behenic	Docosanoic	22 : 0	$C_{22}H_{44}O_2$
Lignoceric	Tetracosanoic	24 : 0	$C_{24}H_{48}O_2$
Oleic	cis-9-Octadecenoic	18 : 1	$C_{18}H_{34}O_2$
Linoleic	cis-9,cis-12-Octadecadienoic	18 : 2	$C_{18}H_{32}O_2$
Linolenic	cis-9,cis-12,cis-15-Octadecatrienoic	18: 3	$C_{18}H_{30}O_2$
Erucle	cis-13-Docosenoic	22 : 1	$C_{32}H_{42}O_2$

xx indicates number of carbons, and y number of double bonds in the fatty acid chain.

Different types of oils have different types of fatty acids. The empirical formula· and structure of various fatty acids present in vegetable oils are given in Table 33.2.

Properties of Vegetable Oils as Fuel

The fuel properties of vegetable oils as listed in Table 33.3 indicate that the kinematics viscosity of vegetable oils varies in the range of 30–40 cSt at 38°C. The high viscosity of these oils is due to their large molecular mass in the range of 600–900, which is about 20 times more higher than that of diesel fuel. The flash point of vegetable oils is very high (above 200°C). The volumetric heating values are in the range of 39–40 MJ/kg, as compared to diesel fuels (about 45 MJ/kg). The presence of chemically bound oxygen in vegetable oils lower their heating values by about 10%. The cetane numbers are in the range of 32–40.

TABLE 33.3
Properties of Vegetable Oils

Vegetable Oil	Kinematic Viscosity At 38°C	Cetane No. (°C)	Heating Value MJ/kg	Cloud Point (°C)	Pour Point (°C)	Flash Point (°C)	Density (kg/l)
Corn	34.9	37.6	39.5	K1.1	K40.0	277	0.9095
Cottonseed	33.5	41.8	39.5	1.7	K15.0	234	0.9148
Crambe	53.6	44.6	40.5	10.0	K12.2	274	0.9048
Linseed	27.2	34.6	39.3	1.7	K15.0	241	0.9236
Peanut	39.6	41.8	39.8	12.8	K6.7	271	0.9026
Rapeseed	37.0	37.6	39.7	K3.9	K31.7	246	0.9115
Safflower	31.3	41.3	39.5	18.3	K6.7	260	0.9144
Sesame	35.5	40.2	39.3	K3.9	K9.4	260	0.9133
Soya bean	32.6	37.9	39.6	K3.9	K12.2	254	0.9138
Sunflower	33.9	37.1	39.6	7.2	K15.0	274	0.9161
Palm	39.6	42.0	-	31.0	-	267	0.9180
Babassu	30.3	38.0	-	20.0	-	150	0.9460
Diesel	3.06	50	43.8	-	K16	76	0.855

Utilization of Vegetable Oils as Fuels

Use of Vegetable Oils as Diesel Fuel

It has been found that this neat vegetable oils can be used as diesel fuels in conventional diesel engines, but this leads to a number of problems related to the type and grade of oil and local climatic conditions. The injection, atomization and combustion characteristics of vegetable oils in diesel engines are significantly different from those of diesel. The high viscosity of vegetable oils interferes with the injection process and leads to poor fuel atomization. The inefficient mixing of oil with air contributes to incomplete combustion, leading to heavy smoke emission, and the high flash point attributes to lower volatility characteristics. These disadvantages, coupled with the reactivity of unsaturated vegetable oils, do not allow the engipe to operate trouble free for longer period of time. These problems can be solved, if the vegetable oils are chemically modified to biodiesel, which is similar in characteristics to diesel.

Use of Biodiesel

Biodiesel is defined as the monoalkyl esters of long-chain fatty acids derived from renewable feedstock, such as vegetable oil or animal fats, for use in compression-ignition engines. Biodiesel has been reported as a possible substitute or extender for conventional diesel and is comprised of fatty acid methyl/ethyl esters, obtained from triglycerides by trans–esterification with methanol/ethanol, respectively. Biodiesel is compatible with conventional diesel and both can be blended in any proportion. Preparation of biodiesel from sunflower oil, used frying oil, jatropha oil, karanji (pongamia) oil, etc. as a source of triglycerides has been reported.

Fuel Properties of Biodiesel

The properties of biodiesel and diesel fuels, as given in Table 33.4, show many similarities, and therefore, biodiesel is rated as a strong candidate as an alternative to diesel. This is due to the fact that the conversion of triglycerides into methyl or ethyl esters through the trans–esterification process reduces the molecular weight to one-third, reduces the viscosity by about one-eighth, and increase the volatility marginally. Biodiesel contains 10-11 % oxygen (w/w), thereby enhancing the combustion process in an engine. It has also been reported that the use of tertiary fatty amines and amides can be effective in enhancing the ignition quality of the biodiesel without having any negative effect on its cold flow properties. However,

TABLE 33.4
Properties of Biodiesel from Different Oils

Vegetable Oil	Kinematic viscosity At 38°C	Cetane No. (°C)	Heating Value MJ/kg	Cloud Point (°C)	Pour Point (°C)	Flash Point (°C)	Density (kg/l)
Peanut	4.9	54	33.6	5	-	176	0.883
Soyabean	4.5	45	33.5	1	K7	178	0.885
Babassu	3.6	63	31.8	4	-	127	0.875
Palm	5.7	62	33.5	13	-	164	0.880
Sunflower	4.6	49	33.5	1	-	183	0.860
Tallow	-	-	-	12	9	96	-
Diesel	3.06	50	43.8	-	K16	76	0.855
20% biodiesel blend	13.2	51	43.2		K16	128	0.859

starting problems persist in cold conditions. Further, biodiesel has low volumetric heating values (about 12%), a high cetane number and a high flash point. The cloud points and flash points of biodiesel are 15–25°C higher than those of diesel.

PROCESS OF BIODIESEL PRODUCTION

Simple Transesterification Reaction

Trans–esterification of vegetable oils with simple alcohol has long been the preferred method for producing biodiesel. In general, there are two methods of trans–esterification.

One method simply uses a catalyst and the other is without a catalyst. The former method has a long history of development and the biodiesel produced by this method is now available in North America, Japan and some Western European Countries.

Chemistry of Trans–esterification Reaction

The overall transesterification reaction is given by three consecutive and reversible equations as below :

Triglyceride + ROH — catalyst — Diglyceride + RICOOR

Diglyceride + ROH — catalyst — Monoglyceride + RIICOOR

Monoglyceride + ROH — catalyst — Glycerol + RIIICOOR,

The first step is the conversion of triglycerides to, diglycerides, followed by the conversion of diglycerides to monoglycerides, and of monoglycerides to glycerol, yielding one methyl ester molecule per mole of glyceride at each step.

The overall chemical reaction of the transesterification process is

```
CH-COORI                              CH2OH     RICOOR
|              + 3ROH - Catalyst      |            +
CH-COORII                             CHOH      RIICOOR
|                                     |            +
CH3-COORIII                           CH2OH     RIIICOOR
Triglyceride Methanol                 Glycerol  Biodiesel
```

where RI, RII and RIII are long-chain hydrocarbons which may be the same or different with R=-CH_3/C_2H_5:

As seen above, the trans–esterification is an equilibrium reaction in which excess alcohol is required to drive the reaction close to completion.

Fortunately, the equilibrium constant favours the formation of methyl esters such that only a 5 : 1 molar ratio of methanol : triglycerides is sufficient for 95-98% yield of ester. It might be anticipated that in such a system, glycerol would play–a major role in achieving conversions close to 100%. Several catalysts were tried for the purpose of trans–esterification by several workers, e.g. magnesium, calcium oxides and carbonates of basic and acidic macro-reticular organic resin, alkaline alumina, phase transfer catalysts, sulphuric acids, p-toluene sulphonic acid, and dehydrating agents as cocatalysts. The catalysts reported to be effective at room temperature were alkoxides and hydroxides.

During methanolysis, two distinct phases are present as the solubility of the oil in methanol is low and the reaction mixture needs vigorous stirring. Optimum reaction conditions for the maximum yield of methvl esters have been reported to be 0.8% (based on weight of oil) potassium hyuroxide catalyst and 100% excess methanol at room temperature for 2.5 h. Glycerol phase separation does not occur when 67% of the theoretical amount of methanol is used. The excess methanol, however, is removed by distillation. Traces of methanol, KOH, free fatty acids (FFAs), chlorophyll, etc., go into the glycerin phase, which can be processed in two stages. Glycerin of 90–95% purity is obtained in the first stage and of 98% purity in the second stage. The basic process schematic of biodiesel production is given in Fig. 33.2. The energetics have indicated that about 50 kW of electricity per tone of biodiesel is required, of which 60–70% is consumed for the production of glycerin. The process requires mixing of vegetable oil with a mixture prepared

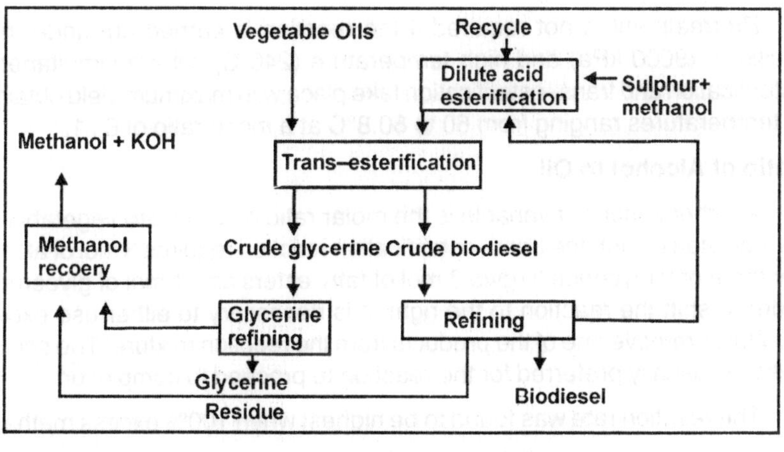

Fig. 33.2 : Basic Technology.

by dissolving KOH catalyst in methanol and heating at 70°C with stirring for 1 h. The mixture is allowed to settle under gravity. The glycerin, being heavier, settles down in the bottom layer and the upper layer constitutes the biodiesel (esters). The glycerin is separated and the esters are washed with water for catalyst recovery. The biodiesel layer is finally dried using silica gel and it is now ready for blending with diesel in various proportions for engine operation. The blend, for convenience, is referred to as Bxx, where XX indicates the amount of biodiesel in percentage in the blend (i.e. B-20 blend is 20% biodiesel and 80% diesel).

PROCESS VARIABLES

The most important variables that influence the trans–esterification reaction are :

1. Reaction temperature.
2. Ratio of alcohol to vegetable oil.
3. Catalyst.
4. Mixing intensity.
5. Purity of reactants.

Reaction Temperature

The literature has revealed that the rate of reaction is strongly influenced by the reaction temperature. However, the reaction is conducted close to the boiling point of methanol (60–70°C) at atmospheric pressure for a given time. Such mild reaction conditions require the removal of free fatty acids from the oil by refining or pre–esterification. Therefore, degummed and deacidified oil is used as feedstock.

Pretreatment is not required if the reaction is carried out under high pressure (9000 kPa) and high temperature (240°C), where simultaneous esterification and trans–esterification take place with maximum yield obtained at temperatures ranging from 60 to 80.8°C at a molar ratio of 6 : 1.

Ratio of Alcohol to Oil

Another important variable is the molar ratio of alcohol to vegetable oil. As indicated earlier, the trans–esterification reaction requires 3 mol of alcohol per mole of triglyceride to give 3 mol of fatty esters and 1 mol of glycerol. In order to shift the reaction to the right, it is necessary to either use excess alcohol or remove one of the products from the reaction mixture. The second option is usually preferred for the reaction to proceed to completion.

The reaction rate was found to be highest when 100% excess methanol was used. A molar ratio of 6 : 1 is normally used in industrial processes to obtain methyl ester yields higher than 98% (w/w).

Catalysts

Alkali metal alkoxides are found to be more effective trans–esterification catalysts compared to acidic catalysts. Sodium alkoxides are the most efficient catalysts, although KOH and NaOH can also be used. Trans–methylation occurs in the presence of both alkaline and acidic catalysts. As they are less corrosive to industrial equipment, alkaline catalysts are preferred in industrial processes. A concentration in the range of 0.5-1% (w/w) has been found to yield 94–99% conversion to vegetable oil esters, and further increase in catalyst concentration does not affect the conversion but adds to extra cost, as the catalyst needs to be removed from the reaction mixture after completion of the reaction.

Mixing intensity

It has been observed that during the trans–esterification reaction, the reactants initially form a two-phase liquid system. The mixing effect has been found to play a significant role in the slow rate of the reaction. As phase separation ceases, mixing becomes insignificant. The effect of mixing on the kinetics of the trans–esterification process forms the basis for process scale-up and design.

Purity of Reactants

Impurities in the oil affect the conversion level considerably. It is reported that about 65–84% conversion into esters using crude vegetable oils has been obtained as compared to 94–97% yields refined oil under the same reaction conditions. The free fatty acids in the crude oils have been found to interfere with the catalyst. This problem can be solved if the reaction is carried out under high temperature and pressure conditions.

SUPER–CRITICAL METHANOL TRANS–ESTERIFICATION

The simple trans–esterification process discussed above is confronted with two problems, i.e. the process is relatively time consuming and it needs separation of the catalyst and saponified impurities from the biodiesel. The first problem is due to the phase separation of the vegetable oil/methanol mixture, which may be dealt with by vigorous stirring. These problems are not faced in the supercritical methanol method of trans–esterification. This is perhaps due to the fact that the tendency of two-phase formation of vegetable oil/methanol mixture is not encountered and a single phase is found due to decrease in the dielectric constant of methanol in the super–critical state. As a result, the reaction was found to be complete in a very short time within 2-4 min. Further, since no catalyst is used, the purification on biodiesel is much easier, trouble free and environment friendly.

The result of trans–esterification of rapeseed oil in the supercritical methanol method has indicated that at temperature of 239°C and pressure of 8.09 MPa, glycerol and methyl esters are obtained as the principal products. Encinar et al. have reported the optimal molar ratio of methanol to cynara oil to be between 4.05 and 5.57, beyond which either the catalytic trans–esterification is incomplete or glycerin separation becomes very difficult. However, a 98% conversion of vegetable oils to methyl esters could be achieved at the molar ratio of 6. When the oil contains a large amount of free fatty acids, a higher molar ratio even up to 45 can be used. It has also been observed that with decrease in molar ratio to a theoretical value of 3, the conversion decreased to 82%.

It has further been observed that under supercritical conditions, the conversion rate of rapeseed oil varies with molar ratio such that a higher molal ratio of MeOH results in increased yield of methyl esters and decreased yields in intermediate products. The study, therefore, concluded that complete conversion with 95% yield took place with a molar ratio of methanol of 42 at a critical temperature of 350°C, whereas a lower molar ratio of 6 or less results in incomplete conversion of rapeseed oil to methyl esters. A study on the effect of temperature at a fixed molar ratio of methanol of 42 indicates that at temperatures of 200 and 230°C, the yield of methyl esters was reported to be about 68 and 70%, respectively, after a reaction time of 1 h. At a temperature of 270°C, the conversion rate is still low, perhaps due to the stability of the supercritical condition (pressure 14 MPa). However, at 300°C, 80% conversion to methyl ester was observed in 240 s. Even at a higher temperature of 400°C, the reaction is almost completed within 120 s, though the decomposition reaction starts taking place due to the thermaldegradation of triglyceride molecules at such a high temperature.

PERFORMANCE OF BIODIESEL IN DIESEL ENGINE

Conventional IC engines can be operated with biodiesel without major modifications. In comparison to diesel, the higher cetane number of biodiesel results in shorter ignition delay and longer combustion duration and hence results in low particulate emissions and minimum carbon deposits on injector nozzles. It is reported that if an engine is operated on biodiesel for a long time, the injection timing may be required to be readjusted for achieving better thermal efficiency. Various blends of biodiesel with diesel have been tried, but B-20 has been found to be the most appropriate blend. Further studies have revealed that biodiesel blends lead to a reduction in smoke opacity, and emission of particulates, unburnt hydrocarbons, carbon dioxide and carbon monoxide, but cause slightly increase in nitrous oxide emissions. It is noteworthy that all the blends have a higher thermal efficiency than diesel and so give improved performance. The effect of the concentration of ester blend on peak thermal efficiency is given in Fig. 33.3. The Figure shows that the ester blend with a concentration of 20% biodiesel gave maximum improvement in peak thermal efficiency, minimum brake specific energy consumption and minimum smoke capacity. Hence, B-20 was recommended as the optimum blend for long-term engine operation.

ENVIRONMENTAL CONSIDERATIONS

In view of environmental considerations, biodiesel is considered 'carbon neutral' because all the carbon dioxide released during consumption had been sequestered from the atmosphere for the growth of vegetable oil crops. Studies have shown that :

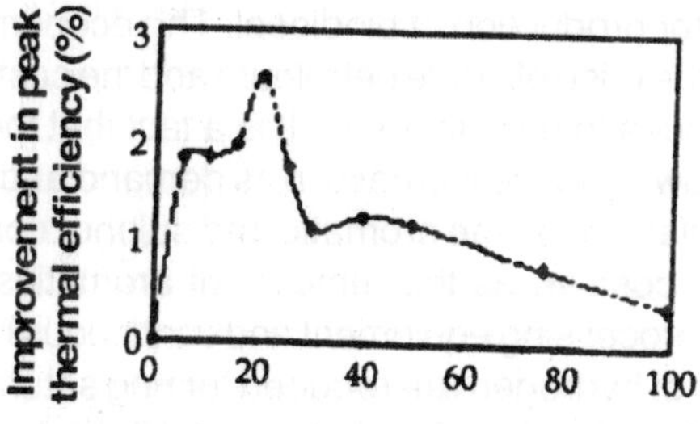

Fig. 33.3 : Improvement in peak thermal efficiency vs. conversion of biodiesel blend.

The combustion of 1:1 of diesel fuel leads to the emission of about 2.6 kg of CO_2 against 1 kg of CO_2/kg of biodiesel, so the use of biodiesel may directly displace this amount of CO_2 when used in engines. The combustion of biodiesel has been reported to emit lesser pollutants compared to diesel. The emission of SO_2, soot, CO, hydrocarbons (HC, polyaromatic hydrocarbons (PAH), and aromatics is given in Fig. 33.4 , which indicates that the engine exhaust contains no SO_2, and shows decreasing emissions of PAH, soot, CO, HC and aromatics.

The NOx emissions are reported to be in the range between G10% as compared to diesel depending on engine's combustion characteristics.

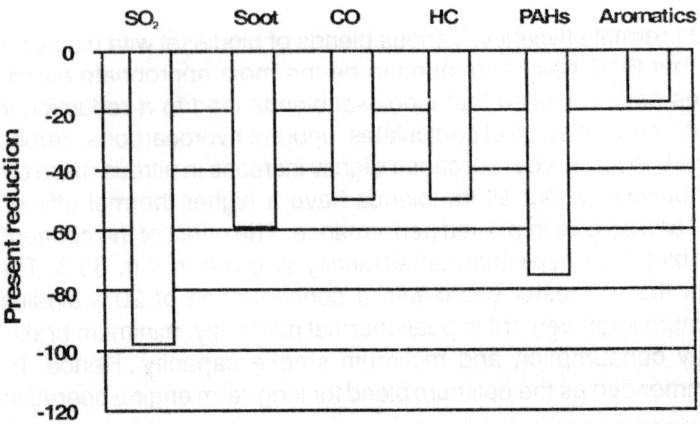

Fig. 33.4 Lower emissions of biodiesel compared with petrodiesel.

ECONOMIC FEASIBILITY OF BIODIESEL

India has rich and abundant resources of edible and non-edible oilseeds, the production of which can be stepped up manifolds if the government provides incentives to farmers for production of biodiesel. The economic feasibility of biodiesel depends on the price of crude petroleum and the cost of transporting diesel over long distances to remote areas. It is a fact that the cost of diesel will increase in future owing to the increase in its demand and limited supply. Further, the strict regulations on the aromatic and sulphur contents of diesel fuels will make diesel costlier, as the removal of aromatics from distillate fractions needs costly processing equipment and continuous high operational cost as large amounts of hydrogen are required for ring saturation. Similarly, reducing the suiphur content is also a big challenge for the industries. Currently, the production of methyl or ethyl esters from edible oils is much more expensive than that of diesel fuels due to the relatively high costs of vegetable oils (about four times the cost of diesel in India). Methyl esters produced from such oils cannot compete economically with diesel fuels unless they are granted protection from tax levies. Under such conditions, tllere is a need to explore alternate feedstocks for the production of biodiesel.

An economic analysis for the production of biodiesel using different types of edible and non-edible oils has been carried out and the results are reported in Table 33.5.

The analysis indicates that linseed oil has the least cost (Rs. 13.56 per litre) and sesame oil has the maximum cost (Rs. 54.00 per litre). The analysis

Table 33.5

Total Cost per litre of biodiesel from various vegetable oils.

Vevetable	Oil cost of vegetable oil per litre (Rs.)	Cost of biodiesel per litre (Rs.)
Groundnut	58	48.28
Mustard	48	38.60
Sesame	64	54.00
Coconut	28	18.61
Safflowe	60	58.26
Soyabean	40	30.26
Sunflower	50	40.26
Linseed	23	13.26
Pongamia oil (non edible oil)	18	10.50
Diesel		22.00

has considered the cost of a plant (Rs. 1,174,000) with an installed capacity 136,500 per year and 10% depreciation.

The operating cost and by-product cost per year are Rs. 4,018,002 and 2,296,000, respectively, with a 10 year life of the plant. Table 33.5 indicates that the cost of biodiesel produced from pongamia oil is the least, i.e. Rs.10.50, followed by linseed oil (Rs. 13.50) and coconut oil (Rs. 18.61) as compared to diesel (Rs. 22) per litre.

The cost can be reduced further if we consider non-edible oils, used frying oils and acid oils instead of edible oils. Non-edible oils from sources such as neem, mahua, pongamia, karanji, babassu, jatropha, etc. are easily available in many parts of the world including India, and are very cheap compared to edible oils. With the mushrooming of fast food centers and restaurants in India, it is expected that considerable amounts of used frying oil will be discarded which can be diverted for biodiesel production, and thus may help reduce the cost of water treatment in the sewerage system and assisting in the recycling of resources. Acid oil, which is cheaper than both raw and refined oils, is a major by-product of the alkali refining industries and is a potential raw material for making biodiesel.

INSTITUTIONS WORKING ON BIODIESEL IN INDIA

Various research institutes are doing R & D on various aspects of resource production, process development and utilization in engines as well as environmental aspects of the use of biodiesel. The following institutions are working in this area :

S. No.	Name of institute/organization	Area of work
1.	Indian Institute of Science, Bangalore (Karnataka)	Promoting cultivation of pongamia.
2.	Central Salt and Marine Research Institute, Bhavnagar (Gujarat)	Cultivation of jatropha.
3.	Indian Institutes of Petroleum, Dehradun (Uttaranchal)	Performance testing of transport buses cultivation of jatropha, neem and karanji.
4.	Delhi College of Engineering, New Delhi	Production.
5.	Harcourt Butler Technological Institute, Kanpur	Production.
6.	Alternate Hydro Energy Centre, Indian Institute of Technology, Roorkee	Kinetics of transesterification.
7.	Indian Oil Corporation Limited, Faridabad	Process development.
8.	Bapuji Institute of Engineering and Technology, Davangere	Engine application.

34

Liquid Fuels from Biomass and Urban Waste

INTRODUCTION

Amongst different technologies for bio-fuels production using renewable sources, the biomass the urban waste gasification process integrated with the Fischer-Tropsch process appears to be the most appropriate one. In order to optimise the feedstock's recovery at the local level, handling and subsequent transportation, a considerable interest has been shown by plants for syn-crude oil (SC) production of medium scale.

The present preliminary study, which is based on precedent study, examine the economics of SC production and co-production of EE from B/W. The plants size has been optimised for local renewable sources using technology either available commercially or near commercialization. Economic analysis has been conducted to investigate the effect of different parameters and variableon the cost of EE and SC. Cost estimation for the EE an SC produced under different solutions investigated.

PLANT SIZE IN ITALIAN CONTEXT

So far plant size is concerned it is to be noted that for such fuels with low energetic density, the transport could affect significant the supplying cost. Therefore, in consideration of studies conducted, an area limited to nearly 50 km has been considered as potential resource of B/W. As see in study an available raw material of nearly 424000 t/y and assuming operation of nearly 7000 hr/y, the overall thermal capacity of plant comes out to be 285 MWt.

BASIC PLANT CONFIGURATIONS

The basic design process are based to achieve maximum SC production or co-generation of SC an dEE. They differ mainly due to the presence of reformer, gas recycling and the energy recovery system. As shown in the Figures 34.1 and 34.2, the plants configurations are based on block schemes a) and b) and comprises :

- B/W pre-processing unit composed by grinder and dryer; gasification unit composed primarily by a BFB gasifier using a mix of O_2/Steam as gasifying agent and dolomite.
- Clean up unit composed mainly of four components : cyclone, bag filter, scrubber, and ZnO guard bed each of which removes one of more contaminants.
- Gas upgradation unit in order permit to feed in correct way the FT unit with a H_2/CO equal 2,083. In the work two solutions have been evaluated the first one has been applied for the co-production of SC and EE without gas re-circulation from FT unit (a1/2) while the second one has been applied to increase SC production with gas re-circulation from FT unit (b1/2).
- FT unit. In this study is evaluated the SC production that will be post processed in the refinery, with use of cobalt catalysts, and slurry-phase reactor at low temperature. The product consist of : water, SC, CO_2, and gas-vapour hydrocabon (less than C_5+).
- Separation unit composed by vapour-liquid separtor, where high pressure UR and some light hydrocabons are removed and sent to the recycle, and liquid-liquid separator, where water and SC are separated.
- Energy recovery unit. The energy recovery are related to : heat from FT unit, heat from SG cooling and chemical energy (CE) of unreacted gas (UR) from FT unit, this last only for scheme a). The steam at high pressure has been produce from FT and Heat Recovery Steam Generator (HRSG) units. The UR for scheme a) feed an heavy-duty gas turbines open cycle, the bottom steam cycle is fed with a steam product at limited pressure of 30 bar_g.
- CO_2 separator unit composed of chemical active absorption based on use of mono-ethanol amine (MEA).

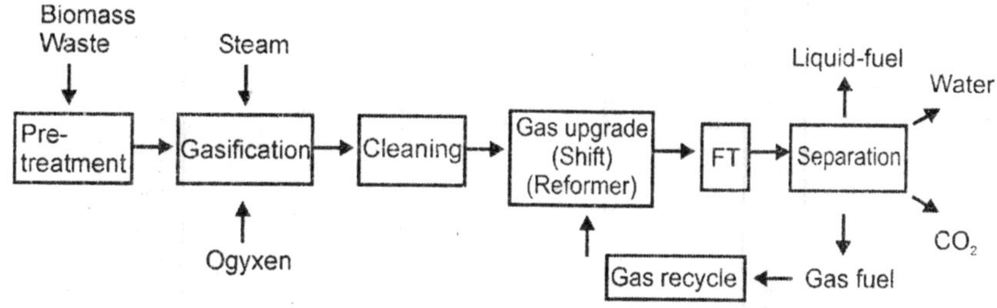

Fig. 34.1 : Plant Configuration, Scheme (a).

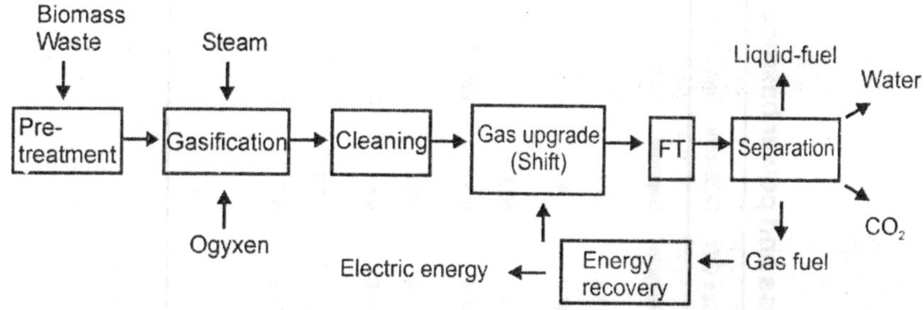

Fig. 34.2 : Plant configuration, Scheme (b).

- Oxygen production unit. The oxygen has been produced or furnished by external provider at purity of 95% (5% N_2, other gas).

The basic plant configuration can have othe two alternative; gasification pressure (atmospheric-pressurised). The combination of these alternatives give four basic configurations, each characterisised by rather distinctive plant features, they are : a1) no recyle, CO_2 separtor, gas turbine (GT) steam turbine (ST); a2) as a1) but a 22 bar_g; b1) recycle with reformer, CO_2 separator, steam turbine (ST); b2) as b1) but a 22 bar_g. Table 34.1 and 34.2 present a summary of mass and power balances and a summary of overall efficiency and field productions for the all plant configurations investigated in the study. The overall efficiency is obtained as energy output (chemical SC + EE), energy in (chemical energy of feedstock's) ratio, if a scheme present a net cnsumption of EE, the overall efficiency is correct with summing of primary energy to produce the EE in energy in.

Tahle 34.1 Mass and power balance

Scheme	Feed stocks	Syn crude	Gas GT/ Recycle	CO2+other Gas Separat.	Gas Turb.	Steam Turb.	Pumping	O2 Prod.	Net EE
(a1) Mass flow [t/hr]	57,4	8,8	13,4	50,1					
Chemi /EE power [MW]	285,0	106,0	85,7	7,4	+24,0	+19,9	-13,5	-6,0	+24,4
(ab) Mass flow [t/hr]	57,4	7,9	14,0	50,9					
Chem/EE power [MW]	285,0	94,9	95,6	8,3	+26,7	+17,3	-2,2	-6,0	+35,8
(b1) Mass flow [t/hr]	57,4	12,5	27,8	60,7					
Chemi/EE power [MW]	285,0	149,9	51,6	4,5	0	+16,4	-18,0	-9,0	-10,6
(b2) Mass flow [t/hr]	57,4	12,4	27,7	57,3					
Chemi/EE power [MW]	285,0	149,5	54,6	4,7	0	+18,3	-3,5	-9,0	+5,8

Table 34.2

Efficiency and Production Field

Scheme	**(a1)**	**(a2)**	**(b1)**	**(b2)**
Production SC field [kgsc/kg/feed]	0,15	0,14	0,22	0,22
Production EE field [kWhe/kg/bio]	0,42	0,62	-0.19	0.13
Overall efficiency (correct)	0,46	0,460,49	(0,45)	0.54

ECONOMIC ANALYSIS WITH DIFFERENT DESIGN SOLUTIONS

The economic investigation has been conducted by analysing various cost terms associated with configurations of the plant studied and hence enables the estimation of the cost of EE and SC produced. The economic analysis was done in a classical mode considering: cost of investment; operating and maintenance costs; depreciation; financing charges.

Cost of Investment (CI) : Cost of investment is the sum of both direct and indirect costs : direct cost comprises of all costs relevant to construction of the plant (cost of the land, preparation of land, different components of theplants for its construction, etc.) whereas indirect cost includes expenses for the plant designing (engineering aspects), testing etc. The costs have been evaluated considering the data available in literature and based upon the values provided for various components by the manufacturers.

Costs of Direct Investment (CID) : Direct costs comprise of all costs relevat to : Acquisition of land; Electro-mechanical work as system for the receipt and storage of biomass; system to feed gasifier; system for the distribution of auxillary fuels; gasification section; filtering section; thermal recovery section; metallic structure and accessories; treatment of feed water, supply and assembling of electrical instruments, mechanical assembling and piping; separation section; O_2 feeding section ; Civil Works as building of control room and offices; floors for the machine and cemented network, preparation of area, roads and platforms, wall enclosures, sewage of water; sewage of dirty water; fire-fighting network.

Cost of Indirect Investment : Cost of engineering and supervision 10-20% of the total cost of direct investment. General costs 5-20% of the total cost of direct investment.

Total Installment cost : Total of Ci is equivalent to 135–123% of CID.

The above-mentioned costs have been estimated by the summation of cost of investment for gasification section; "Shift" section; separation section; oxygen production section; energy recovery section.

Cost of direct investment as a function of plant's potential variation, can be obtained using an exponential relationship based on the existing cost data. If C_1 is the cost of equipment of a part of plant of ability M_1, then the cost of a similar divice, of output M_2, can be calculated by the relationship:

$$C_2 = C_1 \cdot \left(\frac{M_2}{M_1} \right)$$

where the value of the coefficient S depends on the type of equipment or plant.

The corrleation of exponential cost has been development for specific parts and/or sections of plant. In many cases the cost has to be correlated, in terms of parameters related to the plant output.

Direct Cost for Gasification Unit. Cost of gasification plant on pilot scale, uncluding section for heat recovery and cleaning, has been calculated based on the analysis of the cost of pilot plant, 1.3 MW_t. The cost calculation relevant to the plant on large-scale has been done using values obtained from the exploitation the pilot plant as well as literature data.

Direct Cost for Shift Unit. The cost used have taken from the data available in literature that provide the realtionship between the plant cost and actual molar flow rate of $CO+H_2$.

Direct Cost for Reforming Unit. The cost used have been taken from the data available in literature, that provide a relationship between cost of the plant and actual molar flow rate of gas.

Compressin Unit : The cost for the compression section appears to be nearly 900 k€ per kW_e, multistage cooling compressor with compression ratio ß=15-20.

Direct Costs for the Producing Oxygen Unit. The costs used have been taken from the data available in literature that report relationship between cost of theplant and actual daily O_2 production.

Direct Cost for Energy Recovery Unit. The costs for the energy recovery section have been by the taken from the data provided by market analysis of TG generating set and data available in literature.

Table 34.3
Investment Cost

Capital Cost [kε]$_{2001}$	**a1**	**a2**	**b1**	**b2**
Handling, gasification and clean up unit	49084	78327	49084	78327
Shift unit	3810	3939	7647	7977
Reforming unit	0	0	22177	20728
Compression unit	15713	3248	19377	4817
Oxygen production unit	34311	34311	45568	45568
Energy recovery unit	27931	27979	9581	10402
CO2 recovery unit	9170	9277	10763	9940
FT and separation unit	10514	10514	12246	12246
Start cost	7526.65	8379.5	8822,15	9500,25
Total Investment cost	**158059,65**	**175969,5**	**185265,2**	**199505,3**

Direct Cost of FT Unit. The cost has been evaluated by simple calculations considering the volume of slurry reactor (obtained assuming the reaction rate reported in literature and its internals as heat exchange, and settler. All investment costs ae summarised in Table 34.3.

Operational and Maintenance cost. The operational and maintenance costs have been defined as the costs necessary for the functioning fo the plant. The items include : fuels, EE, personal, mateirals etc.

Fuel Cost. The total cost comprises of the mateiral cost (approx. 24 €/t) and the transport cost. Considering average distance of approx –50 km, the overall cost of biomass is approx 30 €/t.

Other Relevant Cost. Such costs include the cost of the relevant chemicals, additives and consumables; mechanical and maintenance operations, etc. On the whole such cost has a fixed value equivalent to nearly 4% of the cost of investment for the realisation of the plant.

Cost of Man-Power Involved. Cost labour involved depends on so many factors such as size of the plant, automatic dependency, different existing norms relevant to the use of different machines, possibilities of realising plants in the already existing industrial areas, etc. It is hypnotised to built autonomous plants or these who does't belong to other industrial plants with number of persons engaged for the all plant equal to 35. The average unitary cost for the staff is of the order of 35 k€.

Electric Energy. The plant have a generating unit, the scheme a1/2 and b2 are net electric producer, only scheme b1 is net consumer for an amount of 74.2 GWh.

Depreciation, Fiscal and Financial Rate. The main fiscal and financial rates adopted in the present study are the inflation rate 2% discount rate 5% and all taxation level 35% depreciation of the plant under investigation is regulated for its fiscal affects under the existing norms of law. The percentage values considered appears to be constant over period of 10 years.

Benefit Derived. The benefits obtained are associated to the sale of EE and SC produced and also the Green Certification (GC). The gain derived from the sale of EE and GC has been assumed to be 85 €/MWh from 90€/MVh, whereas the gain relevant to SC has been assumed to be nearly 430€/t.

RESULTS

The cost of SC or EE has been obtained determining the "Levelised Cost of Energy", $LC_{EE/SC}$ or the effective cost of energy produced as given by

$$LC_{EE/SC} = \frac{(I + L_e + M).\, f_{EE/SC}}{E_{EE/SC} \sum_{t=1}^{n} \frac{1}{(k_n + 1)^t}}$$

wher : I= effective cost of investment; L_e=effective sum of energy cost; M=effectve sum of operation and maintenance costs; E= annual EE or SC production; $F_{EE/SC}$=allocation factors cost with $F_{EE}+F_{SC}=1$. The scheme a1/2 and b2 have two products EE and SC, the allocation of investment, maintenance etc., costs have been made in terms of energy.

Estimation of the $LC_{SC/EE}$ with prominent, determined or assumed economic economic data for the solution investigated, varies respectively between 440.9-601.1€/t and 73.4-78.6 €/MWh as shown in Table 34.4.

TABLE 34. 4

Estimated levelised cost of syn-crude and electric energy and NPV.

	LC_{SC}[€/t]	LC_{EE}[€/MWh]	NPV[k€]
a1 scheme	446,5	74,0	131107,9
a2 scheme	440,9	73.4	181910,9
b1 scheme	562,0	-	-88641,1
b2 scheme	491,9	78.6	28557,39

Sensitivity analysis has been conducted to investigated the cost of $LC_{EE/SC}$ with a variation of on four main parameters, in particular, attention has been focussed ; B/W cost; availability;investment cost, operational cost. The variation assumed has been considered for all the sizes within ±20%. The scheme considered is the b2.

35

Ethanol (Bio-Fuel) Technology

Introduction

Bio–fuel is any fuel that derives from biomass. Thus it could be oils from plants, manure from cows, wood from trees and so on. It is a renewable energy source, unlike other natural resources such as petroleum, coal and nucelar fuels. Agricultural products specifically grown for use as bio–fuels include corn adn soybean, primarily in the United States, and flaxseed and rapeseed, primarily in Europe. Waste from industry, agriculture, forestry, and householdas can also be used to produce bio–energy; examples include straw, lumber, manure, sewage and garbage and food leftover.

The production of bio–fuels to replace petroeleum-based oil and natural gas is in active development. The carbon in bio–fuels is extracted from atmospheric carbon dioxide by growing plants,, so burning it does not result in a net increase of carbon dioxide in the Earth's atmosphere. As a result, bio–fuels are seen by many as away to reduce the amount of carbon dioxide released into the atmosphere by using them to replace non-renewable of energy.

ETHANOL

Ethanol (ethyl alcohol, grain alcohol) is a clear, colourless liquid with a characteristic, agreeble odor. In dilute aqueous solution, it has a somewhat sweet flavour, but in more concentrated solutions it has a burning taste. Ethanol (CH_3CH_2OH) is a group of chemical compounds whose molecule contains a hydroxyl groups, -OH, bonded to a carbon atom. Ethanol made from cellulosic biomass materials instead of traditional feedstocks (starch crops) is called bioethanol.

The Clean Air Amendments of 1990 mandated the sale of oxygenated fuels in areas with unhealthy levels of carbon monoxide. Since that time, there has been strong demand for ethanol as an oxygenated blended with gasoline. In the United States each year, more than 1.5 billiion gallons are added to gasoline to increase octane and improve the emission quality of gasoline. In some areas ethanol is blended with gasoline to form an E10 blend (10% ethanol and 90% gasoline), but it can be used in higher concentrations such as E85 or in its pure form.

PRODUCTION

The production phases in Ethanol production are shown in the following line diagram (Fig. 35.1).

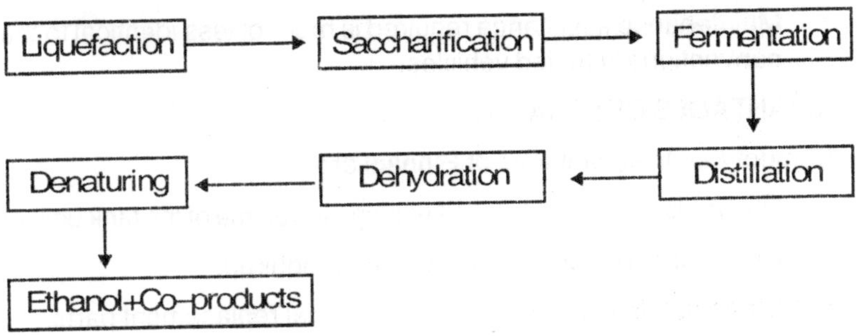

Fig. 35.1 : Ethanol Production Process.

A recent Australian study with E10 gives the following emission results.

- Decreased emission of CO by 32%.
- Decreased emissions of HC by 12%.
- 1% increase in NOx.
- Decrease in non-regulated toxics; 1-3 butadiene decrease by 19% benzene decrease by 27%, toluene decrease by 30% and xylene decrease by 30% and xylene decrease by 27%.
- Increase in non-regulated toxics: acetaldehyde increase by 180% and formaldehyde increase by 25%.

Recent Australian life-cycle analysis work has revealed that E10 blends are considered greenhouse neutral. The same study revealed that E10 decreased tail pipe emissions of hydrocarbons and NOx (25x and 15%

ADVANTAGES OF ETHANOL

Some of the advantages of Ethanol as an automotive fuel are :

- It reduces our dependence or imported fuels.
- It reduces air polution.
- Ethanol is renewable.
- Refueling is akin to that of gasoline or diesel.
- Is applicable for both light and heavy-duty vehicles.
- More energy density compared to gasoline with optimized compression ratio.
- Maintenance assistance required is more of less identical to that of conventionally fueled vehicles.

DISADVANTAGES OF ETHANOL

Someof the disadvantages of Ethnaol are :

- Demands frequent refueling keeping the volume of the tank unaltered.
- Use of special compatible lubricants required.
- Ethanol, especially E85 requires special replacement parts.

OPERATION AND PERFORMANCE

- High energy density compared to gasoline.
- No loss in power, acceleration and payload.
- Special lubricants are required.
- Special parts required.

INDIAN INITITATIVES ON ETHANOL

In the year 1980, IIP an IOC, R & D conducted a study with ethanol as the fuel in some 13-passenger cars including army vehicle. The test included city driving, highway driving and hill driving conditions. Some of the findigns of this study are :

Loss in volumetric fúel economy of 1% and 3.9% with E10 and E20 fuels respectively under city driving conditions and 3.5% and 4.3% under highway driving conditions.

Cold starting and driveability demerits found higher with ethanol blends.

ADVANTAGES OF ETHANOL

Some of the advantages of Ethanol as an automotive fuel are :

- It reduces our dependence or imported fuels.
- It reduces air polution.
- Ethanol is renewable.
- Refueling is akin to that of gasoline or diesel.
- Is applicable for both light and heavy-duty vehicles.
- More energy density compared to gasoline with optimized compression ratio.
- Maintenance assistance required is more of less identical to that of conventionally fueled vehicles.

DISADVANTAGES OF ETHANOL

Someof the disadvantages of Ethnaol are :

- Demands frequent refueling keeping the volume of the tank unaltered.
- Use of special compatible lubricants required.
- Ethanol, especially E85 requires special replacement parts.

OPERATION AND PERFORMANCE

- High energy density compared to gasoline.
- No loss in power, acceleration and payload.
- Special lubricants are required.
- Special parts required.

INDIAN INITITATIVES ON ETHANOL

In the year 1980, IIP an IOC, R & D conducted a study with ethanol as the fuel in some 13-passenger cars including army vehicle. The test included city driving, highway driving and hill driving conditions. Some of the findigns of this study are :

Loss in volumetric fuel economy of 1% and 3.9% with E10 and E20 fuels respectively under city driving conditions and 3.5% and 4.3% under highway driving conditions.

Cold starting and driveability demerits found higher with ethanol blends.

No compatibility problems observed with metallic and non metallic component

Moreover a committee to look into all the aspects of introduction of Ethanol-Gasoline blend as an auto fuel was constituted by the Ministry of Petroleum and Natural Gas. The committee was heading with the preliminary aim to introduce ethanol blends in the NCR but considering the economics and logistics, the committee could not mandate the introduction sometimes in the year 1999.

Ministry of Petroleum and Natural Gas launched three pilot projects in the country. The first project at Mirja was initiated on 15.4.2001; the 2nd at Bareilly on 22.6.2001 and the 3rd was launched at Manmad on 24.6.2001. Other technical and R & D activities are also been carried out in various parts of India.

Based on the experience of the pilot projects, Government of India on 29.11.2001 has tanken a decision to introduce petrol blended with 5% ethanol for use in motor vehicles all over the country in a phased manner. In the first phase, the 5% ethanol blended petrol will be introduced in the States of Andhra Pradesh, Gujarat, Haryana, Karnataka, Maharashtra, Punjab, Tamil Nadu, and Uttar Pradesh, Rest of the States/Union Territories will be taken up in the second phase.

On the other hand, India is also working to blend 10% ethanol in petrol. The pilot projects and R & D initiatives are also lined up to study the feasibility of 10% ethanol-gasoline blend. Amendments in BIS specification to accommodate this 10% blend is being pursued.

ALL FOLLOWING PROJECT REPORTS ARE READILY AVAILABLE

- Calcined Petroleum Coke
- Calcining Of Magnesite & Dead Burnt Magnesite
- Calcium Aluminate
- Calcium Based Grease
- Calcium Carbide
- Calcium Carbonate
- Calcium Carbonate (Precipitated) From By Product (Lime Slurry & Carbon Dioxide)
- Calcium Carbonate (Activated & Precipitated)
- Calcium Chloride
- Calcium Gluconate
- Calcium Nitrate
- Calcium Silicate Bricks
- Calcium Stearate By Fusion Process
- Camphor Powder (Synthetic)
- Construction Chemicals (With Detailed Market Survey And Formulae Etc.)
- Carbon Dioxide
- Carbon Black From Fertilizer Waste
- Carbon Black (Petroleum Based)
- Carboxy Methyl Cellulose (Cmc)
- Casein And By Products
- Casein From Milk
- Cationic Softner (Stearic Acid Based)
- Caustic Soda
- Caustic Soda From Soda Ash By Soda Lime Process
- Caustic Soda (Liquid) By Electrolytic Process
- Caustic Soda From Trona
- Caustic Soda, Chlorine And Hydrogen Gas By Electro-Lysis Of Brine Solution
- Cellulose Acetate Moulding Powder
- Cellulose Powder & Micro Crystalline Cellulose Powder
- Cement Admixture
- Cement Colour
- Cement Water Proofing Compound
- Cement From Fly Ash & Lime
- Cement Tiles (Glazed)
- Chlorinated Paraffin Wax (Cpw)
- Citric Acid From Lemon
- Citric Acid From Molasses
- Double Firing (Heating)
- Chelated Zinc (Zn Edta)
- Chemicals From Prawn Head
- Chitin & Chitosan From Prawn Shell Waste
- Chloral Hydrate
- Chloramphenicol
- Chromic Acid (With Pollution Control)
- Chromic Acid (Oxide) & Blue Oxide
- Chlorinated Paraffin Wax (Cpw)
- Chromic Acid
- Cement Paint & Distemper
- Citric Acid From Lemon
- Citric Acid From Molasses
- Cleaning Of Cooling System And Boiler
- Coal Tar Distillation
- Coal Washing Plant
- Cobalt Octoate
- Compost For Mushroom
- Construction Chemicals
- Copper Oxychloride
- Coolant (Engine)
- Copper Phthalocyanine Blue & Green
- Correction Fluid
- Cupric Chloride
- Crude Oil Bleaching For Petroleum Jelly
- Cutting Oil
- Cyanuric Chloride
- Cyanoacrylate Adhesive
- Cutting Oil
- Defoaming Agent For Paper Industry
- De-Nickeling (Electrolytic Process)
- Detergent Cake & Powder
- Detergent Powder
- Detergent Concentrate (Idet 10)
- Dextrose Monohydrate & Dextrose Anhydrous Powder From Tapioca Starch
- Di-Basic Lead Stearate
- Di Calcium Phosphate
- Diclofenal Sodium Slow Release (Sr) Tables 100mg.
- Di Ethyl Oxalate
- Di Methyl Orthophthalate
- Di-Methyl Phthalate
- Diclofenac Gel
- Dioctyl Phthalate (Dop)
- Di Phenyl Glycerine
- Di Phenyl Oxide
- Dinitro-Chloro Benzene
- Distillery
- Distilled Water
- Dodecyl Benzene Sulphonate
- Dustless Chalk
- Edta & Its Salts
- Electroless Nickel Plating On Plastics
- Electrolyte (Like Sulphuric Acid) For Lead Acid Dry Rechargable 5.5.Ah. Battery
- Electropolishing On Gold Jewellery
- Electropolishing On Various Metals
- Endosulfan
- Enzyme Based Detergent Powder
- Ephedrine Hydrochloride
- Epoxy Resin Based Compound
- Ethanol (Biofuel)
- Ethyl Alcohol From Molasses
- Ethyl Acetate
- Ehtyl Ether
- Ethyl Alcohol (Potable Liquor)
- Ethyl Hexanol
- Extra Temperature Lubricating Grease
- Extraction Of Essential Oils By Sugar Critical Fluid (Carbon Dioxide) Method From Flowers, Herbal & Spices
- Fabric Stain Remover
- Fatty Acid
- Ferric Alum
- Ferric And Non Ferric Alum (Aluminium Sulphate)
- Ferro Chrome Ligno Sulphonate
- Ferro Manganese
- Ferro Silicone

Contact EIRI for required Project report apart from this list.

- Ferro Vanadium From Vanadium Sludge
- Ferrous Silicate
- Ferrous Sulphate
- Ferrous Sulphide
- Fertilizer From Animal Blood & Leather Waste
- Fluorescent Tube Light Powder
- Foamed Pvc Compounding & Its Products
- Formaldehyde
- Food Grade Grease Or Lubricant
- Fractional Distillation Of D.M.O (Dementholized Oil)
- Fractional Distillation Of Essential Oil & Medicinalplant Extract
- Friction Dust (Liquid & Powder) From Cnsl
- Fruit Flavours
- Furfural From Rice Husk
- Fumaric Acid
- Gas Filling Of Lpg Cylinder
- Garlic Acid
- Ginger And Garlic Paste
- Ginger Processing
- Gasket Shellac Compound
- Gear Oil
- Gibberellic Acid
- Glass Putty
- Gluconic Acid
- Glucose D- Powder
- Glycerine
- Gossypol (Poly Phenol) From Cotton Seed Oil
- Greases (Lithium Based)
- Guar Gum Powder
- Hair Fixer (Hair Gel Type)
- High Temerature Grease
- Hard Grease
- H - Acid
- Henna Paste Making
- Henna Powder Repackaging
- Heptal Dehyde
- Herbal Beer
- High Carbon Ferro Chrome
- Humid Acid
- Hydrated Calcium Silicate Brick
- Hydrated Lime From Sea Shell
- Hydrochloric Acid
- Hydro Fluoric Acid
- Hydrogen Peroxide (By Auto-Oxidation Process)
- Ice Packs (Solutions Type, White Gel Type, Violet Semi Solid Polymer Type)
- Improving Drop Point Paraffin Wax From 45-50°c To 75-80°c
- Industrial Alcohol

Market Survey Cum Detailed Techno Economic Feasibility Report on all Projects are available Contact.
"ENGINEERS INDIA RESEARCH INSTITUTE". 4449, Nai Sarak (D), Main Road, Delhi-110006 (India)
Ph. : 09811437895, 91-11-23918117, 23916431, 45626431, 64727385 Fax : 91-11-23916431
E-mail : eiriprojects@gmail.com, eiribooks@yahoo.com • website: www.eiri.in, www.eiriindia.org

ALL FOLLOWING PROJECT REPORTS ARE READILY AVAILABLE

PAINT, ENAMEL, SOLVENTS, THINNERS, INKS & VARNISH
PAINT, ENAMEL, SOLVENTS, THINNERS, INKS & VARNISH

- Acrylic Emulsion Paints
- Acrylic Cement Paint (Dry Powder)
- Aluminium Paint
- Automobile Paints
- Ball Point Pen Refill Ink
- Bituminious Road Emulsion
- Bitumen
- Bituminious Felts For Water & Damp Proofing
- Bituminious Road Emulsion Rapid Medium & Slow Setting
- Buffing & Polishing
- Cement Paint For White & Grey Cement
- Dispersant
- Dry Distemper
- Dry Distemper & Cement Paint
- Duplicating Ink Black For Gestner Duplicator
- Emulsion Paints (Water Based)
- Hammertone Paint
- Insulating Varnish & Wire Enamel
- Iron Oxide Pigments
- Insulating Varnish (Poly Vinyl Butyral Based, Ffc Grade)
- Lime Colour (Cement Colour)
- Synthetic Red Oxide For Floorings
- Solvent & Thinners
- Marking Inks (Water Proof)
- Metal Naphthanate (As Drier For Paints)
- N.C.Putty
- Offset Printing Ink
- Oil Bound Distemper Paint
- Paint Brushes
- Paint Manufacture For Rolling Coating Of Aluminium And Steel Coil
- Paint Removers
- Paint Industry
- Paint & Varnish
- Picture Varnish
- Powder Coating Paint
- Printing Inks (Offset,Flexo & Roto Gravure)
- Primer Paint & Enamel Paint
- Putty & Water Proofing Paint
- Printing Inks (Flexo-Graphic Ink)
- Putty (Metal Casement)
- Red Oxide Primer (Anti Corrosive)
- Refractory Paint (Graphite Based)
- Screen Printing Inks
- Silk Screen Printing Ink Formulation For Plastic, Paper, Cloth
- Stamp & Pad Ink
- Stoving Paint
- Spirit Soluble Maleic Resin
- Texture Paint
- Thinners And Its Allied Products
- Toner Ink
- Varnish Thinner (Solvent)
- Vacuum Metallizing Lacquers
- Wood Primer

PHARMACEUTICAL, DRUGS, AYURVEDIC/HERBAL COSMETICS & MEDICINES, HOMOEOPATHIC MEDICINES, HOMOEOPATHIC MEDICINES, DISPOSABLE SYRINGE, DENTAL COLLEGE & FINE CHEMICALS ETC.
MEDICINES, HOMOEOPATHIC MEDICINES, DISPOSABLE SYRINGE, DENTAL COLLEGE & FINE CHEMICALS ETC.

- Aromatic Pills
- Alumina From Bauxite
- Aspirin
- Ayurvedic Pain Balm Ointments
- Ayurvedic Churan And Tablets
- Ayurvedic Tablets (Hajmola Type)
- Ayurvedic/Herbalpharmacy
- Ayurvedic Sherbats
- Ayurvedic Products
- Bulk Drugs (E.O.U)
- Blood Bags
- Calcium Gluconate
- Capsule, Tablet & Injection With Modern Instruments
- Cashew Feni
- Chloroquinone Phosphate (Bulk Drugs)
- Clinical Thermometer
- Dental Clinic
- Dental College
- Dental Grade Eugenol
- Dextrose Monohydrate, Liquid Glucose
- Dehydrated Onion & Onion Powder
- Dextrose Powder (Anhydrous From Starch)
- Dextrose Saline Solution
- Distillery (I.M.F.L)
- Disposable Needles For Syringes
- Disprin
- Distilled Water
- Empty Hard Gelatine Capsules
- Fairness Cream
- Filling & Packing Of Capsules
- Glucose - D - Powder
- Glycerine
- Hair Colour Mate (Formulations And Process Only)
- Herbal Cosmetics
- Herbal Shampoo
- Herbal Shampoo And Cream
- Herbal Hair Oils (Ayurvedic)
- Homoe & Bio-Medicines With Mother Tincture
- Homoepathic Medicines
- Hypodermic Needles
- I.V. Fluids
- Ibuprofen
- Infusion & Transfusion Sets (I.V. Set)
- Injectable For Pharmaceuticals
- Injection Ampoules Packaging Box
- Integerated Surgical Cotton
- Ice Making Plant
- Ice & Cold Storage
- Lactose & By Products Processing From Milk
- Lichen (Jatamansi Charila)
- Liquid Glucose And Its By-Products
- L-Lysine Monohydro Chloride
- Liquid Glucose From Potatoes
- Medical College
- Methanol (Hpcl Grade)
- Nicotine From Tobacco Waste
- Ointment-Ayurvedic (Yellow & White)
- Pharmaceutical And Food Grade Gelatine
- Pharmaceutical Industry (Tablets, Capsules, Liquid, Gel, Ointment Powder Injectable)
- Pharmaceutical Unit (Eou) With Formulations, Injectables, Etc.
- Pyridine & Derivatives
- Salt (Iodized Salt)
- Saline & Injection Water
- Saline Water & Dextrose Solution (I.V.Fluid In Plastic Bottles)
- Sorbitol
- Starch (Maize)
- Surgical Adhesive Plaster
- Surgical Bandages
- Surgical Gloves
- Surgical Cotton
- Surgical Cotton And Bandage
- Synthetic Camphor Powder
- Tablets & Capsules
- Tissue Culture
- Tincture From Rectified Spirit
- Trimethopime
- Veterinary College With Hospital
- Veterenary Medicines (Only Formulations)
- Vitamin 'C', Sorbitol' Anhydrous Dextrose, Starch

Market Survey Cum Detailed Techno Economic Feasibility Report on all Projects are available Contact.
"ENGINEERS INDIA RESEARCH INSTITUTE". 4449, Nai Sarak (D), Main Road, Delhi-110006 (India)
Ph. : 09811437895, 91-11-23918117, 23916431, 45626431, 64727385 Fax : 91-11-23916431
E-mail : eiriprojects@gmail.com, eiribooks@yahoo.com • website: www.eiri.in, www.eiriindia.org